URBAN DEVELOPMENT
IN
NORTH-EAST INDIA
POTENTIALITY AND PROBLEMS

URBAN DEVELOPMENT
IN
NORTH-EAST INDIA
POTENTIALITY AND PROBLEMS

Dr. B. Datta Ray
Dr. A.K. Neog
H.K. Mazhari

RELIANCE PUBLISHING HOUSE
NEW DELHI-110008

First Published 1999

ISBN: 81-7510-094-X

Published by :
Dr. S.K. Bhatia *for*
RELIANCE PUBLISHING HOUSE
3026/7H, RANJIT NAGAR
NEW DELHI-110 008
PH. : 5722605, 5737377. FAX : 5772748

Composed by :
COMPUTRA COMMUNICATION
9, GOPALPUR, DELHI-110 009
PH. : 765 2321

Printed by :

ACKNOWLEDGEMENTS

The papers included in this volume were presented to a seminar on Potentiality and Problems of Small Towns in North-East India Council for Social Science Research on 20-21 November 1995. The basic perimeter of the seminar was framed by Dr. A.K. Neog. The seminar was inaugurated by His Excellency Mr. M.M. Jacob, Governor of Meghalaya who pointed out the administrative and economic compulsions which led to the growth of new towns. Professor B. Pakem, Vice-Chancellor, North Eastern Hill University who presided over the inaugural session said that the 74th Amendement Act to the Indian Constitution added a new dimension to urban affairs and their management.

We are grateful to Government of Meghalaya, Government of India and Indian Council of Social Science Research, North-Eastern Regional Centre, Shillong for giving us generous support to undertake this study.

We would like to record our sincere appreciation of service of Mr. H.K. Mazhari for his support to urban studies. To the publishers of this volume M/s. Reliance Publishing House, we owe a debt of gratitude for aggreeing to publish this volume which is an important in put to North-East India study.

B. Datta Ray
Secretary
North-East India Council for Social Science Research
Shillong-793003

INTRODUCTION

The urbanisation process had a late start in North-East India but it gained momentum since 1971. The urban population in the country stood at 217.61 million in 1991 and is expected to touch 300 million by 2002 A.D. But the level, rate and pattern of urbanization are not uniform over time and space in North-East India. There is palpable intra regional variation the range being maximum of 46.1 per cent in the hilly Mizoram and minimum 11.1 per cent in the plains of Assam suggesting fast pace of urbanisation in the hilly semi-subsistent triable states and slow and low in plain area as of Assam. The Census of 1991 reveals that the highest percentage of urban population is recorded by Kamrup district (32.76), whereas the lowest percentage is found in the Dhemaji district (1.86). In the Barak Valley though Silchar city accounts for 1.1 lakh population, the level of urbanization is low. It is because of the fact that the percentage of rural population is relatively high in the absence of many towns with small size of population. The spatial pattern of urbanization in North-East India is characterized by unequal distribution of urban population.

The 1991 census reveals that in the entire North-East India there are 183 towns, of which 87 towns (47.5 per cent) are in Assam, 30 in Manipur, 22 in Mizoram, 18 in Tripura, 10 in Arunachal Pradesh, 9 in Nagaland and 7 in Meghalaya. Of the 8 Class I towns, with population above one lakh, 4 in Assam

(Guwahati, Dibrugarh, Silchar and Jorhat) and one each in Manipur, Meghalaya, Mizoram and Tripura. In the Class II category with population of 50,000 to 99,999, there are 6 towns in the region, with 4 in Assam (Dhubri, Nagaon, Tezpur and Tinsukia) and 2 in Nagaland (Dimapur and Kohima).

Physical limits in the horizontal expansion of geographical area in class I and II towns in North-East India seem to have already been approached. Problems of over-crowding, slum dwelling, population, drainage and sewage disposal, water scarcity, power supply, public health and sanitation, education and medical facilities are experienced actutely in all towns of North-East India. All the problems are detrimental to urban civic life which in turns retard the economic health of these towns.

Administrative compulsions, economic necessities, social attitudes and strategic requirements determined the setting up and growth process of towns. Throughout the history of urbanisation of North-East India, towns have been imposed on rural landscape for administrative and strategic purposes without any major consideration of urban potentiality. An urgent need to assess the urban potentiality both in macro and micro levels have been felt. It is necessary to assess the carrying capacity of urban centres and study the rural hinterland of each town. As most of the urban centres of the region have come up unplanned, there is serious lack of infrastructures, transport and communication linkage, training and servicing facilities.

Due to lack of agricultural and large scale industrial potentialities for towns in this region, attention has to be paid to small and medium size manufacturing units including servicing industries for small towns's growth and viability. Trade, marketing and transport facilities are to be planned in conformity with the regional character.

Planned Human Resource Development is the prime requisite for any socio-economic advancement of North-East India. Nearly sixty percent of the people arc illiterate. To cope with this dismal situation open schooling system with vocational facilities should be explored to make the small towns vibrant, active and healthy nodal points in the urban settlement pattern.

Growing urbanization would exert stress on local environment and threaten the quality of life. Most of the poor in the next century would likely be in urban centres and their living conditions would be worse than those of rural poor.

Poverty is a direct and growing threat to the urban future. The sheer numbers of poor are threatening to overwhelm the urban settlements. Unlike the people belonging to other income groups, the standard of living of urban poor is going to be worse when compared to the rural poor. The poor in the small towns in North East do not have the means to meet the basic needs of shelter, water, health and education. Thousands of urban poor children are plagued by problems like school drop-outs, loabour and sexual exploitations. For women, urban life is fraught with insecurity with the threats to them and their families and scarcities of health care and educational facilities which could have enabled them to escape from poverty.

The Eco-systems in North-East India are already at the risk from unplanned urban development. Proper planning for municipal services and urban engineering are badly needed to find a lasting solution to severe environmental pollution and health hazards in all towns in North East India which stand on delicate ecological balance.

The concept of modern strong villages with balanced growth and development may be examined in the context of North-East India's urbanisation spread. Raising the living standard of rural areas through radical land reforms and rational land relations might help to restore ecological and economic balance.

B. Datta Ray
H.K. Mazhari
A.K. Nsog

CONTRIBUTORS

1. *Dr. Pabitra Giri*/Centre for Urban Economic Studies, Calcutta University, Calcutta-700027
2. *Dr. N.N. Bhattacharyya*/Department of Geography, Gauhati University, Guwahati-781014
3. *Dr. Surendra Singh*/Department of Geography, North-Eastern Hill University, Shillong-793014
4. *Dr. Prabin Baisya*/S.B.M.S. College, Sualkuchi, Assam
5. *Dr. A.K. Agarwal*/'Department of Economics, North-Eastern Hill University, Aizwal Campus, Aizwal, Mizoram
6. Dr. Zahid Hussain Anthropological Survey of India, Shillong-1
7. *Dr. Jogomaya Saikia*/Regional Engineering College, Silchar, Cachar
8. *Dr. Amaresh C. Dubey*/Deptt. of Economics, North-Eastern Hill University, Shillong-14
9. *Ms. W. Syiem*/Deptt. of Urban Affairs, Shillong
10. *Mr. Kshirode Marak*/Scholar, Tura, West Garo Hills
11. *Mr. H.K. Mazhari*/Deppt. of Urban Affairs, Shillong
12. *Mr. B.K. Kar*/Deppt. of Geography, Gauhati University, Guwahati-14
    Dr. M.M. Das/Deptt. of Geograhy, Gauhati University, Guwahati-14
13. *Dr. S.K. Agnihotri*/Administrative Reforms Commissioner, Govt. of Meghalaya, Shillong

14. *Dr. Neelam Sinha*/National Open School/HRD, New Delhi
15. *Dr. Kishore Bhattacherjee*/Deptt. of Folklore Research, Gauhati University, Guwahati
16. *Dr. S.K. Barpujari*/Formerly of Deptt. of History, Gauhati University, Guwahati.
17. *Dr. R.P. Athparia*/Anthropological Survey of India, Shillong-1
18. *Mr. H.C. Khaund*/Town & Country Planning Officer, Jorhat, Assam
    Dr. A.K. Borah/Deptt. of Sociology, Dibrugarh University, Dibrugarh, Assam
    Dr. Manurl Hussain/Deptt. of Political Science, Guwahati University, Guwahati-14
19. *Dr. P.C. Dutta*/Deptt. of Statistics, S.S. College, Hailakandi, Assam
    Mr. B.C. Pradhan/S.S. College, Hailakandi, Assam
20. *Mr. R.P. Bhattacharjee*/North Eastern Regional Institute of Science & Technology, Itanagar, Arunachal Pradesh
21. *Dr. H. Kamkhenthang*/Jt. Director of Tribal Development & Backward Class, Govt. of Manipur, Imphal-1
22. *Dr. Mahadev Chakravarti*/Deptt. of History, Tripura University, Agartala-799004, Tripura

CONTENTS

	Acknowledgements	*v*
	Introduction	*vii*
	Contributors	*ix*
1.	Role of Small and Medium-sized Towns in the Development of North-East India/ *Pabitra Giri*	1
2.	The Role of Small Towns in the Development Process of North-East India/ *N.N. Bhattacharyya*	25
3.	Towns within Town-System—A Case study of North-East India/*Surendra Singh*	30
4.	Urbanisation in the North-East Towns of Assam—With Reference to Two Small/ *Prabin Baishya*	50
5.	Potentiality and Problems of Small Towns in North-East India/*A.K. Agarwal*	63
6.	Hill Town Planning/*Zahid Husain*	69
7.	Socio-Technological Problems in the Growth of Small Towns in the North-East India/*Jogomaya Saikia*	83
8.	Urbanization in Meghalaya—Growth and Prospects of Small Towns/*Amaresh C. Dubey*	85
9.	Planning and Development for Small and Medium Towns in Meghalaya/*W. Syiem*	96
10.	Growth of Towns in Garo Hills/*Kshirode Marak*	103
11.	Urban Solid Waste Management in a Small Town/*H.K. Mazhari*	113

12. Spati-Temporal Pattern and Characteristics of Small Towns in Assam/ *B.K. Kar and M.M. Das* 118
13. Municipal Management in Small Towns/ *S.K. Agnihotri* 132
14. Open Schooling—A Viable Solution for Small Towns of the North-Eastern States/ *Neelam Sinha* 140
15. Small Towns and Socio-Cultural Change in Assam—The Necessity of Oral Historical Approach/*Kishore Bhattacharjee* 154
16. Haflong—Past and Present/*S.K. Barpujari* 160
17. Problems of Small Towns in the Hill Area of Assam—A Case Study of Diphu Town/ *R.P. Athparia* 170
18. Ecology of Small Town—A Case Study of Mariani Town of Assam/*H.C. khaund, A.K. Borah, M. Hussain* 181
19. Problems of Community Integration in Small Towns of Barak Valley Districts of Assam—A Case Study of Lala Town/*P.C. Dutta & B.C. Pradhan* 194
20. Potentiality and Problems of Small Towns in Arunachal Pradesh—A Case Study of Bomdila Town/*R.P. Bhattacharjee* 207
21. Lamka (Churachandpur) Town/*H. Kamkhenthang* 214
22. Small Towns in Tripura in the Past and Present/*Mahadev Chakravarti* 226

LIST OF TABLES

Chapter 1

Table 1: Level and Rate of Urbanisation in Eastern India 5

Table 2: Average annual exponential growth rate of population 6

Table 3: Size-Distribution of Towns in North-East India 7

Table 4: Growth rate of common towns in different-size classes 9

Table 5: Percentage distribution of birth place urban male migrants by types of movements, North-East India, 1961, 1971, 1981 10

Table 6: Number and population of UAs/Towns having services as the predominant/leading function according Mono, Bi and Multi-functional categories in the North-East India, 1991 12

Table 7: Percentage of inhabited villages for selected population sizes and distance ranges from the nearest town, 1981 14

Table 8: The Structure of Workforce in North-East India, 1991 15

Table 9: The Structure of Urban workforce in North-East India, 1991 16

Appendix 1: Change in the functional classification of selected North-East India Towns, 1961 to 1991 21

Chapter 3

Table 1: Percentage Decadal Variation of Urban Population in the N.E.R. (1901-11 to 1981-91) 34

Table 2: Number of Towns in various Town-Classes according to their Population Sizes (1981 & 1991) 36

Table 3: Number of Towns according to Town Orders (1991) 40

Table 4: Occupational Structure of Different Town-Orders (1991) 48

Chapter 4

Table 1: Growth of Urban Areas & Population—1951-1991 51

Table 2: Urban Areas by Population Size, 1991 53

Chapter 8

Table 1: Urbanization Trend in Meghalaya Total and Urban Population of Meghalaya (District-wise) 87

Table 2: Total and Urban Population of Meghalaya (District-wise) 89

Table 3: Urbanization at District Level 90

Table 4: Decadal Varation of Urban Population (District-wise) 90

Table 5: Size-class Distribution of Towns in Meghalaya 91

Table 6: Population of Towns by Size-class in Meghalaya 91

Table 7: Decadal Growth of Population of Towns by their Size-class 92

Table 8: Percentage Distribution of Total Urban Population by Size-class 92

Chapter 9

Table 1: Density of Population, Sex Ratio and Growth of Population in Meghalaya by Districts 97

Chapter 12

Table 1: Trend of Urban Population in Assam, 1901-1991 121

Table 2: Catagorywise Distribution of Urban Centres in Assam, 1991 123

Table 3: Distribution of Small and other Urban Centres in respect of Population Growth Categories during 1971-1991 in Assam 126
Table 4: Occupational Pattern of Urban Centres in Assam, 1971 and 1991 129
Chapter 14
Table 1: Literacy rates in Decending Order 142 1991
Table 2: Dropout rates 1994-95 142
Table III(a) 151
Table III (b) 152
Chapter 19
Table 1: Population of Lala Town 198
Table 2: Lala Rural College 199
Table 3: Educational Institution: 1995 199
Table 4: Income Expenditure Statement of Lala Town Committee 199
Chapter 20
Table 1: Urban Population and Size-class in Arunachal Pradesh 208
Table 2: Workers Classification of Bomdila Town in Board Sectors (Percentage) 210
Table 3: Literacy-rate of Bomdila Town 211
Chapter 22
Table 1: List of Small Towns in Trimpura 227
Table 1A: Population of Agartala (now class I) 227
Table 1B: Growth of Urban Population in Tripura Since 1901 228
Table 2: Different classes of Towns in Tripura 231 from 1901 to 1981
Table 3: Literacy Rates and Ranks by Rural-Urban Residence for Tripura in 1981 and 1991 232
Table 3A: Literates and Literacy Rates in Tripura, 1991 232

LIST OF FIGURES

Chapter 3
Fig. 1 38
Fig. 2 41
Chapter 12
Fig. 1 122
Fig. 2 124
Fig. 3 127

Chapter 1

ROLE OF SMALL AND MEDIUM-SIZED TOWNS IN THE DEVELOPMENT OF NORTH-EAST INDIA

Pabitra Giri

INTRODUCTION

A town serves as a central place to its hinterland; at the same time, it is a point of link between the hinterland and the rest of the world. The role of small towns in the urbanisation process determines and gets determined by the pattern of development in the long run. It would be worthwhile, therefore, to discuss briefly the development process in the North-East India, before we take up the small town issue.

Geographically, the North-East India stands in relative isolation from the rest of India, owing to (*i*) distance from the rest of the country, (*ii*) closure of relatively short-distance and cheap transport routes through Bangladesh after Independence and (*iii*) inadequate development of rail and road transport facilities. However, the relative isolation has not led to an inward-looking development process. Rather the development in the area is by and large an example of outward-looking enclave type of development for historical and other reasons.

Historically, under the colonial rule, the

development process started in this region with the export oriented tea plantation, exploitation of forest resources and oil. These industries have relatively weak production linkages with the rest of the economy. Most of the inputs are imported from and output produced are exported to outside the region. Besides, ownership and control of these activities and also of wholesale trade and commerce were, and still are, at the hands of the migrants from the outside the region (Planning Commission, 1981, p. 5). Consequently, investible surplus is siphoned out of the region.

Secondly, the region is neither homogeneous nor integrated in terms of market. It lacks of physical, social as well as economic integration. While poor physical integration is due to topographical barriers, social integration is lacking because the population comprises a large number of tribal groups. These communities are mostly engaged in traditional low productivity farming. Therefore, the rural economy in the region is largely a collection of subsistence economies and lacks market integration. Besides, the region has recently been subdivided into a number of political units, which although fulfilled the demand of self-control of the major ethnic groups in the region, might adversely affect the economic integration of the region (Ganguly, 1978, p. 40).[1]

Thirdly, in view of its strategic location, the region has received a substantial amount of central government help in terms of funds and jobs. However, centarl government investments are made more from the strategic perspective than from the long term regional development perspective. Money injected into the region by the central government raises the purchasing power of a privileged few but fails to strengthen the local income and employment generation process. This is primarily because of underdeveloped supply conditions in both farm and non-farm production activities. Consequently, a large majority of the local people are left out of the purview of the current development process.

The pattern of enclave type development has contributed to the social and political tension observed in the recent years in the North-East. The situation has been aggravated by the population growth, largely due to in migration from both inside and outside the country (Planning Commission, 1981, p. 4). The migrants, more endowed than the local people, have obtained more than proportionate share in the non-farm employment. Local people have to depend primarily on agriculture, but there is not much scope for additional employment in view of limited availability of cultivable land and lack of modernisation.

In this context, it may be noted that the future development scenario of North-East India outlined in many of the writings, put emphasis, either explicitly or implicitly, on the outward-oriented industrial growth. Accordingly priority areas identified are transport, power and human capital development. The agricultural development is taken into consideration just for improving the economic conditions of the rural people, but not as a precondition for the overall economic development of the region (See for example, Munshi, 1978, p. 11; Ganguly, 1978, p. 44). However, unless the regional market expands and becomes sizeable, modern industries, even if located in the region, cannot be competitive with the industries in other parts of India. Improvement in the transport link with the rest of India by itself will not be able to ensue a sustainable broad-based development process in the region. It will only facilitate the drain of the natural resources of the region and perpetuate the enclave type of growth.

One may think of an alternative development scenario that would be primarily inward-looking with emphasis on the utilisation of local resources and expansion of local markets. In the initial phase, priority will be given to the development of rural sector by improving agriculture and allied activities. Concomitantly efforts will be made to diversify the rural economy and strengthen rural-urban relationship.[2] Once the regional market develops, relatively large scale and export-oriented industries, in which the region would acquire comparative advantage, will be established.

The role of small and medium-sized towns in the North-East India will be discussed here in the perspective of the alternative development scenario. Section 2 will analyse how the emerging pattern of urbanisation in the North-East India is by and large related to the enclave type of development and its deficiencies. Section 3 will examine the prospects of the small and medium-sized towns in the North-East with reference to the alternative development scenario.

It will be useful at this point to address briefly the definitional issue. There is no formal definition of what is a small town and what is a medium-sized town. census of India classifies the towns into six categories and treated class II (with population 99,999-50,000) and class III (49,999-20,000) towns as medium-sized and towns with less than 20,000 population as small (Census of India, 1986, p. 351).[3] Although 20,000 population seems to be a reasonable cut off point for small towns in view of the small average size of villages in the North-East India, it has no analytical justification as such.[4] Given a natural growth rate of around two percent a year, small towns of today will cross this cut off point in future. Indeed, when we talk about small and medium-sized towns, we are concerned actually with the lower order towns in urban hierarchy. So we will discuss here about the lower order towns in general rather than using a specific cut off point. The relevant data will be reported in terms of the census size categories.

URBANISATION IN NORTH-EAST INDIA—TRENDS & PATTERNS

The level of urbanisation in the North-East India was less than half of the all-India level in 1971. During the last two decades the rate of urbanisation in the region as a whole was faster compared to the all-India rate, although the level of urbanisation was less than the all-India average in 1991 (Table 1).

Table 1: Level and Rate of Urbanisation in Eastern India

	Urbanisation Level			Urbanisation rate		Share of Urban pop.
	1971	1981	1991	1971-81	1981-91	1991
Arunachal	3.70	6.56	12.21	77.31	100.97	2.41
Assam	8.82	9.88	11.08	12.07	12.35	56.71
Manipur	13.19	26.42	27.52	100.33	4.16	11.61
Meghalaya	14.55	18.07	18.60	24.19	2.93	7.55
Mizoram	11.36	24.67	46.10	117.18	86.84	7.28
Nagaland	9.95	15.52	17.21	55.91	10.95	4.82
Tripura	10.43	10.99	15.30	5.32	39.21	9.62
N-E India	9.43	11.75	13.90	24.59	18.31	100.00
All India	19.91	23.44	25.72	17.29	10.20	—

Source: Census of India 1991, Paper 2 and 1991, Provisional population Totals: Rural-Urban Distribution.

'—' = not applicable

However, the rate of urbanisation was neither uniform across the states nor stable (excepting in Assam) over the decades. The highter rate of urbanisation was primarily experienced by the smaller states. For instance, during 1971-81, in both Manipur and Mizoram, rate of urbanisation was more than 100 percent, but during 1981-91, the rate for Manipur dropped to 4.16 percent only (a number of small towns were declassified), while in case of Mizoram the rate of urbanisation slowed down but it was still quite high at 86.84 percent. In contrast in Tripura, the rate of urbanisation was quite low (5.32 per cent) during 1971-81 but increased to 39.21 percent in the following decade. The unstable rate of urbanisation in the North-Eastern states indicates, perhaps, that urbanisation in this region is not linked to broad based economic progress but to administrative and other contingent factors, like political movement and forced migration.

Table 2: Average annual exponential growth rate of population

	Urban		Rural		Urban-rural growth differential	
	1971-81	1981-91	1971-81	1981-91	1971-81	1981-91
Arunachal	8.74	9.28	6.03	6.84	6.03	6.84
Assam	3.27	3.27	1.27	1.29	1.27	1.29
Manipur	9.76	2.98	1.16	2.34	8.60	0.62
Meghalaya	4.95	2.74	2.36	2.77	2.59	–0.03
Mizoram	11.71	9.57	2.37	0.07	9.34	9.64
Nagaland	8.50	5.58	3.42	4.29	5.08	1.29
Tripura	3.29	6.19	2.41	1.61	0.58	3.78
N-E India	n.a.	n.a.	n.a.	n.a.	n.a.	n.a.
All India	3.83	3.09	1.78	1.80	2.05	1.29

Source: Census of India 1991, Paper 2 of 1991.
n.a. = not available.

As mentioned earlier, the North-East India is not a homogeneous region. In terms of topography, excepting Assam and Tripura, all others states are predominantly hilly area. This has its impact on the urbanisation pattern. In the hill areas, for ecological reason, villages are small and scattered; and village people mostly depend on subsistence 'jhum' cultivation. In such a situation urban settlements will be few in number and small in size. Apart from towns on the hill, there are another category of small towns, located at the base of hills. These are essentially enlarged form of the traditional market places, where hill people trade their products with people from plains. In contrast, in Assam, particularly in the tea growing areas, the small urban settlements are developed as nodal point of transport and trade to cater the needs of the tea gardens, which are scattered over the area. Besides, agricultural surplus from the settled cultivation in the plains of Assam has contributed to the grwoth of small towns. In recent decades, with the expansion of administrative set up, a new category of small towns has emerged in hills and elsewhere also. These towns are imposed administrative centres, with some trading activities catering to the purchasing power injected through the public sector employment.

Thus, in the urban structure of the North-East, the small and medium-sized towns are predominant both in terms of number and the share of urban population (Table 3.) In 1991, 72 percent of the towns in North-East India are small towns (with less than

Table 3: Size-Distribution of Towns in North-East India, 1991

	I	II	III	IV	V	VI	Total
Arunacnal	—	—	—	5	5	—	10
Assam	4	4	20	32	15	12	87
Manipur	1	—	3	5	17	4	30
Meghalaya	1	—	2	2	2	—	7
Mizoram	1	—	2	3	5	11	22
Nagaland	—	2	2	3	2	—	9
Tripura	1	—	4	7	4	2	18
N-E India	8 (38.2)	6 (9.1)	33 (23.1)	52 (17.3)	50 (9.2)	29 (3.1)	183 (100)
All India*	300 (64.9)	345 (11.0)	947 (13.3)	1167 (7.9)	740 (2.6)	196 (0.3)	3696 (100)

Source: Census of India 1991, Paper 2 of 1991.

* Excluding Jammu and Kashmir

Note: Figures in parenthesis indicates percentage share of total urban population.

20000 population) accounting for 29.8 percent of

urban population and 24 percent towns are medium-sized accounting 32.2 percent of urban population. If we look at the all-India (excluding Jammu and Kashmir) figures, small and medium-sized towns together accounted for 92 percent of all towns but only 35 percent of the total urban population. It appears that though in the North-East the small and medium-sized towns accounted for a larger share of urban population, such towns are relatively less in absolute number. Another disquieting feature is that the relatively small urban system is dominated by one or two large urban centres, which is largely due to the enclave type development. From the ecological point of view, further expansion of these cities are not desirable.

Another notable aspect of urbanisation in the North-East India is that, during the last three decades the small and medium-sized towns are growing steadily (excepting in Tripura), while the cities has experienced relatively slow growth, particularly during 1981-91 (Table 4). Although apparently this trend is satisfactory, we must note, firstly, that many of these towns are very small in size; the high rate of growth is due to the very low base, while absolute expansion is relatively small. Secondly, many of the small towns are new administrative centres; the initial growth impulse, largely due to the administrative jobs, is unlikely to continue in future.

The process of urbanisation in the North-East India is largely due to migration. Both rural and urban population growth rates are higher than the natural growth rate and urban growth rate exceeds the rural growth rate in most cases (Table 2). To go by Census of India migration data, in 1981, in the North-Eastern states 40 to 60 per cent of urban male population are migrants, excepting in Manipur (Table 5). Moreover, a large proportion 40 to 70 percent of urban migrants are out-of-state migrants, again Manipur being the exception. This indicates that rural-urban interaction is weak in the region.

Table 4: Growth rate of common towns in different-size classes

State	Years	Size-classes						
		I	II	III	IV	V	VI	All
Arunachal	71-81	—	—	—	—	78.64	49.30	57.98
	81-91	—	—	—	—	85.51	44.30	80.76
Assam	51-61	—	—	54.07	54.42	59.91	76.67	56.27
	61-71	45.00	37.39	56.61	26.03	46.90	49.62	46.29
	71-91							
Manipur	51-61	—	—	—	—	—	2266.07	2666.1
	61-71	—	48.21	—	—	—	—	48.21
	71-81	56.05	—	—	—	133.73	121.99	77.82
	81-91	28.09	—	38.47	41.93	44.82	20.59	33.36
Meghalaya	51-61	—	34.75	—	—	—	847.12	43.19
	61-71	—	21.01	—	113.94	- 62.19	—	25.27
	71-81	42.32	—	—	127.63	44.73	—	39.98
	81-91	27.23	—	29.55	60.28	28.47	163.77	36.36
Mizoram	51-61	—	—	—	—	105.14	—	105.14
	61-71	—	—	—	122.63			122.63
	71-81	—	—	134.70	—	186.01	—	142.85
	81-91	—	107.19	—	106.82	104.60	—	106.50
Nagaland	51-61	—	—	—	—	—	75.66	75.66
	61-71	—	—	—	—	168.28	—	168.28
	71-81	—	—	59.39	70.62	—	—	65.93
	81-91	—	—	63.71	50.72	68.83	—	60.46
Tripura	51-61	—	—	28.84	—	—	—	28.84
	61-71	—	82.70	—	27.33	29.70	—	57.64
	71-81	31.84	—	—	17.71	14.82	—	26.27
	81-91	19.25	—	24.47	15.75	23.30	28.96	19.47
All India	51-61	31.01	26.49	25.42	25.49	27.07	50.48	28.51
	61-71	36.07	33.79	33.33	31.58	33.40	35.26	34.43
	71-81	37.16	37.33	38.47	36.47	40.04	48.14	37.56
	81-91	34.49	31.60	29.57	28.41	30.02	43.88	32.81

Source: (1) Cencus of India, Occasional Paper 1 of 1986, Study on Distribution of Infrastructural Facilities in Different Regions and Levels and Trends of Urbanisation, pp. 354-356;

(2) Census of India 1991, Series 1 India, Paper 2 of 1991, Provisional Population Totals: Rural-Urban Distribution, pp. 419-425.

Notes: (*i*) All India figures for 1971-81 excludes Assam, and that for 1981-91 excludes both Assam and Jammu-Kashmir.

(*ii*) For computing 1981-91 figures an Urban Agglomeration is treated as a single entity.

'–' = nil

Table 5: Percentage distribution of birth place urban male migrants by types of movements, North-East India, 1961, 1971, 1981

		within district	inter district	inter state	from outside India	total	% of male migrant in popn.
Arunachal Pradesh	1961	—	—	—	—	—	—
	1971	13.9	1.8	60.5	23.8	100.0	84.2
	1981	16.1	5.3	63.9	14.7	100.0	60.0
Assam	1961	19.2	13.6	30.1	37.1	100.0	59.0
	1971	23.5	15.1	31.9	29.5	100.0	53.2
	1981	na	na	na	na		na
Manipur	1961	43.4	—	34.4	22.2	100.0	15.0
	1971	50.2	10.6	30.0	9.2	100.0	15.0
	1981	39.6	31.7	25.6	3.1	100.0	9.1
Meghalaya	1961	20.7	19.7	26.4	33.2	100.0	59.1
	1971	22.3	0.7	49.8	27.2	100.0	46.2
	1981	28.3	8.8	50.5	12.4	100.0	46.9
Mizoram	1961	75.0	7.6	4.4	13.0	100.0	55.8
	1971	89.1	5.6	3.6	1.7	100.0	62.7
	1981	75.8	9.3	13.3	1.6	100.0	59.4
Nagaland	1961	43.3	0.4	41.8	14.5	100.0	61.7
	1971	15.6	5.0	66.7	12.7	100.0	79.0
	1981	23.1	27.4	44.2	5.3	100.0	68.6
Tripura	1961	8.4	—	6.4	85.2	100.0	60.0
	1971	7.4	4.1	7.3	81.2	100.0	52.6
	1981	10.3	8.0	9.6	72.1	100.0	41.3
All India*	1961	26.8	31.1	28.5	13.6	100.0	43.7
	1971	26.3	33.3	29.9	10.5	100.0	37.5
	1981	27.7	36.3	28.6	7.4	100.0	34.9

Source: Census of India, 1981 (Census Monograph No. 2), Internal Migration in India, 1961-81 (An Analysis), (S.K. Sinha), 1986. n.a. = not available

* Excludes Assam.

In short, in spite of the relatively high share in the total urban population, the number of small and medium-sized towns is inadequate and their high growth rates over past three decades seems to be transient in nature. This points to some of the basic deficiencies of the small and medium-sized towns: Firstly, the small and medium sized towns do not have strong and diversified economic base. Secondly, the have relatively weak linkages, both physical and economic linkages, with the rural sector.

ECONOMIC BASE OF TOWNS IN THE NORTH-EAST INDIA

To examine the economic base of towns in the North-Eastern India, we look at the functional classification of towns and urban agglomerations in 1991. On the basis of the proportion of workers engaged in nine industrial categories, Census of India 1991 has classified towns into five function groups (Census of India 1991, Occasional Paper No. 3 of 1994):

1. Primary (comprising industrial categories I-IV),
2. Industry (V & VI),
3. Trade (VII),
4. Transport (VIII) and
5. Services (IX.

The leading function of a town is the fuction having the largest proportion of workers. Moreover, in terms of the degree of diversification of function, towns are classified into three groups: mono-functional (if the leading function accounts for more than forty percent), bi-functional (if 60 percent of more workers are in two of the five functions) and multi-functional (if 60 percent or more workers are found in three functions).

Table 6 shows the number of 'service' towns (towns with service as the leading function) for each state in the North-East India and the share of the service towns in urban population. It can be observed that the urbanisation process in the North-East India is predominantly based on the 'service' towns. It may be noted, here, that the service activities largely consist of government financed services, *e.g.*, public

Table 6: Number and population of UAs/Towns having services as the predominant/ leading function according Mono, Bi and Multi-functional categories in the North-East India, 1991.

States		All		Mono-func.		Bi-func.		Multi-func.	
		No.	% Pop*	No.	% Pop	No.	% Pop	No.	% Pop
Arunachal	(10)	9	92.8	9	100.0	0	0.0	0	0.0
Assam	(87)	28	59.5	6	5.5	14	81.7	8	12.8
Manipur	(30)	2	41.3	1	97.1	0	0.0	1	2.7
Mighalaya	(7)	6	96.4	3	91.2	2	6.4	1	2.4
Mizoram	(22)	2	53.1	2	100.0	0	0.0	0	0.0
Nagaland	(9)	9	100.0	8	72.5	1	27.4	0	0.0
Tripura	(18)	16	89.9	11	72.9	3	16.3	2	10.8
N-E India	(183)	72	**	40	**	20	**	12	**
All India	(3697)	736	26.7	250	22.2	180	42.9	306	34.6

Source: Census of India 1991, Occasional Paper No. 3 of 1994, Functional Classification of Urban Agglomerations/Towns of India 1991, p. 56.

Note: Figures in brackets show the total number of Urban Agglomeration/town.

* Percentage of population with respect to the total urban population.

** Figures not reported, needs detail estimation.

administration-including defence, education and health services. Besides, many of these service towns are mono-functional. In Manipur and Mizoram, although the importance of service towns in urban population is relatively low (41 and 53 per cent respectively), the non-service towns are predominantly agricultural towns. In Manipur, for as many as 26 towns (accounting for 55 per cent of urban population) primary sector is the predominant function, while in Mizoram for 20 towns (accounting for about 47 percent of urban population). Only in Assam, the towns have some sort of a diversified economic base: 35 towns are trading towns accounting for about 25 per cent of urban population and another 12 towns are industry-oriented (having 6.44 percent share of urban population).

To relate the functional character with the size-class of towns, most of the lower order towns (below 50,000 population) in the North-East states, of course, excepting Assam, are 'service' towns. In Assam, there are 79 lower-order towns in 1991, of which 22 are 'service' towns but they are bi-functional or multi-functional in nature, with trade and commerce being the next important function. Another 33 are trading towns and two are 'transport and communication' oriented towns. All 12 'industrial' towns are lower order towns.

What is more significant is that the functional classification of the towns are not changing much over the decades. In Assam, out of 54 towns in 1961, functional classification changed for 18 during 1961-71 and for only 8 during 1971-91. In Meghalaya, Mizoram and Tripura there was no change at all during 1961-91 (Appendix 1).[5]

SMALL AND MEDIUM-SIZED TOWNS AND RURAL-URBAN RELATIONSHIP

Not only the economic base of the small and medium-sized towns is not diversified but their linkages with the villages are relatively weak. This is partly due to the hilly terrain and small and scattered villages, but more important is the fact that the average road density (per sq. km area) in the North-East India is lower than the all-India average. The large majority of villages are not only away from the towns, but also not connected by surfaced roads. From Table 7 it may be seen that a very high percentage of villages are having population less than 500. Most of them are situated more than 20 km away from a town and not accessible by any all-weather surfaced road.

The situation can be accounted for, at least in

Table 7: Percentage of inhabited villages for selected population sizes and distance ranges from the nearest town, 1981

State	Percentage of villages inhabited with persons		% of inhabited villages with distance from nearest town		Inhabited villages with pucca road connection (percentage)
	200	< 500	< 500	> 20 km	> 50 km
Arunachal	80.79	94.75	96.10	91.59	3.73
Assam	25.27	55.62	50.90	15.69	19.55
Manipur	50.10	74.53	59.65	35.37	13.30
Meghalaya	69.63	93.50	91.30	57.00	7.29
Minoram	n.a.	n.a.	n.a.	n.a.	n.a.
Nagaland	34.79	68.65	88.85	71.77	9.17
Tripura	63.33	83.79	72.08	36.20	8.76
All India	n.a.	n.a.	n.a.	n.a.	25.13

Source: Census of India, Occasional Paper 1 of 1986, Study on Distribution of Infrastructural Facilities in Different Regions and Levels and Trends of Urbanisation.

n.a. = not available

part, by to the fact that the existing road network (National and State Highways) are laid primarily to serve the interest of defence rather than regional development. The surfaced roads are away from the large rural settlements, which are presumably in agriculturally potential areas (as can be seen from the maps and data provided with the Census village directory). So the small and medium-sized towns, which has been established as administrative centres given the existing road network, are away from the large villages. It is quite likely that many of the existing small service towns would not fit as ideal central places of a 'generative' rural-urban relationship.

As observed earlier, in the North East India, the small and medium-sized towns are relatively less in number and town density per square kilometer area is realtively low compared to all-India averages. But in view of the terrain conditions and consequent difficulties in realising the economies of scale, the region should have a greater number of lower order towns. Further, there are many pockets, including some parts of Assam, where few towns exist. In these areas paucity of small towns and subsistence agriculture are complementary to each other.

The physical access to a town is only a necessary but not sufficient condition for the formation of rural-urban linkages. Links are forged between the two sectors through trade, input-output links, flow of funds and flow of information. The data on the structure of work force show that in the North-Eastern states proportions of workers engaged in trade and manufacturing are much less than that at the all-India level (Table 8). Further, the proportion of workers engaged in trade in less in rural areas

Table 8: The Structure of Workforce in North-East India, 1991

(percentage)

State	Agri-culture	Mining	Manufac-turing	Cons truction	Trade	Trans-port	Ser-vices
Arunachal	67.26	0.18	2.68	5.98	3.31	1.13	19.47
Assam	73.50	0.49	3.99	1.57	6.84	2.50	11.11
Manipur	69.97	0.03	8.11	1.55	3.83	1.21	15.30
Meghalaya	74.21	0.60	2.15	1.59	5.26	1.45	14.75
Mizoram	65.77	0.22	2.61	2.47	5.19	1.14	22.61
Nagaland	75.20	0.06	1.71	1.77	3.19	0.89	17.19
Tripura	63.79	0.29	4.94	1.47	7.68	2.77	19.06
N-E India	72.19	0.41	4.02	1.76	6.23	2.19	13.19
All India	66.92	0.61	10.03	1.94	7.45	2.80	10.25

Source: Compiled from Census of India 1991, Primary Census Abstract (Data provided in floppies).

compared to urban areas indicating, perhaps, a weak trading network between the rural and urban sectors (Table 9). This is an outcome of various interacting factors, like absence of physical infrastructure, paucity of agricultural surplus, lack of diversification of the rural economy and also the motivational deficiency among the native people.

Table 9: The Structure of urban workforce in North-East India, 1991

(percentages)

State	Agri-culture	Mining	Manufac-turing	Cons truction	Trade	Trans-port	Ser-vices
Arunachal	8.85	0.00	5.64	13.18	12.02	3.94	56.36
Assam	8.72	1.06	13.75	5.66	28.61	11.50	30.69
Manipur	43.02	0.07	13.99	3.27	10.79	2.67	26.19
Meghalaya	8.58	0.68	7.98	5.73	19.15	6.14	51.73
Mizoram	40.69	0.51	5.35	3.97	10.87	2.45	54.94
Nagaland	14.30	0.26	4.75	5.54	15.97	4.25	54.94
Tripura	10.15	1.08	9.22	3.86	20.19	8.10	47.39
N-E India	15.80	0.80	11.50	5.31	22.45	8.42	35.73
All India	13.34	1.12	25.07	5.07	21.99	8.28	25.12

Source: Same as in Table 8.

THE PROSPECT OF SMALL AND MEDIUM-SIZED TOWNS AND THE NEED FOR RURAL-URBAN INTEGRATION

Urbanisation level in the North-East India is low but the rate of urbanisation is high. Therefore, it is expected that in the coming decades a good number of small and medium-sized towns will emerge. Besides, in the hill areas, topography warrants that the small and medium-sized towns rather than the large cities should be the vehicle of urbanisation. More importantly, the small towns growth is complementary to the inward-looking development, which, as discussed earlier, is the only sustainable process of development in the North-East India at this stage. The prospect and potentiality of small town development should be considered in light of this alternative scenario of development and the concomitant need for transforming the rural economy through a process of integration between the rural and urban sector.

Under the inward-looking development scenario, the broad priority areas are almost similar as under the outward-looking scenario, namely, transport, power, industry, agriculture, and human capital development. But the difference will be in detail, in the focus, in the sequencing of priorities over time and space. Thus, in the choice of transport links, preference should be given not so much for inter-regional transport links, as for intra-regional transport links, linking the villages with the small towns by all-weather surfaced road. For efficient utilisation of scarce resources, priority should be given to those small towns which have maximum potentiality for rural-urban linkages, for instance towns at hill-foot, towns with large and resourceful hinterland. Hopefully, several such towns could be identified from the existing service towns. Their links with the rural hinterland may be strengthened not only through construction of link roads, but also by the way of provision of other facilities and services, including health, education, information and technical services at the small and medium-sized towns.

Concomitantly, the surrounding rural economy has to be developed and diversified, by extension of modern agricultural and allied practices, *e.g.*, the sericulture, horticulture etc. To attain this goal, emphasis should be given on the provision of related infrastructural services.

The composition of production activities in the urban area is an important determinant of the rural-urban linkage and diversification of the rural economy. At the initial stage, the urban production should have link with the demand from local agriculture and allied activities and rural households, and on supply side with locally available resources. Not only this will help in developing input-output linkages and income generation at the local level, but also expose a large number of people to relatively advanced technology and practices.

Last but not least in importance is the role of

rural-urban integration in changing socio-cultural set-up and human capital development. The processes are slow, particularly so in the North-East because of ethnic heterogeneity, and interacting. The agricultural development and rural-urban integration ensures that the process will embrace the majority of population.

However, it will not be easy to move toward the alternative development scenario as it would mean not merely changes in the infrastructural set-up and the location matrix of urban system, but also a different social equation emerging in the process of rural-urban integration. The rural people, including various ethnic groups, will demand for an increasing share of urban jobs and facilities. There will be a conflict of interest between the cities on the one hand and the small and medium-sized towns and rural areas on the other. Greater share of resources for agriculture and smaller towns means less for the cities. As the interest of the existing privileged groups are bound to be affected at least in the short run, they, being mostly city based and more organised compared to rural people, would try to undermine the required change in the policy direction. Of course, in the absence of broad-based sustainable expansion of the regional economy, in the long-run the conflicts and tensions between various interest groups would increase rather than decrease.

To conclude, in the North-East India, the need for an urban system supporting a broad-based development process will be furfilled provided small and medium-sized towns are integrated with the rural economy, facilitating integration of agriculture and non-farm activities at local level. There is scope for pursuing an active policy to achieve the goal. The various problems of small towns, *e.g.*, availability and improvement of civic amenities, financing of local urban bodies should be addressed from this overall perspective.

NOTES

1. Of course, the North-Eastern Regional Council has been established to facilitate the physical and economic integration of the region, but one cannot be very sure about its effectiveness (See, Dass, 1985; Agarwal, 1985).

2. See Mathew (1981) for studies indicating the feasibility of rural diversification.

3. Since towns with one lakh or more population is treated as city, it would be at least consistent with the convention if we set 99,9999 as the upper limit the population range for the small and medium-sized towns. However, under the Eighth Five Year Plan, the coverage of the Integrated Development of Small and Medium Town scheme has been extended to towns with less than three lakh population (Planning Commission, 1992).

4. Of course, accepting 20,000 as the cut off mark saves a lot of computation as we can use data made available by Census of India in six size-classification of towns.

5. The functional classification used in Appendix 1 is different from what is used in Table 5. Functional classification used in Appendix 1 is based on the proportion of workers in the non-agricultural workers only. For the methodology of this type of classification see Mitra (1981).

REFERENCES

Agarwal, A.K., 1985, "North-East Region: NEC through Economic Perspective", in K. Alam (1985), pp. 242-251.

Alam, K., ed., 1985, Planning in North-East India, New Delhi.

Census of India, 1986, Occasional Paper 1 of 1986, Study on Distribution of Infrastructural Facilities in Different Regions and Levels and Trends of Urbanisation.

Census of India 1991, 1994, Occasional Paper No. 3 of 1994, Functional Classification of Urban Agglomerations/Towns of

India 1991.

Dass, S.K., 1985, "Regional Planning in North-East India: The Role of NEC", in K. Alam (1985), pp. 223-231.

Datta Ray. B. (ed.), 1978. Social and Economic Profile of North-East India, New Delhi.

Ganguly, J.B., 1978, "Prespects for Integrated Development of the North-Eastern Region", in B. Datta Ray (1978), pp. 39-50.

Mathew, T., (ed.), 1981, North-Eastern Hill Regions of India-Problems and Prospects of Development, New Delhi.

Mitra, A. et. al., 1981, Shifts in the Functions of Cities and Towns in India, 1961-71, New Delhi.

Munshi, S., A. Guha and S.K. Chanbe, 1978, "Regionalization and integrated economic development in North-East India", in B. Datta Ray (1978), pp. 1-38.

Planning Commission (Government of India), 1981, Report on development of North-Eastern Region. (National Committee on the Development of Backward Areas).

Planning Commission (Government of India), 1992, Eighth Five Year Plan 1992-97, Vol. 2. Delhi.

APPENDIX

Appendix 1: Change in the functional classification of selected North-East India Towns, 1961 to 1991.

State	Town	Sc71	MFT61	MFT71	MFT91	FST61	FST71	FST91	M61	T61	S61	M71	T71	S71	M91	T91	S91
Assam																	
	Gauhati	I	S	M	T	SS	MMf	TTg	37	18	45	40	30	30	21	41	38
	Silcher	II	T	T	T	TTg	TTg	TTg	20	42	38	19	45	36	20	45	35
	Dibrugarh	II	T	T	T	TTg	TTg	TTg	20	42	38	20	51	29	22	46	32
	Nowgong	II	S	T	T	SS	TTg	TTs	‘20	37	43	22	46	32	28	45	28
	Tinsukia	II	T	T	T	TTg	TTg	TTg	25	39	36	25	39	36	27	51	22
	N. Lakimpur	III	S	T	T	SS	TTg	TTg	23	33	44	21	46	33	23	43	33
	Jorhat	III	S	T	T	SS	TTg	TTg	19	37	44	16	51	33	18	51	31
	Pandu	III	T	T	*	TTg	TTg		8	73	19	16	79	15			
	Hojai	III	T	T	T	TTg	TTg	TTg	26	43	31	18	55	27	20	56	23
	Dhubri	III	S	T	T	SS	TTg	TTg	23	37	40	29	42	29	29	40	31
	Sibsagar	III	S	M	M	SS	MMg	MMg	32	23	45	43	31	26	41	34	25
	Karimganj	III	T	T	T	TTg	TTg	TTg	15	43	42	20	45	35	19	42	39
	Lumding	III	T	T	T	TTg	TTg	TTg	8	83	19	5	80	15	18	58	23
	Barpeta	III	M	T	T	MA	TTg	TTg	51	28	21	23	49	28	23	40	36
	Tejpur	III	S	S	T	SS	SS‘	TTg	24	30	46	24	37	39	24	41	35
	Kharputia	IV	T	T	T	TTg	TTg	TTg	19	57	24	22	64	14	21	64	16
	Mariani	IV	T	T	T	TTg	TTg	TTg	21	62	17	26	59	15	27	59	15
	Dhing	IV	T	T	T	TTg	TTg	TTg	17	50	33	25	49	26	26	43	31
	Digboi	IV	M	T	M	MMf	TTg	MMf	43	23	34	35	45	20	40	39	21
	Kokrajhar	IV	S	T	T	SS	TTg	TTg	29	31	40	26	39	35	27	34	38
	Radhakish Orepure	IV	S	S	*	SS	SS		30	28	42	15	36	49			

Town	Sc71	MFT61	MFT71	MFT91	FST61	FST71	FST91	M61	T61	S61	M71	T71	S7	1M9	1T91	S91
Doom Dooma	IV	T	T	T	TTg	TTg	TTg	31	40	29	28	50	22	22	56	22
Barpeta Rd	IV	T	T	T	TTg	TTg	TTg	31	45	24	25	53	22	25	56	19
Gauripur	IV	T	T	T	TTg	TTg	TTg	20	45	35	35	38	27	29	40	30
Kailasahar	IV	S	S	S	SS	SS	SS	24	23	53	10	30	60	8	28	64
Golaghat	IV	S	T	T	SS	TTg	TTg	23	31	46	21	43	36	22	46	32
Mankachar	IV	T	T	T	TTg	TTg	TTg	17	49	34	31	50	19	26	50	24
Hailakandi	IV	S	S	S	SS	SS	SS	23	33	44	24	37	39	20	38	42
Bongaigaon	IV	T	T	T	TTg	TTg	TTg	29	48	23	25	58	17	18	65	18
Nalbari	IV	S	T	T	SS	TTg	TTg	33	31	36	23	47	30	24	42	34
Mangaldai	IV	S	S	S	SS	SS	SS	28	26	46	27	36	37	24	37	39
Goalpara	IV	S	T	S	SS	TTg	SS	18	32	50	23	44	33	26	36	39
Bilasipara	IV	T	T	T	TTg	TTg	TTg	31	43	21	36	48	16	34	46	20
Digboi OT	IV	M	M	M	MMf	MMf	MMf	75	6	19	65	16	19	58	14	28
Naharkatia	IV	M	T	T	MMg	TTg	TTg	43	31	24	36	45	19	34	47	19
Dhekiajuli	IV	T	T	T	TTg	TTg	TTg	13	49	38	22	54	24	21	49	31
Sualkuchhi	IV	M	M	M	MA	MA	MA	78	13	9	73	13	14	72	12	16
Abhayapuri	V	T	T	S	TTg	TTg	SS	30	36	34	23	39	28	26	34	40
N-Gohati	V	M	S	S	MA	SS	SS	43	31	26	32	34	34	22	28	50
Sarthebari	V	M	M	M	MMf	MA	MA	77	11	12	48	35	17	38	34	28
Bihpuria	V	T	T	T	TTg	TTg	TTg	34	38	28	20	53	27	19	54	27
Badarpur	V	T	T	T	TTg	TTg	TTg	1	95	4	25	51	24	11	64	25
Haflong	V	S	S	S	SS	SS	SS	16	23	61	19	29	52	21	20	59
Rangia	V	S	T	S	SS	TTg	SS	18	38	44	17	55	27	13	38	49
Sapatgram	V	T	T	T	TTg	TTg	TTg	26	46	28	40	47	13	39	44	18
Tangla	V	T	T	T	TTg	TTg	TTg	27	44	29	22	60	18	19	58	22
Dergaon	V	S	S	S	SS	SS	SS	15	13	72	12	23	65	10	20	71
Kamakhya	V	S	S	*	SS	SS		22	25	53	19	40	41			
Nazira	V	M	T	M	MMf	TTg	MMf	47	23	30	31	38	31	38	32	30

State Town	Sc71	MFT61	MFT71	MFT91	FST61	FST71	FST91	M61	T61	S61	M71	T71	S71	M91	T91	S91
Lakhipur	VI	T	T	S	TTg	TTg	SS	22	57	21	26	51	23	28	35	37
Chabua	VI	T	T	T	TTg	TTg	TTg	24	48	28	25	51	24	23	55	23
Amingaon	VI	T	T	M	TTg	TTg	MMf	31	60	9	16	65	19	37	36	28
Tihu	VI	M	T	T	MMf	TTg	TTg	43	31	26	35	43	22	19	43	38
Palasbari	VI	M	T	T	MA	TTg	TTg	50	27	23	30	49	21	30	44	26
Manipur																
Imphal	II	M	M	S	MA	MA	SS	53	21	26	40	29	31	29	25	46
Meghalaya																
Shillong	II	S	S	S	SS	SS	SS	10	19	71	17	28	55	18	29	53
Mawlai	IV	S	S	S	SS	SS	SS	23	20	57	32	31	37	18	26	56
Nongthmmai	IV	S	S	S	SS	SS	SS	8	12	80	15	16	69	13	23	64
Tura	IV	S	S	S	SS	SS	SS	15	14	71	12	21	67	17	26	57
Jowai	V	S	S	S	SS	SS	SS	28	18	54	32	22	46	12	27	61
Shillong (Cant.)	IV	S	S	S	SS	SS	SS	4	9	87	24	37	39	15	26	59
Mizoram																
Aijal	III	S	S	S	SS	SS	SS	38	16	46	21	26	53	22	24	55
Nagaland																
Kohima	III	S	S	S	SS	SS	SS	7	10	83	10	9	81	12	12	77
Dimapur	IV	S	T	T	SS	TTg	TTg	7	46	47	25	44	31	22	43	35
Mokokchung	IV	S	S	S	SS	SS	SS	21	8	71	8	10	82	17	26	57
Tripura																
Agartala	II	S	S	S	SS	SS	SS	22	30	48	12	30	58	12	29	59
Belonia	IV	S	S	S	SS	SS	SS	24	26	48	17	35	48	10	32	58
Khowai	V	S	S	S	SS	SS	SS	18	34	48	12	38	50	11	32	57

Notes: Sc 71 = Size-class in 1971
MFT 61 = Main Function type 1961
M = Manufacturing with Mining and Construction
T = Trade & Commerce & Transport & Communication
FST 61 = Functional sub-type in 1961
MA = Manufacturing-household
MMf = Manufacturing-nonhousehold
MMg = Manufacturing-mining

S = Services TTg = trading and commerce
TTt = Transport and Communication

M61 = percentage of non-agricultural workers in manufacturing, mining and construction in 1961
T61 = percentage of non-agricultural workers in trade and commerce & transport and communication in 1961
S61 = percentage of non-agricultural workers in services in 1961
* merged with other city/town

Sources: 1961 and 1971 values are from Ashok Mitra et al. (1981), Shifts in the functions of cities and towns of India, 1961-71;
1991 values are computed from 1991 census data using Mitra's method.

Chapter 2

THE ROLE OF SMALL TOWNS IN THE DEVELOPMENT PROCESS OF NORTH-EAST INDIA

N.N. Bhattacharyya

As per 1991 census about 65 per cent of India's urban population lived in class I cities having population of 100,000 and above, including 23 million cities and the remaining 35 per cent of the urban population lived in class II (50,000-99,999), class III (20,000-49,999), Class IV (10,000-19,999), class V (5,000-9,999) and class VI (below 5,000) towns. This uneven spatial distribution of urban population has resulted in highly irregular concentration among different categories of urban centres. In North-East India there were 183 urban centres, of which 87 were in Assam, 30 in Manipur, 22 in Mizoram, 18 in Tripura, 10 in Arunachal Pradesh, 9 in Nagaland and 7 in Meghalaya in the year 1991. The distribution of urban population at the state level shows greater imbalances in North East India. Although Assam has the highest number of urban settlement, Mizoram with 46.2 per cent is the most urbanized states of the region. The least urbanized part of North-East India is Assam (11 per cent). In the states of Manipur (28 per cent), Meghalaya (19 per cent), Nagaland (17 per cent), Tripura (15 per cent) and Arunachal Pradesh (12 per cent), the proportion of urban population to total population is higher than that of Assam. Thus the growth of urban centres and urban population in North East India is rather slow and insignificant. This is mainly due to its rural economy and a poor level of industrialization. The urban population of North East India stands at 4.3 million and it comes to about 14 per cent of the total population as against the country's 26 per cent. This accounts for only 2 per cent of India's urban population. The 1991 census has given one lakh plus status to eight urban centres of North East India, namely Guwahati (677,571), Shillong (222,273), Imphal (200,165), Agartala (157,636), Aizwal (154,343), Dibrugarh (123,885), Silchar (115,045) and Jorhat (111584). The city of Guwahati which achieved such status in 1961 continues to be largest city in the entire North East India. The six towns which were grouped under class II were Nagaon (93,324), Tinsukia (73,760), Dhubri (65,861), Dimapur (56,918), Tezpur (54,999) and Kohima (53,122). Nearly 47 per cent of the total urban population of the region live in these cities and major towns and the rest 53 per cent of the urban population live in 169 towns which are small in size. These small towns are not evenly distributed among the states of North East India. Assam has the highest number of such towns (79), Manipur (29), Tripura (17), Mizoram (21), Arunachal (10), Nagaland (7) and Meghalaya (6). These small towns have special significance for the entire region because they can play a greater role in the process of social and economic development and thus in securing a better quality of life.

The urban system of India has evolved during the past 100 years under the impact of colonial economic and administrative policies in a lopsided manner. Kingsley Devis and his followers shared a great concern over the rapid urban growth and massive rural urban migration in India as early as 1960 and they strongly advocated local autonomy planning and steps to bring about dispersed urban industrial development. Similarly in 1967 McGee coined the term 'pseudo urbanisation' to describe the phenomenal growth of large urban cities in south and southeast Asia on the face of mounting unemployment, lopsided occupational structure, mushrooming of squatter settlements, inadequate transport and sanitation facilities and so on. All these problems are detrimental to the civic life of the major urban centres which create a serious threat to the quality or urban life in the country.

It is mentioned that there are 169 small urban centres in North East India. These small towns have a predominantly rural economic base, and a substantial segment of its work-force being in agriculture. Agriculture is a space consuming activity and it is labour intensive. It requires fertilizers, processing plants, distribution depots and marketing facilities etc. Similarly the rural people require economic and social services. All these facilities and services cannot be provided everywhere. These may be provided in a rational manner in the small towns. It is to be noted that the small towns appear in a hierarchy because there are different grades of demands from the villages, each having different thresholds of population and ranges of goods. Such a urban hierarchy should be properly developed without gaps so that every area and everyone can get equal opportunities. These hierarchy of towns not only provide services for the increased production in the rural sector of economy, but also provide new innovations. Thus they work as catalysts of social change. Therefore, stress should be given to small towns because they are closer to rural people and hence will have a greater impact on the lower strata of the society. Besides, these small towns will be able to avoid pitfalls of inhuman environment that exist in the major towns and cities like Guwahati. Thus it can be concluded that the resource-based small towns may enliven the local economy, generate more employment opportunities for the rural people and also give a positive check on the migrants from the rural areas and small towns to the major towns and cities.

An examination of the settlement hierarchy in North East India shows that there is a discordance between 14 major urban centres and 35998 villages. There is very little generative link between urban and, rural sectors of economy in the settlement system of the region. The growth of cities and major urban centres is essentially a 'centre-down' strategy of development in India and hence this strategy has no appeal for the 'bottom-up' or development from below. But small urban centres constitute some important elements in the development process for both centre-down and bottom-up strategy which are now gaining currency everywhere. In the entie north-eastern region of India there are 169 small urban centres and most of there are potential growth centres. These small urban centres have a significant role in the face lift of the countryside especially to their surrounding rural areas. But forcible shift of activities and services from the major urban centres to the minor or small towns witout having the required resource base and infrastructural facilities should be avoided Economic viability and the future distribution of demand should be primary consideration for adopting a policy on planning for growth centres and regional development of North East India.

REFERENCES

Bhattacharyya, N.N., 1991, 'A Strategy for Rural Development in North East India', in Samanta, R.K. (ed), *Rural Development in*

North East India—Perspectives Issues and Experiences. Uppal Publishing House New Delhi. pp. 312-315.

Bhattacharyya, B., 1994 'Urban Agglomeration, Quality of Urban Life and the Issue of Urban Decentration in India', North Eastern Geographer. Guwahati, Vol. 25. No. 1 and 2, pp. 32-42.

Bhooshan, B.S., 1980 (ed.) *Towards Alternative Settlement Strategies*, Heritage Publishers, New Delhi.

Singh, S.B., 1995 (Ed.), *Emerging Frontiers of Urban Settlement Geography*, M.D. Publications Pvt. Ltd., New Delhi.

Chapter 3

TOWNS WITHIN TOWN-SYSTEM—

A CASE STUDY OF NORTH-EASTERN REGION

Surendra Singh

INTRODUCTION

There are numerous studies on different aspects of population dynamics, trends of urban growth, regional dimensions of demographic characteristics, functional hierarchies and morphology of towns of the North-Eastern part of the country (Chittaranjan 1978, Goel 1983, Gopalakrishnan 1991, Taher 1993, Borthakur 1993, Sharma 1995). Some studies are also conducted on the specific problems of urban settlement structure, internal dynamics and land use changes in the town-morphology (Mahanta 1986, Sarma 1989, Chakraborty N. 1991, Chakraborty S. 1991, Chakraborty, et. al. 1995, Singh I. 1995, Singh L. 1995). In fact, town do not grow in isolation. There require proper infrastructure and strong surroundings to grow properly. Therefore, the parameters of town growth and urban dynamics are not only concerned with the internal assemblages of the town structure but also related to the external linkages with the other towns of higher orders in its spatial as well as vertical arrangements. Thus, a strong and well-organised town-system of a region leads towards its well-balanced development and fast growth. Towns are having multidimensional characteristics with in the town-system and accelerate various developmental processes through them. Threfore, the strategies of socio-ecnomic development are expected to be prepared on the basis of optimisation of town-systems of an area through organising properly the urban space following 'growth centre approach' of development (Sen *et. al.* 1975, Bhat *et. al.* 1976, Whyte 1979, Misra & Sundram 1980). As a result, towns which are main elements of town-systems are considered as interaction points of socio-cultural activities, the market point as places of exchange of commodities, the functional nodes for the tertiarisation of rural economies because they also act as the centres of raw material processing and absorption of surplus labour available in their surroundings. Therefore, the growth, demographic composition and functional characteristics of towns are directly or indirectly dependent on the parameters which are related to the functional hierarchy and ordering of the spatial arrangement of towns.

So far as spatial organisation of towns of the North-Eastern Region is concerned, there is general observation of the planners, administrations, geographers and regional economists regarding the urban dynamics and spatial linkages of socio-economic activities of the region that the organisation of urban agglomertions over space is too weak to collapse because of inherent conflicting nature of economic as well as demographic forces. The North-Eastern Region of the country is socio-culturally rich, however, there are social conflicts and tensions because of weak interactions and, consequently, the tribal societies of the hill areas have been living in isolation since long. Nagaland is a case of complete social isolation, while the starting stage of socio-economic interaction through town-organisation can be seen in the states of Assam and Tripura (the plains of the region). Immigaration, in-flow of essential commodities and out-flow of raw and unprocessed resource materials of the area, weak foreward and backward linkages of regional economies and weak core-periphery relations of spatial interactions and space-economy are main causes of weakening the town-organisations of the region. As a result, town-system might be working only to diffuse or distribute the essential commodities trading from outside the region. Therefore, the functional structure of even lower order towns of the system which are much closer to the resource structure of the region might also be emerging on the basis of 'push forces' of spatial organisation of the economy rather then the processings of local resource base. There are, thus, many and varied aspects to be studied regarding space economy and regional development of the North-Eastern Region in light of transformation of economic space through town-system, elements and processes of space-economy of the region and the physical and functional structures of towns at different hierarchic orders. However, study of the size-growth, rank-size regularities and the emerging patterns of towns over economic landscape of the North-Eastern Region is equally important in understanding the underlying processes of socio-economic changes and role of towns in the development of regional economies of the region. These aspects of towns-systems are dealt here with the present piece of research.

URBAN GROTH AND MIGRATION

Third World Countries' population has been called 'demographic transition and even for some countries, it is called demographic revolution'. These changes have become increasingly evident in the past thirty to forty years. It is true in case of India and specially the

North-Eastern Region where repid population growth at annual average rate of 2.81% from 4.27 million to 10.26 million persons during 1901-1951 and 5.19% rate from 10.26 million to 31.55 million persons during the 40 years of the last half-century 1951-1991 have been recorded. it is the consequence of two demographic factors:

(i) *the natural growth* of population because of a large gap of 19.8% between birth rate (30.5%) and death rate (10.8%) specially in the plains of Assam during 1990-92, though this gap has been slightly reducing in the region from 21.6% to 19.8% during the last decade (1981-83 to 1990-92) (Registrar General of India 1994), and

(ii) *the immigaration* from the other parts of the country as well as outside country specially during the 1950s when decadal variations of population figures has been recorded 34.3% during 1951-61 with a reduction of upto 30.5% per 1981-91. It is interesting to note here that these figures of decadal variations of total population have always been higher than the national averages (that are 21.5% for 1951-61 and 23.8% for 1981-91).

So far as acceleration of urban processes in the North-Eastern Region is concerned, it is obvious from the urban population trends that there has been a significant increase in urban population from its negligible volume of 1901 to a big volume of 4.38 million in 1991. As a result, a record rate of decadal variation of urban population has been figured which is higher than the decadal variation of total population in almost all the states of the region during all the decades of the century (Table 1). The decades of the mid century (specially the 1950s) are of significant

Table 1. Percentage Decadal Variation of Urban Population in the N.E.R. (1901-11 to 1981-91)

(Figs., in %)

Decades	*Name of the States*							
	Arunachal Pradesh	*Assam'*	*Tripura'*	*Mani pur*	*Megha laya*	*Mizo ram*	*Nagal*	*All India*
1901-11	—	20.55	6.48	3.34	41.76	—	-21.66	0.35
1911-21	—	36.80	13.35	7.17	26.13	—	15.15	8.27
1921-31	—	27.58	23.72	7.25	54.25	—	-1.11	19.12
1931-41	—	28.30	84.69	16.21	43.93	—	27.11	31.97
1941-51	—	65.73	140.74	-97.13	53.20	—	17.62	41.43
1951-61	—	126.57	141.81	2226.07	100.78	105.14	364.41	26.41
1961-71	—	65.01	57.64	108.95	25.27	164.85	168.28	38.23
1971-81	139.63	58.79*	38.93	165.36	63.98	222.61	133.95	46.14
1981-91	167.04	39.58*	86.69	34.67	36.76	161.02	73.18	36.47

N.B. * the growth rates have been worked out on the interpolated population figures for 1981.

Sources: 1. Census of India 1991, Series-1, paper 2 of 1992, the *Final Population Tables.*

2. *Basic Statistics of North-Eastern Region-1995*, NEC publication Shillong. Table 3, p. 45.

records when the highest degree of decadal variation of urban population of more than 100% has been marked in the North-Eastern Region. During the decade 1951-61, a record decadal growth of 2,226. 07% was marked in the state of Manipur. Further, another fact regarding the acceleration of urban processes can be highlighted by comparing the figures of the population share residing in the urban areas of the region. In spite of faster growth of urban population in the North-Eastern Region of the country, the percentage share of urban population is still marked very low *i.e.*, 13.89%, nearly half of the national average, *i.e.*, 26.13% in 1991. In the state-wise distribution of this share, Mizoram ranked on first which occupies a markable share of 46.1% as recorded the most urbanised state of the region in 1991. It may be a misleading fact. It is figured highest urbanised because of misinterpretation of the census definition of urban areas and even small villages of about 2,000 population size have been declared as urban centre by the state government. Infact, it is obvious that the process of urbanisation in the North-East is being accelerated fast at its very low level of urban standards. It means there is an initial stage of urbanisation following the 'take-off' stage of its acceleration which would influence the functional as well as socio-economic structure of towns of the region. These facts of urbanisation may further be examined by analysing the growth of towns in its regional frame.

GROWTH AND POPULATION SIZE OF TOWNS

Town-growth is true reflection of intensification and diversified nature of socio-economic activities (*i.e.*, agglomeration of human activities forms a force of attraction for the growth of towns), increasing degree of spatial interactions (*i.e.*, expension of the influencing zones of towns) and continuum in spatial organisation of concentrated activities of the area (*i.e.*, core-periphery concavities). On account of these established relationships of the socio-economic parameters of town-growth over spacc, towns always follows 'principle of allometric growth*' in its towns-system. it means bigger towns of the system have higher growth rate with their increasing diversity in the socio-economic structure and strong spatial interactions and *Vice-Versa.* These regularities of towns may be tested considering the town-classes of the

* The concept of allometric growth is based on the log-linearity of the distribution of town, *e.g.*, $Y = ax^b$, which can be written as log $Y = \log a + b \log X$, where b refers to rate of change of towns w.r.t. the cnage of whole system. This is as—

$$b = (\Delta \log Y/\Delta \log X).$$

It is proportionate change. It can be rewritten as

$$b = \{(\Delta Y/Y) \div (\Delta X/X)\}.$$

North-Eastern Region of the country.

The study of town-growth can be made in two ways—(a) the changes in the number of towns over time in different town-classes, and (b) the hierarchic ordering of towns within the town system. Going through the general observations of Table-2 regarding changes occuring in various town-classes, there seems a clear cut quality in the growth and increase the number of towns in the North-Eastern Region during the last decade (1981-1991). Table 2 reveals that, on

Table 2. Number of Towns in various Town-Classes according to their Population Sizes (1981 & 1991)

States	Very large (> 100,000)		Large size (100,000-50,000)		Medium (50,000-20,000)		Small (20,000-10,000)		Very small (10,000>)		Total No. of Town	
	1981	1991	1981	1991	1981	1991	1981	1991	1981	1991	1981	1991
(A) The Plains:												
1. Assam	4	4	5	4	12	20	22	32	23	27	66	87
2. Tripura	1	1	—	—	1	4	4	7	4	6	10	18
(B) The Hills:												
3. Arunachal	—	—	—	—	—	—	—	5	9	5	9	10
4. Nagaland	—	—	—	2	2	2	2	3	3	2	7	9
5. Manipur	1	1	—	—	2	4	4	5	25	20	32	30
6. Meghalaya	1	1	—	—	1	2	1	2	4	2	7	7
7. Mizoram	—	1	1	—	—	2	1	3	4	16	6	22
Total	7	8	6	6	18	34	34	57	72	78	138	183

Sources: 1. Census of India, 1981.

2. Provisional Population Tables, paper 2 of 1991, census of India 1991.

one hand, a fast increase has been recorded in the medium, small and very small size towns (below 50,000 population size); there is a record increase of 16 towns (from 18 to 34) in the middle size class (50-20 thousand population size), 23 towns (from 34 to 57) in the small size class (20-10 thousand population) and 6 towns at very small size class (of below 10 thousand of population) in the North-Eastern Region of the country during the 1980s. While on the other hand, a stationary condition of change in the number of towns has been observed in the large and very large size classes (above 50 thousand population) in entire region during the same period, though there may be a significant record growth of population of the individual towns in the region. The state-wise distribution of large size towns (100,000-50,000 population) shows interesting features of distribution that the plains of the Bramputra valley and the Mizoram Hills have lost one large size town in each state during 1980s, while the state of Nagaland has transformed two medium size towns to larger ones. Thus, the larger order towns are maintaining their strength, however, there are record changes in their distributional patterns and placements. Moreover, the individual position of towns within the town-system can be examined by placing the strength of town according to their ranks. The 'rank-size regularities' of town distribution would explain the tendency of proportionate (*i.e.*, allometric) growth. Putting towns according to their ranks for the states of North-Eastern Region, it can be concluded that, though there is higher degree of spatial interaction in the well-matured higher order town-systems emerging in the plains of Assam and Tripura on account of direct impact of migration influx from rural to urban and from the other parts of the country, however, one can find 'primacy' in the town distribution in these areas. The similar features of distribution are also emerging in the hill areas of Meghalaya, Manipur and Mizoram where the state capitals are growing faster than the other towns of lower-orders (Fig. 1). The middle size class towns are stagnant with insignificant growth in these states. As a result, rank-size curves are more concave for these states. But, the cases of Arunachal Pradesh and Nagaland are different with less concavity in their

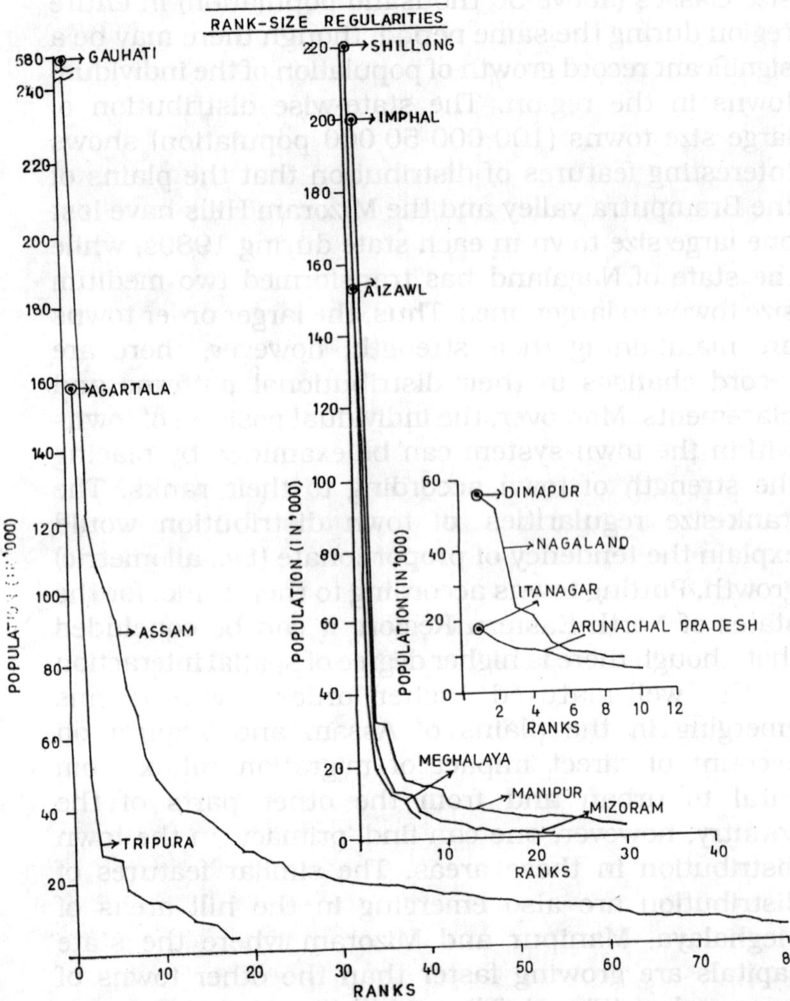

RANK-SIZE REGULARITIES
GAUHATI
SHILLONG
IMPHAL
AIZAWL
AGARTALA
DIMAPUR
NAGALAND
ITANAGAR
ARUNACHAL PRADESH
ASSAM
MEGHALAYA
MANIPUR
MIZORAM
TRIPURA
POPULATION (IN '000)
RANKS

town distribution. It may be because of the initial stage of their socio-economic development and town-growth which minimises the gaps between the sizes of higher and lower order towns. In general, it can be said that a significant gap between higher and lower order towns within the town-system has been existing due to some irregularities in the town-growth. This gap in the distribution increases the degree of primacy by weakening the smooth functioning of town systems. Therefore, there is a fundamental fallacy in the distribution and growth of the towns of the North-Eastern Region. It can be explained implicitly by analysing the spatial arrangements of town systems.

SPATIAL ORGANISATION OF TOWNS

The spatial arrangement of towns at different orders as shown by Table 3 is an emergence of *five* higher order town-systems within which the groups of three to seven middle order towns are categorically emerging. Each middle order town is linked with a group of nearly eight lowest order towns of the organisation (Table-3). Further more, this arrangement of towns in the region can be studied by taking into account the main functional parameters of towns as the elements of spatial system. For instance, if the towns are considered as the *nodes* of areal forces because they are working with integrating the backward and foreward linkages of production processes and the transport routes are recognised as *channels* of radiating the spread effects of developmental activities in the spatial organisation of towns, then the developmental processes in the region are operated through the combination of geographical forces of the town surroundings, which are bound up tightly through the central place constraints, form a functional hierarchy. If these elements of the spatial organisation are working loosely in the areas of

Table 3: Number of Towns according to Town Orders (1991)

Name of Higher/Middle order towns.	*No. of lower order towns within*
I. Bogaigaon Town System (Higher order):	
1. Kokrajhar (Middle order)	5
2. Dhubri (Middle order)	4
3. Golpara (Middle order)	6
4. Bogaigaon (Middle order)	8
II. Guwahati Town System (Higher order)	
1. Rangia (Middle order)	8
2. Tejpur (Middle order)	5
3. Nogaon (Middle order)	5
4. Dimapur (Middle order)	8
5. Lumding (Middle order)	5
6. Shillong (Middle order)	4
7. Guwahati (Middle order)	6
III. Dibrugarh Town System (Higher order):	
1. Tinsukhia (Middle order)	12
2. Lakhimpur (Middle order)	5
3. Jorhat (Middle order)	9
4. Dibrugarh (Middle order)	4
IV. Silchar Town System (Higher order):	
1. Agartala (Middle order)	18
2. Aizawal (Middle order)	12
3. Lunglai (Middle order)	9
4. Silchar (Middle order)	7
V. Imphal Town System (Higher order):	
1. Imphal (Middle order)	5
2. Thaubal (Middle order)	18
3. Churachandpur (Middle order)	7

N.B.: 13 towns have not been included in this system of classification.

functional attraction, there is a need to strengthen them optimally through accelerating the decision making processes for geo-space development. There are following salient features of spatial organisation of towns emerging in the North-Eastern Region of the country (see Fig. 2)

1. SPACING AND SPATIAL ARRANGEMENTS OF TOWNS

(a) The town-organisations of the lower

TOWN-SYSTEMS

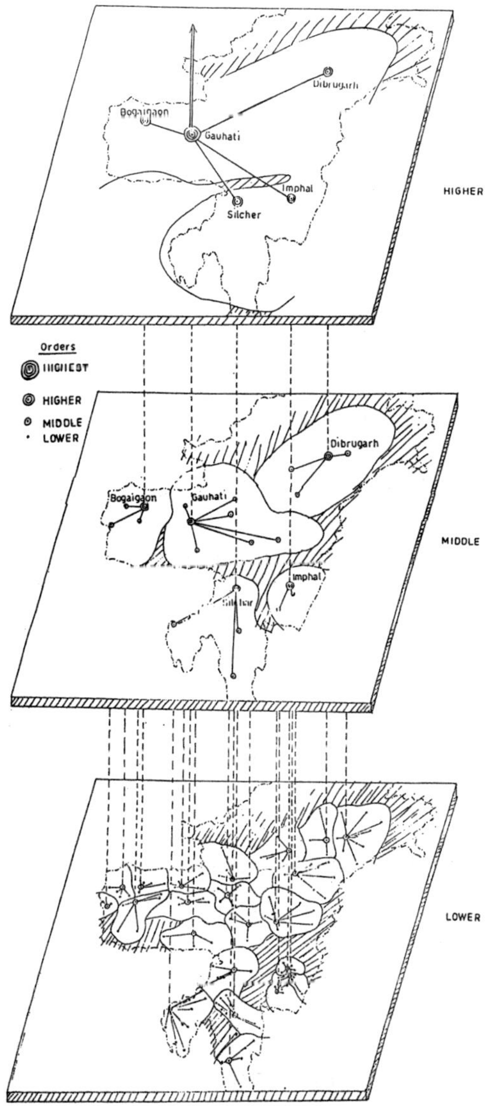

Brahamputra valley of the Assam state and the Agartala plains of Tripura follow weak ordering and very less spacing among various orders because of the fast growth of higher order towns and the effects of immigration specially during partition.

(b) Tura and Shillong town ordanisations of Meghalaya, Aizwal of Mizoram, Itanagar and Pasighat organisations, emerging in Arunachal pradesh which have enough space because of their growth in the hill and Mountainous areas of the North-East, are weak in their nodality character and inter-connectivity.

(c) organisations based on Jorhat, Dimapur and Tezpur towns have been growing fast because of their rich resource background of two type of ecological niches of the middle Brahamputra plains and surrounding hill areas of western Arunachal pradesh and Naga hills.

(d) The Dibrugarh and Tinsukia town-organisations of upper Brahamputra valley are having complex functional structure of oil-based industrial development.

(e) The Guwahati based town-organisation is well-matured because of the biggest trade town of the region.

(f) the emergence of Silchar-based organisation in based in the carridor-growth of smaller towns between two types of hill geo-ecology.

2. FUNCTIONAL HIERARCHY AND TOWN ORDERING

In fact, internal functional dynamism of the towns, espeically of hill areas of the region, does not have much influence on the regional economies because of diffused and dependent development of urban centres. However, the external functional linkages of town growth which lead to the functional hierarcy and spatial ordering, are noticeable in this connection (Chakraborty et. al. 1994).

The validity of functional hierarchy and its weaknesses can be highlighted by putting the towns and delineating regional boundaries of spatial organisation with considering the interaction patterns of various functions of the region and connectivity of the towns especially at lower order where town growth is recorded remarkable. On account of non-availability of data for such parameters of towns, the studies on functional linkages are not available. However, nearest-neighbour conditions of spatial interactions can be imposed for establishing functional hierarchy and town-ordering. Adopting shortest distance criteria for for the demarcation of trade zones of towns, it is found that the town-organisation of the North-Eastern Region follows 'administrative principle' (*i.e.*, k = 7), rather than 'Market or Transport Principle' with the distortion of shape and size of trade areas. It may be because of the impact of historical and cultural backgrounds of towns which are emerging on the rich resource-space intensive agricultural landscape in the plains, and tribal subsistence agricultural landscape of the hills and mountains.

3. OCCUPATIONAL DIFFERENTIATIONS

In fact, there are significant differentiations in the occupational structure of towns at various orders. The following conclusions can be drawn from the Table 4 which shows variations of demographic and occupational parameters of the towns.

(a) The average size of population of lower order towns is nearly 8.2 thousand which is approximately ten times lesser than the size of middle order towns which have more than one lakh average size of population, while the highest order town (*i.e.*, Guwahati

Urban Agglomeration one in number) is more than five times larger than the middle order towns having a population size of 5.77 lakhs in 1991.

(b) The average annual growth rate of these towns is higher at higher order and *Vice Versa.* Say for example, the average annual growth is recorded 2.7% of lower order towns, 3.5% of higher order towns and 9.4% of the highest order town, while the sex ratio is inversely related to the size as well as growth of the towns. The sex ratio is low (783 female per 1000 males) at the highest order town in 1991, while it is recorded medium (834 female per 1000 male) at middle order and high (883 female per 1000 male) at lower order towns. The higher growth rate of population with low sex ratio at higher order towns is a clear indication of male-dominated immigration of the rural population towards these towns.

(c) Dependency ratio is recorded highest in the higher order towns (2.36). It means the share of children and aged persons are proportinately higher in these towns which destroy the shape of age-sex pyramids.

(d) The functions which are being performed in the lower order towns are agriculturally dominated and more than one-fifth share of total working force is still engaged in primary activities (agriculture and allied services) while this proportion is very low at higher order towns (Table 4). Further, it is interesting to note that the tertiary sactor (trade, transport and services) in dominating at all the town-orders and has strong increasing percentage share of working force from lower order (60.2%) to the higher order (78.7%) and then to the highest order (83.8%). But the manufacturing sector is very weak in all town-systems. Within manufacturing sector, household and cottage industries are having significant places at lower order towns and, consequently, ratio of the work force employed in household industries with other than household industries is higher (.1532) aqt lower order towns. This ratio has been recorded highest (1.60) on a newly emerged town (namely Lamlai) of Churachandpur town-system emerging in the Manipur valley of agriculturally dominated economic landscape.

CONCLUSIONS

Of course, the study of town-system is very much useful for preparing an integrated-device for the developmental stategies of an area/region. In fact, lower order towns of the town-system, which are emerging over economic space with different socio-economic characteristics at the threshold of established town-systems throughout the country, act as 'growth-points' through which the new chennals for the transmission of developmental impulses are possible (Misra 1973). Likewise, lower order towns of the town-system existing in the North-Eastern Region (that may be called newly emerging growth points of the region) are also different in their demographic as well as socio-economic characteristics. An obvious duality can be observed in the structural features of town-system existing in the North-East. Higher order towns have peculiar characteristics of fast growing population with male dominated immigrants coming in from lower order towns and near surroundings of rural areas. The proportion of dependents (*i.e.*, children and too aged persons) is higher with strong tertiary sectors of these towns. On the other hand, lower-order growing towns of the North-East (below 10,000 population) are characterised with the dominance of rural immigrants of active female agricultural labour force (because of persistance of low dependency ratio with low sex ratio in most of the towns of this order). It can be observed as direct shift of occupational structure from primary activities to service sectors. Industrial sector is weak and insignificant. As a result, jobs which are being generated on those towns are main attraction for rural migrants. It plays a dominant role in socio-economic transformation of these towns.

ACKNOWLEDGEMENTS

The author gratefully acknowledges the help rendered by the Research Scholars of the Department of Geography of our University specially Mr. Tarun Kumar for compilation of data and Mr. L. Sunil Singh for preparation of maps and diagrams used in this article.

REFERENCES

Bhat, L.S. et. al. (1976): *Micro-Level Planning, K.B. Publication*, New Delhi.

Borthakur, Munjula (1993): *The Periodic Market System*, unpublished Ph.D. these, Department of Geography, NEHU, Shillong.

Chacraborty, N. (1991): *Rural-Urban Linkages and Interactions*, Unpublished M.Phil Dissertation, Deptt. of Geography, NEHU, Shillong.

Chakraborty, N. et. al. (1994): peripheral Urban Development-An Analytical Model with special reference to Shillong, in J.B. Ganguly (ed): *Urbanisation and Development in North-East India.* Deep & Deep Publications, New Delhi, pp. 224-236.

Chakraborty, S. (1991): *Impct of Geomorphology on the Urban landuse*, Unpublished M. Phil Dessertation Deptt. of Geography, NEHU, Shillong.

Chittaranjan, P. (1978): *Urbanisation in North-East India,*Unpublished M. Phil Dissertation, Deptt. of Geography, NEHU, Shillong.

Goel, N.P. (1983): Demographic Structure of North-East India, Unpublished Ph.D. thesis, Deptt. of Geography NEHU, Shillong.

Gopalakrishnan, R. (1991): *The North-East India-Land, Economy and People*, Har-Anand Publications, New Delhi.

Misra, R.P. (1973): Growth Foci as New Channels for the Transmission of Development Impulses in space, in Mathur.

O.P. & R.P. Misra (ed.) *Planning for the Backward Areas-Some Contributions*, (Dev. Studies No. 9) Inst. of Dev. Studies, Uni. of Mysore, pp. 30-57.

Misra, R.P. & K.V. Sundram (1980): *Multi-Level Planning and Integrated Rural Development in India*, Heritage Publishers, New Delhi.

Registrar General of India (1994): *Sample Registration Bulletin* Vol. XXVIII (No. 1 & 2).

Sarma, S. (1989): *Growth Problems of Gauhati and its Regional Impact*, Unpublished Ph.D. these, Deptt. of Geography, NEHU, Shillong.

Sharma, H.N. (1995): Social Profile of North-East India, in A. Ahmad (ed): *Social Structure and Regional Development*, Rawat publications, Jaipur, pp. 219-238.

Singh, A. Lalit (1995): The Periodic Markets as Rural Service Cenres *Hill Geographer*, Vol. XI (No. 1 & 2) pp. 46-61.

Singh, S. Ibochaoba (1995): Development Patterns and Potentials of A Rural Service Centre, *Hill Geographer*, Vol. XI (No. 1 & 2), pp. 62-70.

Sen, Lalit K. *et. al.* (1975): *Growth Centres in Raichur*, National Institute of Rural Development, Hyderabad.

Taher, M. (1993): *Social Geography-Concepts and Theories*, North-Eastern India Geographical Society, Guwahati.

Whyte, R.O. (1979): *The Spatial Geography of Rural Economics*, Oxford University Press.

Table 4: Occupational Structure of Different Town-Orders (1991)

Name of the Order/ Town		Total Population (1991)	M/F Ratio (F per 1000 M)	20 years Growth rate (%) (1971-91)	% of main workers Total Population	Dependency Ratio	% of share of workers in				Household	
							Agricultural Activities (1 + II)	Mining Plantation Fishing (III + IV)	Manufacturing (Va + Vb)	Trade Transport (VI + VII VIII)	Other Services (IX)	Other then HH (HH/O)
Highest Order:												
Guwahati (U.A)		5,77,591	783	188.25	33.60	2.00	2.39	1.90	11.80	46.52	37.30	.05822
Higher Order:												
Bogaigaon		48,907	834	96.02	29.58	2.34	0.93	0.79	12.45	68.15	17.67	.0656
Tinsukhia		73,760	742	34.33	34.21	1.90	3.40	1.43	26.81	54.13	13.36	.0473
Silcher		1,12,045	919	118.73	28.98	2.44	1.18	2.71	9.97	51.37	34.75	.0681
Imphal (MC)		1,98,535	949	56.18	26.74	2.78	3.10	3.77	17.30	31.06	44.65	.6047
		1,08,313	834	69.30	30.02	2.36	2.15	2.51	16.63	51.18	27.61	.1964
Middle Order Representative:												
Bogaigaon Town-Order Towns												
Kokrajhar	Gosaigaon	11,316	842	—	30.40	2.28	13.40	4.15	7.70	43.98	30.75	.0601
Dhubri	Golakganj	6,220	916	—	2858	2.46	10.69	1.12	18.22	49.83	20.24	.2196
Golpara	Bohari	7,583	910	—	23.92	3.13	13.72	2.42	22.32	45.26	15.88	.5399
Bogaigaon	Pathsala	7,236	820	44.11	28.26	2.48	18.29	3.96	12.76	38.29	26.96	.0611
Gauhati	***Town-Order:***											
Rangia	Bokakhat	6,997	820	—	3075	2.23	16.30	4.74	13.94	39.17	27.23	.0963
Tejpur	Dhakjuli	'15,459	873	48.25	31.99	2.17	15.36	1.82	21.03	43.84	25.80	.1075
Nogaon	Jagi Road P. Mill	3,790	812	—	33.90	1.94	9.33	0.15	91.98	1.94	6.15	.0000
Dimapur	a. Bakajan	11,008	830	—	30.33	2.30	17.97	1.23	27.46	35.34	18.33	.0540
	b. Phek	8,432	644	—	40.22	1.47	17.92	3.71	2.12	1.06	63.50	.2807
Lumding	Maibong	5,802	738	—	34.64	1.92	4.28	4.29	3.98	47.26	40.05	.4107
Shillong	Jowai	20,713	981	90.28	33.06	1.96	2.00	0.80	7.53	30.23	59.42	.0617
Guwahati	Jagi Road	13,582	828	—	33.11	2.02	12.29	1.40	31.73	41.74	15.23	.2227

Name of the Order/ Town		Total Population (1991)	M/F Ratio (F per 1000 M)	20 years Growth rate (%) (1971-91)	% of main workers Total Population	Dependency Ratio	% of share of workers in Agricultural Activities (1 + II)	Mining Plantation Fishing (III + IV)	Manufacturing (Va + Vb)	Trade Transport (VI + VII VIII)	Other Services (IX)	Household Other then HH (HH/O)
Dibrugarh Town-Order;												
Tinsukhia	a. Naharkatu	15,037	808	39.57	33.50	1.98	6.25	11.9	16.18	47.64	18.01	.0516
	b. Roing	7.271	657	—	33.53	1.36	6.35	4.35	3.20	30.76	54.18	0.833
Lakhimpur	Bihpuria	8,506	866	61.83	33.38	2.17	17.83	1.57	1.20	46.83	22.18	.0278
Jorha	Majira	8,336	854	50.20	27.59	2.64	10.52	20.26	8.69	33.48	26.52	.2922
Dibrugarh	Moranhat	3,978	861	57.61	28.30	2.52	3.82	4.17	19.89	49.82	25.84	.0419
Silchar Town-Order:												
Agartala	Seronura	8,135	922	27.51	—	—	—	—	—	—	—	
Aizawal	Sairang	3,532	840	—	—	—	—	—	—	—	—	
Lunglai Baiti		2,331	1004	—	—	—	—	—	—	—	—	
Silchar Lala		8,031	954	55.9	27.89	2.97	24.11	0.94	8.93	38.26	26.92	.3846
Imphal Town-Order:												
Imphal Andro		6,796	977	—	27.91	7.45	90.94	0.32	2.59	1.32	4.78	.5454
Thaubal	Wangjing	5,305	1,036	18.87	—	—	—	—	—	—	—	—
Churachandpur	Lamlai	3,606	905	—	33.50	3.11	76.82	0.33	5.38	5.62	11.42	1.6000
Averages		8,292	883	54.12	33.53	2.12	19.39	3.72	16.34	33.54	26.96	.1532

Source: 1. Census Operation Offices of various States through NICNET.
2. Provisional Population Tables, Paper 2 of 1991, Census of India, 1991.

Chapter 4

URBANISATION IN THE NORTHEAST: WITH REFERENCE TO TWO SMALL TOWNS OF ASSAM

Prabin Baishya

INTRODUCTION

Urbanisation is a stage of economic development where a non-agricultural population concentrated in a locus is supported by agricultural surplus arising in the peripheral areas. The extraction of the surplus implicitly denotes the emergence of transport of and trade in commodities to feed the non-agricultural population in the seats of courts or capitals of the countries while trade itself leads to the growth of mercantile settlements around ports, harbours and other transport junctions as well as in places of pilgrimages where commerial depots for sale and purchase appear.[1]

In the North-East, modern urban areas like Guwahati, Shillong, Kohima, Imphal, Aizwal and Agartala are mainly the creation of the British colonialists as administrative headquarters. While Western industrial cities like Manchester and Lancashire emerged as a result of the industrial revolution, the urban areas in the North-East are mostly the trading and commercial centres inhabited by wholesellers and retailers side by side with people engaged in other services sector. The most important trade centres in the region during the 1st decade of the present century were Goalpara, Barpeta, Guwahati, Tezpur, Nagaon, Golaghat, Jorhat, Dibrugarh and Sadiya in the Brahmaputra Valley, Habiganj, Ajmirganj, Sunamganj, Chattak, Balaganj, Sylhet (now all in Bangladesh) and Silchar in the Surama Valley.[2]

GROWTH OF URBAN AREAS

North East India is the least urbanised region of the country. The 1951 Census Report had observed that erstwhile Assam which included Nagaland, Meghalaya and Mizoram was the 'least urbanised' among the Indian States with only 4.6 p.c. urban population while Manipur was 'almost cent percent rural' with barely 0.5 p.c. urban inhabitants as against Tripura's 6.7 p.c. in only one town—Agartala in contrust to 17% of Indian population living in towns and cities.[3] The situation has, however, changed notably during the last 40 years from 1951 to 1991 as seen from Table I.

Table 1. Growth of Urban Areas & Population—1951-1991

State	Urb. Popu. in lakhs	P.C.	No. Towns	Urb. Popu. in Lakhs	P.C.	No. Towns	Urb. Popu.	P.C.	No. Towns
	1951			1971			1991		
Assam	4.14	4.6	28	12.89	8.82	73	24.70	11.10	87
Arunachal	—	—	—	0.17	3.70	4	1.04	12.80	10
Meghalaya	—	—	—	0.47	14.55	5	3.29	18.60	7
Mizoram	—	—	—	0.83	11.36	2	3.17	46.10	22
Nagaland	—	—	—	0.51	9.55	3	2.10	17.27	9
Manipur	0.03	0.5	1	1.42	13.19	8	5.05	27.52	30
Tripura	0.42	6.7	1	1.62	10.43	6	4.18	15.30	18
Total	4.59		30	18.48	9.44	101	43.53	13.86	183

Source: Different Tables in Census of India, 1951, Assam etc., Census of India, 1971, Assam & Basic Statistics, NEC, 1980 & 1992.

In 1951 undivided Assam had 28 urban areas

with a population of 4.14 lakhs while adjusted number of towns in the present area of Assam[4] was 24. The 1971 and 1991 census data show that while the number of towns in the N.E.R. increased from 101 to 183 (1.8 times) urban population had risen sizeably from 18.46 lakhs to 43.53 lakhs, *i.e.*, by 2.8 times over the 20 year period. The 1991 census figures show that with the largest number of urban areas and highest number of urban population Assam is the least urbanised state in the region with only 11.10% of her population living in 87 towns preceeded by Arunachal Pradesh (12.80%) in 10 towns while Mizoram occupies the top position with 46.10% of her population residing in 11 towns and 11 concentrated villages treated as class VI towns. In the North-East as a whole only 13.86% out of the total population of 313.80 lakhs are urban residents as against all India average of 25.73 p.c.

NEW CLASSIFICATION OF URBAN AREAS

The 74th Constitutional Amendment of 1992 classifies the urban areas according to population size into 3 categories, viz. Nagar Panchayats or Town Councils with a population of 5,000-20,000 treated as transitional urban areas, Municipal Councils having 20,000-3,00,000 population and Municipal Corporations with a population exceeding 3 lakhs. While 135 urban areas of the North East come under the first category and 47 under the 2nd. Only one city viz. Guwahati with a population of 5.57 lakhs comes under the perview of Municipal Corporation. The above classification under the provisions of the 74th Constitutional Amendment is intended to provide political and fiscal powers to the local bodies. But the state governments are yet to adopt a uniform policy about the population size classification.

Table 2. Urban Areas by Population Size, 1991.

State	5000-20,000	20,000-3,00,000	above 3,00,000	Total Areas
Arunachal	10	—	—	10
Assam	58	28	1	87
Manipur	26	4		30
Meghalaya	4	3	—	7
Mizoram	19	3	—	22
Nagaland	5	4	—	9
Tripura	13	5	—	18
Total	135	47	1	183

Source: Calculated from Table 12 of Basic Statistics, NEC, 1992.

URBAN SCENARIO IN ASSAM

As evident from Table 2, Assam contains 58 small urban areas with a population up to 20,000, while 28 areas have more than 20,000 but less than 3 lakhs and only one city, viz. Guwahati contains 5.57 lakhs residents. Out of the 58 small towns again 12 areas have less than 5,000 population while 27 areas have a population up to 10,000 and the remaining 19 areas have more than 10,000 but less than 20,000 residents. It may be recalled that under the existing system of local government in the urban areas, 43 localities containing 4.61 lakhs population forming 18.66% of the total urban population are administered by Town Committees, 24 areas providing residence to 16.39 lakhs residents constituting 66.32% of the urban population are under Municipal Boards including the Guwahati Municipal Corporation (GMC) and 3.70 lakhs population (15.02%) are residing in 20 Census Towns which are administered by Gaon Panchayats. It may also be observed that only 3 urban areas, viz. Dibrugarh, Jorhat and Silchar each has a population exceeding one lakh and only one city, viz. Guwahati provides habitation to 5.57 lakhs.[5] But from the point of view of provisions for amenities of life, there is little difference between some areas having Town Committees or Municipal Boards or areas without having them in the Census Towns as it will be evident from our case studies.

As regards characteristics of the urban areas. In economically advanced countries urbanisation is both an antecedent and a consequence of higher standard of living achieved by increasing division of labour and specialization in skill, technology and productivity arising out of industrial growth.[6] But in Assam as well as in the entire North East region there are only a few towns like Guwahati, Bongaigaon, Digboi, Tinsukia, Namrup, Mirza-Palasbari etc. having industries registered under the Factories Act. Most of the other towns emerged as centres of trade and commerce at the transport nodal points like railway stations, bus stops on road junctions, river ports etc. and/or administrative headquarters of a revenue circle, a district sub-division or of a district. The non-agricultural population of all these business centres is heavily concentrated in wholesale and retail trades, hotels and restaurants, gorcery and stationery shops, Pan shops and street shops intercepted by some tailoring services, bicycle, radio etc. repairing services and one or two rice mills; most of them working outside the perview of the tax net although income of some of them engaged in grey business might exceed those of salaried persons paying income tax there. In this cntext it may be recalled that from the angle of economic growth, trade and commerce do not produce any real commodity, rather being motivated by what the American economist Thorstein Veblen[7] called 'predatory instinct' the merchants, rentiers and speculators pick the pockets of their fellow citizens for 'producing money' in the transections. In the urban areas of Assam, this trading class consisting of 2.16 lakhs forms 28.61% of the urban main workers as against 13.75% engaged in manufacturing, processing, repairing and servicing sectors as per

1991 census records. The remaining 57.64% are engaged in agriculture (9.77%), construction (5.67%) and transport & communications, storage and other services (42.20%).[8]

The growth of urban areas in the N.E. region as a whole from barely 30 in 1951 to 183 in 1991 and their population rising from a mere 4.59 lakhs to 43.53 lakhs and in Assam from 24 to 87 urban areas with the number of residents rising from only 4.14 lakhs to 24.70 lakhs shows quantum jumps. This rapid growth of urban areas and urban population has thrown challanges in two different directions. The most important one is that it has created problems of providing basic amenities of life like roads, transport and communication, shelter, street light, drinking water and public health and sanitation facilities. It has also posed challenges to the eco-system by denuding the neighbouring forests and occupying the green lands under the plough for constructing residential houses, besides, polluting the biosphere by effluents, sewages and solid wastes. Regulation and control of all these problems as well as renewal of the environment call for massive investment in the social sector.

Fast growing urban areas, however, have also some very important positive aspects for agricultural societies requiring transfer of agricultural surplus population to the secondary and tertiary sectors. The urban areas have provided avenues for occupational shifts of a segment of the agricultural population particularly to the services sector as evidenced by 42.20% engaged in the sector in Assam. Apart from the question of income out flow from the peripheries to the centres, the urban areas have also opened agricultural marketing facilities to the surrounding villages and helped monetisation of the rural economy. The growth of small urban areas and their linkages with big towns and cities through transport and communication has also checked to a great extent the drift of population to the cities. This aspect also demands more social investment in the small urban areas.

CASE STUDIES

With the above background we digress now to illustrate some features of two small urban areas, viz. Sarthebari and Sualkuchi in Assam. While Sarthebari is situated at a distance of 97 km. to the West of Guwahati via Nalbari in the Barpeta District, Sualkuchi stands to the West at a distance of 35 km. from Guwahati on the north bank of the Brahmaputra. Both the localities were originally *Craft villages*, the former specialising in Bell Metal industry and the latter as the cenre of Pat and Muga silk fabric production in Assam. While Sarthebari provides residence to about 12,000 population (according to 1991 Census 9707) in 1132 holdings in a 2.90 sq. km. areas with a density of 410 persons as per a Town Committee Report, Sualkuchi contains in 3.44 sq. km. area a population of 20,528 in 4048 households with a density of 590 as per Sualkuchi Development Block records (1991 census population was 14,310). In Sarthebari a Town Committee was formed as early as 1955. But the people of Sualkuchi resisted several attempts for the formation of a T.C. in apprehension of the imposts of taxes and as such, the locality is administered by three Gaon Panchayats.

It is, however, interesting to observe that from the angle of providing the basic amenities of life, there is little difference, as has already been hinted, between a locality having a Town Committee, a Municipal Board or a Municipal Corporation and other urban areas administered by Gaon Panchayats. For example, all the 19 km. roads excluding 5.8 km. covered by the PWD in Sarthebari as well as all the roads, lanes and byelanes in Sualkuchi except nearly 10 km. ill managed roads under the PWD are unmetalled clay roads. In Sarthebari, however, the clay roads remain free from muds during the rainy season due mainly to sandy quality of the soil whereas in Sualkuchi they remain plustered by ankle-deep mud. These are, however, not the peculiarities of the roads in Sualkuchi alone; the conditions of the roads in the interior outgrowths like Hangarabari, Hatigaon, Jatiya, Kahilipara etc. under the Guwahati M.C. are no better; during the rainy season they also remain under water and mud and what is surprising, the Corporation authorities do not have even trace maps of the new roads constructed by the residents themselves, leave aside improving them.

The Sarthebari T.C. is reported to have prepared a scheme, as this writer was told by the Chairman during his visit in Oct. 1995 (the writer is a resident of Sualkuchi since (1964), for earth works, gravelling, black topping and brick drainages, but for paucity of funds (total annual revenue collection is around Rs. 2.5 lakhs as against a monthly recurring expenditure of Rs. 20,000), nothing could be done although it could repair 9 roads and place 25 RCC pipes for drainage with a government finance under Flood Damage Repair scheme during 1993-94. The T.C. there, has, of course, been maintaining 125 street lights, cleaning the streets and a market place while the streets in the already mentioned outgrowths in Guwahati as well as those in Sualkuchi remain dark and uncleaned. Water logging during the rainy days is a common feature in almost all the urban areas in the Assam plains. While Sarthebari has remained free from this problem thanks to the marshy surroundings, the northern side of Sualkuchi suffers the most from water logging due to filling up of the swamps by the road sides for construction of residential houses.

With regard to public health and sanitation, the

Sarthebari T.C. has failed during its 40 year life to provide safe drinking water and the residents are depending on private tube wells or ring wells. The majority of the residents of Sualkuchi has, of course, received drinking water thanks to a rural water supply project undertaken by the Public Health Engineering Deptt. While the Sarthebari T.C. could provide for 132 low cost sanitation units during 1992-93 and 1993-94 and had been maintaining 5 public toilets, there is no authority to look after this important aspect in Sualkuchi. In the medical sector, both the urban areas have one public health unit each without beds while the construction of a 50 bed hospital at Sualkuchi remained incomplete during the last decade. However, the people of Sualkuchi may take advantage of the medical facilities at Guwahati for its nearness while the residents of Sarthebari may avail of the limited services available at Nalbari, 20 km. to the east.

CULTURAL MILIEU

Urbanisation as a way of life implies concentration of population both in size and heterogeneity which speed up the process of socialisation of the inhabitants. But the residents of both Sarthebari and Sualkuchi being original homogenous groups and their exposure to differential contact and association remaining limited, are conservative and conventional in outlook and ideas particularly in the context of economic development which demands the emergence of *Social Deviants* to introduce innovations in industry and other enterprises. To cite concrete examples; the educated older and younger generations of Sualkuchi take pride in the Silk industry by calling the locality 'the Manchester of India'. No doubt, there is similarity between the Weaving Industry of Manchester and that of Sualkuchi, but while Manchester, a 17th century town of not more than 9 or 10 thousands population, emerged as the textile centre of the world by the end of the 18th century due to application of scientific inventions[9], 'the age-old weaving industry of Sualkuchi remained at the same pre-Newtonian technological level' meeting only a small fraction of the demand for traditional fabrics in Assam[10]. Likewise the bell metal industry of Sarthebari as well as the brass metal industry of Hajo, another craft village with the ancient Hayagrib Madhab Temple and the Sufi shrine Powa Mecca, 35 kms. to the north-west of Guwahati, remained at the same Pre-Newtonian traditional level through ages and are decaying for lack of modernisation[11].

The population of these urban areas clustered in the village segments bearing the old names like Chupa, Tola, Tol and Para are maintaining organic solidarity exhibiting the *Mores*, taboos and folkways in their behavioural norms and life style due to absence of higher cultural contact. But in spite of the conservatism of the olders, the younger generations are found torn between the impulses of tradition and modernity and are subject to contradictory pressures. In an emerging situation of *Anomie*, the youth has been caught by the maelstrom of the new culture of elitist consumerism, the craving for rock music, gadgets and cola drinks even without having the financial access has swept high the imagination of the mofussil youth even in interior Naga villages[12] and have made them restless for want of leadership to channelise their energy towards reconstructing the socio-economic system for dispensation of social justice.

CONCLUSION

The occupational pattern of the population in the urban areas shows that most of the towns are trading and/or administrative centres and they are not industrial agglomerations. While the people of the small towns too aspire for higher material culture, they have neither the means nor the psyche for organising production on modern lines with a view to raising their productivity and income. Regulation of industrial location in the metropolis may, however, help industrial dispersal to the suburbs and mofussil areas. In this context examples cited from Communist China[13] where numerous 'township enterprises' like food product factories, feed processing plants, repair and spare parts workshops, clothing factories and tailoring workshops, general storage, book stalls etc. are set up in small towns may not be tasteful to the neo-laissez-faire economists of our country. But the citadals of laissez-faire theory like England also have their regulatory measures like the Special Areas (Development and Improvement) Act, 1934, the Distribution of Industries Act, 1945 and the Country Planning Act of 1947 through which 'work is taken to the workers'[14] in the semi-urban areas and the countryside. In Japan, a regulation for introduction of Industries into Rural Areas (1971), a Law for Redevelopment of Traditional Industrial Act (1974) and such other measures were introduced for preventing the concentration of factories in large urban areas with a view to integrated development of relatively underdeveloped areas[15]. The instances show that in developed countries the market forces are not allowed to make their hey-day. As a matter of fact, sustainable development of a society with long-term vision, observes The Club of Rome, 'would never arise within a world economy which relied exclusively on the operation of the market forces...'[16]

The small towns are also playing the role of shock-absorbers by preventing population migration to the big towns and cities. Given the amenities of life like all weather roads, quick transport and communication, health, sanitation and recreational facilities these small urban areas help the residents by commuting to the work place to enjoy family and community oriented life while avoiding the humdrum of city life. But the local bodies of these small urban areas are found constrained to invest in the social sector due to paucity of funds. No doubt, the local bodies, particularly The Nagar Panchayats and Gaon Panchayats have been given sufficient powers to levy, collect and appropriate taxes, duties, tolls and fees; but while imposing the imports they should also see to the paying capacities of the residents as well as to the collection costs. It is generally found that most of local authorities are apprehensive of annoying the local population by imposts of taxes and tolls while they are also to pocket the criticism for their failure to provide the basic amenities of life. The state governments are also starving the local bodies by not allocating the funds due to them. For example, the Sarthebari T.C. was not paid a single paise during the last two years out of the proceeds of Motor Vehicle Tax, land revenue and amusement tax collected by the Barpeta District authorities, leave aside other general grants. All this calls for setting up of a State Finance Commission in every state as provided by the 73rd and 74th Constitutional Amendments for ensuring devolution of funds from the State to the local governments in the urban as well as rural areas.

REFERENCES

1. Gadgil, D.R., The Industrial Revolution of India in Recent Times, Oxford, 1924/1985, pp. 6-8.
2. Provincial Gazetteer of Assam, Cultural Publishing House, Delhi, 1906-1983, p. 64.
3. Census of India, 1951, Assam, Manipur, Tripura, Vol. XII, pt. 1-A, pp. 147-48.

4. Census of India, 1971, Asam, General Report, Table IV-10.
5. Calculated from Table 1.04 of the Statistical Hand Book, Assam, '94.
6. Hauser, Philip M., Social, Economic & Technological Problems of Rapid Urbanisation, Paper in Hoselitz, B.E. et al (Ed), Industrialisation and Society, UNESCO, Mount, 1966, pp. 202-04.
7. Screpanti, E., et. al., An Outline History of Economic Thought, Clarendon Press, Oxford, 1993, p. 281.
8. Statistical Hand Book, Assam, 1994, Tables 1.09 and 1.10.
9. Mantoux, Paul, The Industrial Revolution in the Eighteenth Century, Janathan Cape, London, 1948, pp. 865-66.
10. Baishya, P., Small & Cottage Industries: A Study in Assam, Manas Publication, Delhi, 1989, p. 134. Also for detail- Sualkuchir Resham Udyog: Prayuktir Sthavirata in Sutradhar, April, 1-15, 1996, pp. 20-22.
11. Baishya, P., ibid, pp. 129-33.
12. Horum, M. (A) Naga Polity, Low Price Publications, Delhi, 1975/92, pp. 134-35.
13. Yuan Bao-min, China: Development of Small Towns in the Delta of Yangtze River, Paper in Dantwala, M.L. et. al. (ed), Asian Seminar on Rural Development, Oxford & IBH, 1986, pp. 420-21.
14. Brown, A.J., Regional Economics with special reference to United Kingdom, paper in Surveys of Applied Economics, Royal Economic Society, Macmillan, 1976, Vol. I, pp. 29-30.
15. Yaso Maikwa, Rural Industries in Japan, Paper in Misra, R.P., (Ed.), Rural Industrialisation in Third World Countries, Sterling, 1985, pp. 204-05.
16. King, Alexander et. al., The First Global Revolution, A Report by the Council of the Club of Rome, Orient Longman, 1993, p. 34.

Chapter 5

POTENTIALITY AND PROBLEMS OF SMALL TOWNS IN NORTH EAST INDIA

A.K. Agarwal

City growth in developing countries is not a new phenomenon may be due to either rapid population growth in the adjacent areas in the face of limited farm acreage pushes landless labour into the cities, or unusually strong economic forces pull migrants into the cities. In absence of matching expansion of industrialisation and other productive activities it has been observed that over a period of time the rising migration to the city is associated with high and even rising rates of urban unemployment (Todaro, 1969). Migrants in developing countries do compromise with inadequate shelter and try to make a living through ingenious-though not particularly remunerative activities. Thus as Brian Berry (1973) observes, rapid urbanisation has not been accompanied by a rise in economic development, as was the case in Europe and North America, and instead has been associated with unemployment, low level of life expectancy, poor nutritional status, and low levels of education.

Mills (1991) opines that cities are crucial for economic development, their size and density permit economies of scale and scope that are pre-requisites to growth. The best jobs and highest earnings are found there. The growth of urban areas makes efficient production possible and encourages the adoption of new technology. The development of modern industrial, service and non-profit sectors takes place there.

Mills further observes that the attraction of cities are not restricted to activities in for-profit sectors. In most developing countries that best educational and cultural institutions are located there, as are the largest and most diversified financial institutions. Government agencies usually find the city desirable for the same reason. Cause and effect run in both directions regarding government agencies; proximity ficilitates interaction with commercial firms and other government organisations, but it is equally important for private businesses to be close to government agencies to obtain licences, loans, and so on. However, in the present scenario of liberalisation era and considerable autonomy to the states it may not be the case exactly with India but certainly some factors do play their role in congestion of states' capital towns.

Development of cities, district headquarters and to some extent emergence of small towns particularly the adjacent rural areas to the big cities coupled with some administrative headquarters at the block level is the out come of the influx of intra-state migration of rural people to these cities/towns. It is a common belief that the best centres of education for higher and professional standards, the best hospitals, the most efficient water supply and waste disposal system, and the best roads and highly subsidised public transit system are found in the capital towns and district headquarters. All these play an important role in attracting people living under comparatively less advantageous conditions to these towns equipped with better living conditions and better job opportunities. It is not necessary that all the migrants will be settled with best living conditions available but majority of them have to compromise with low level of living standards alongwith inadquate infrastructure amenities making their lives worst than before.

Emergence of small towns as a result of state government policy to elevate some rural areas to the status of lowest category of urban areas without considering the minimum norms required for in terms of employment in secondary and tertiary sectors and other essential infrastructural facilities put enormous pressure on the capacity of the government agencies involved in urban affairs to provide such infrastructure such as schools, housing, roads, water and transportation. Under the circumstances these towns remain rural in character in real term. Simultaneously this lead to a phenomenon of rising prices for urban land and shelter, overcrowding and shortage of public services, price rise in general due to a mismatch of demand and supply. The worst affected people of this unthoughtful over night urbanisation belong to the low income group.

Infrastructure refers to predominantly government owned capital that provides vital services to residents and businesses, including water supply and waste disposal system, trnasportation system (roads, and public transit system), health and educational facilities and utilities (gas, electricity and telecommunication). Not all such facilities are government owned but some are privately manged. However, in small towns such facilities are purely the responsibility of the government as private investment is completely absent. Moreover the infrastructure facilities provide people of great direct importance at a much lower cost by the government, every body wants more especially if it is paid for by someone else.

Discrimination against rural areas in infrastructure provision is a major reason for differences in standard of living in small towns and cities. The right solution is to improve infrastructure services in small towns and neighbouring rural areas to ehnance their viability and reduce the incentives for migration.

People prefer to migrate in search of best economic opportunities available for the educated/skilled and semi-skilled people. This create shortage of required manpower in small towns and adjacent rural areas and the resultant high in wages for short run which is neutralised by increased cost of living over a period of time. Direct benefits of high wages are also not reaped by the migrants over a long period of time as the urban labour supply tends to expand as fast as—if not faster than—demand, limiting the growth of wages and incomes, especially for unskilled labour.

All production and consumption activities generate wastes that are discharged to the air, water, or land. Waste disposal is polluting to extent that it impairs the value of the discharge medium for use by others. In absence of any proper waste disposal system as available in big cities, water borne diseases are the most serious environmental and public health problem in small towns. Although it is a debatable question but in general it appears that life expectancy at present appears to be longer in cities than in rural areas, in part because of pollution control programmes, and in part because urban residents have higher incomes, better nutrition and health care. It will be appropriate to mention here that the pollution control measures are almost at the same level everywhere except for state's capital. There is no well specified system for drainage and sanitation in small towns of north east.

In case of introducing Panchayati Raj system by some states of north east the responsibility of local governments will extend to build and operate local infrastructure (schools, transportation, water supply and waste disposal) and administer a variety of regulatory programmes such as land use control. The local institutions often have little or no autonomy in infrastructure planning, government is responsible for managing infrastructure at the local level. Shortage of funds and short supply of trained manpower to execute such programmes and added to it the government pressure to keep the taxes and charges down promising local resident to provide adequate services will result in widening the gulf between needs and services in these town areas in large.

Available resources and technology define a production possibility frontier for each city, but achieving that frontier requires a careful balance between business and government. In moving cities to their production possibility frantiers, government, must establish conditions that enable the private sector to function efficiently (Mills, 1991). In absence of private sector at large as observed in the north eastern hilly towns it becomes the government responsibility to make sincere efforts to serve these towns as the vehicles by which the low income people may improve their living standards instead of forced living ina detriorating environment.

The government must invest in physical infrastructure to provide services that are essential to residents. This is more so important for reasons of health and environmental quality to arrest migration to capital towns. Enhancing the capacity of individuals and municipal authorities, if any, for resource mobilisation locally constitutes perhaps the most pressing challenge of the state. The structural adjustment is vital to promote productive entrepreneurship especially in the informal sector. It is through creative policy initiatives directed at these enterprises that a new era of production and prosperous urban development will dawn. Development of small towns is all the more important from view point of balanced development of all parts of the state and to avoid congestion and overcrowding in capital towns. The vicious circle of slum dwellers and poverty ridden people can only be broken by a planned development of small towns adjacent to the big cities and the places of importance of business and trade.

REFERENCES

Barry Brian J.L., 1973: The Human Consequences of Urbanization: Divergent paths in the Urban Experience of the Twentieth century, New York, St. Martin's Press.

Edwin S. Mills, 1991: "Urban Efficiency, Productivity, and Economic Development", Proceedings of the World Bank Annual Conference on Development Economics, 1991.

Todaro Michael, 1969: "A Model of tobor, Migration and Urban Unemployment in Less Developed Countries", American Economic Review, 59: 138-48.

Chapter 6

HILL TOWN PLANNING

Zahid Husain

Urbanisation is an indicator of development and progress of socio-economic and cultural evolution of people and landscape of an areas. Urban centres are nodal and growth points of a region where take place secondary and tertiary functions and activities connected with the centre itself and its 'hinterland' as well. Many civilisations of the world reached pinnacle of their development with flourishing/blooming of urban centres, *e.g.*, Indus, Mesopotamia, Nile, Greek, Roman etc.

In evolutionary process of culture, economy, land use, and landscape urban system sprouts from a developed rural system. Both the systems are interconnected and interdependent. These are two distinct wheels of economy and landscape, and one can not be understood without other, particularly the urban system. On the basis of secondary and tertiary sector activities, size of population, land use and function a settlement can be adjudged as urban. The towns are centres of 'conjunctive urban functions' and land use; and also of assimilation and dispersal of knowledge. The structure and function of towns have internal and external linkages (both are weak in towns of Northeast India, especially of the hilly region).

As the hills and plains are endowed with different and diverse potentialities for urbanisation, so are the problems in their towns. This necessitates separate town planning for hills and plains. Town planning in the hills has to be exclusively based on potentiality of hills and should address problems of hill towns. Due to ruggedness of terrain, lack of suitable sites for human settlements (particularly big size urban agglomerations) and various environmental constraints many difficulties are faced in construction and maintenance of towns in the hilly region. These all make 'hill town planning' as a distinct and challenging task. Therefore, this paper tries to examine potentialities and problems of development of hill towns, and then attempts on 'town planning' in the Northeastern Hills of India.

POTENTIALITY

To evaluate potentiality of hills for towns, first of all the historical, evolutionary and locational process of origin and growth of urban centres in the world has to be understood clearly, so that assessment can be accurate, useful and practical. Before doing so, it is worth to note in brief some relevant points connected with relationship between rural and urban systems. (1) Rural system plays a determining role in formation, functioning and sustenance of urban system. (2) Coming up of towns is a turning point in the growth of human settlements, land use, culture, economy and landscape. (3) Villages and towns form a well-knit system of spatio-temporal-functional organisation in the matrix of settlement pattern and land use in a region which gives specific character to its landscape. (4) Both rural and urban systems depend on local resources base, though degree varies. (5) Interplay, interaction and interdependence between rural and urban systems are but natural.

The world history of urbanisation tells us that towns are product of basically two distinct process—

engodgenous and exogenous. (1) In *Endogenous* process urban centres/towns come into existence as a result of two factors: (1) Due to 'excess agriculture products', in which a village gradually grows into an urban centre where surplus agriculture products are brought/assembled from surrounding villages due to various reasons for transaction. These centres can be called market or *mandi* towns where inter-related secndary and tertiary activities start consequently. In this case, strength of an urban centre depends on supply of products from the hinterland. The urban system will break consequent to weakening of rural system. Probably it happened in the decline to Harappan towns, because on-set of dry climate in Thar desert off-set the rural system, in turn affected health of Harappan towns. (b) Non-agriculture product based towns which emerge due to endogenous locational factors viz., halting places on trade routes/ highways and mountain passes, sea and river ports; centres of—learning, pilgrimage, administration, strategic location, recreation etc. (c) Increase of polulation of a village beyond carrying capacity of agriculture system, where its inhabitants diversity means of subsistence from primary to secondary and tertiary sectors. It such cases a village automatically acquires an urban character.

(2) In *Exogenous* process urban centres come up due to external locational factors such as establishment of towns for specific purposes—Industry, mining, administration, medical, tourism, power stations, transport junctions etc. In this process towns emerge first then follows development of rest of urban facilities. They appear to be grafted/planted settlements on rural fabric. Such towns do not grow from the rural systems, rather in course of time influence the rural system to its own benefit. Survival of such towns is externally controlled.

Broadly the first category of urbanisation (endogenous can be associated with the agricultural or pre-industrial society and the second (exogenous) with the industrial society. One more urbanisation has been witnessed by mankind and that belongs to 'post-pollution' or 'post-sick urbanisation' period. It appears that the Harappans and Romans also faced 'post-pollution' phase. 'Post-sick urbanisation' period has started now as evident from shifting of place of residence by urbanites from towns to country sides in want of good land, space and environment. In this process urbanism is now carried to rural areas. Some parts of Africa and Asia are experiencing this process, whereas Europe and America might have seen it earlier. But in 'post-industrial urbanisation' the evolutionary process is reversed. First town is established, then follow growth and urban-rural interaction, which are seldomly smooth. Moreover, spatio-temporal-functional linkages and hierarchy are not ensured in it, which are but natural in the 'pre-industrial phase'.

As late as 1960s the entire Northeastern Hills remained exclusively rural in character with typical exception of Shillong and to some extent Tura, Kohima, Haflong and Aizawl (Imphal is in the intermountain valley). The rural economy never reached to surplus stage to generate endogenic urbanisation. Though intra and inter village barter/exchange of products used to exist, but markets or *'hats'* developed only in the foothills throughout the North-East Indian Sub-continent, where hill and plain dwellers used to exchange excess products from their respective ecosystem. Archaeological evidence of Ita fort, Malinathan, Rukmaninagar (Sadiya) and Dimapur are examples of historic towns which grew in the foothills.

Despite existence of old trade routes across the

hills of North-Eastern India no village turned into a market-town because these hills are not so broad (vast) necessitating halting places of a town's prominance. On the far east we have Rima (on the trade route connecting Assam and China) after crossing the high mountains of Lohit, whereas Wallang, Minutang and Hayuliang on this side remained mere villages only. An important trade route connected Lhasa (Tibet) to Udalguri (Assam) via Tsona Monastery, Tawang, Dirang, Rupa, Shergaon or Kalaktang, but no town did emerge enroute.

In the Garo Hills cotton used to be a commercial product from *jhum* fields, but it was carried to foothills for sale. In the adjacent Khasi Hills, iron smithy was once at pcak and iron and its implements were marketed far and near in this part of the Indian sub-continent. But no market place developed in these hills to carry out transaction inside the hills. Instead, these items were carried down the hills to be sold in the *'hats'* and nearby market centres of the plains. In the Indo-Burma ranges, Imphal was the only exceptional town being seat of administration. When towns could not come up despite presence of some endogenous factors, question of coming up of gowns due to exogenous factors does not arise as it is altogether a different proposition in context of Northeastern hills. In this case, industralisation is conspicuously absent in the hills as a major exogenous locational factor due to lack of potential for it. Simply lack of industrialisation is not only factor behind non-emergence of hill towns.

The point stressed here is that the entre hill ccosystem of the North-Eastern India has not provided sufficient potential for urbanisation, question of big or small towns is different. On the other hand, whatever number, size and types of hill towns we see today most of them are product of exogenous forces in which townships appear as planted one on the rural fabric without any real inter-connection with the villages. Such urban agglomerations are generally seats of modern administration having few office building, residential quarters, schools, hospitals and a typical 'Bazaar Line'. Neither they have all urban amenities nor various urban functions and land use operate there. Whatever centres of administration are thrust upon the hills, they lack 'hinterland' in true sense, thus they do not act as nodal/growth points. Of course, some sort of urban-rural interaction starts after formation of such towns, but that is not enough to create spatio-temporal-functional hierarchy and pattern in human settlements and land use of the area. Moreover, in the beginning such towns create burden on rural system/economy instead of boosting it.

Whatever may be causes of origin and growth of towns in the hills of North-Eastern India (whether due to endogenous or exogenous reasons), presence of such towns has to be critically examined and analysed on the following points. (1) What process(s) has been responsible for origin and growth of a town? (2) Is it suitably located, established and developed keeping well being of man and environment in mind? (3) What are the type, nature, function, relevance and dimensions of a town? (4) How far it can be allowed to grow and expand? (5) What is its role in regional settlement hierarchy and pattern? (6) Whether inter-relatedness and interdependence between rural and urban systems are functioning or dysfunctioning? Each town has to be studied on these lines to ultimately put the findings at regional and sub-regional levels to assess state and stage of urbanisation in its true sense. Mere coming up of towns does not mean urbanisation where urbanism, a way of life opposite to and different from rural life, is absent.

In the light of the points discussed under potential it can be said that there is *'Pre-mature urbanisation'* in the North-Eastern India, as it is case in all developing countries. It is similar to 'over urbanisation'. McGee termed it 'pseudo urbanisation'. It means more people live in towns in comparison to economic development, and towns come up before time. That's why towns are not fully developed, and prone to problems. In North-Eastern Hills of India the economy is not well rpien to support towns as development of agriculture and industry is at infancy stage. Urbanisation is evident in census figures only, but not in life style (urbanism), infra structure (development) and facilities (functions and amenities) of towns. Though many of the existing towns are result of exogenous process, but had time being allowed to lapse, then the local economy would have definitely progressed to that stage where towns would have sprang automatically through endogenous process. Even location of most of these 'pre-mature' towns would have remained same. It means, exogenous process has hastened occurrence of towns in the North-East India, particularly in its hilly part.

The towns of North-Eastern India have poor functional and spatial organisation. Surendra Singh (in this volume) has concluded that growth of middle, small and very small towns is rapid while that of big towns is stationary; and there is a big gap between growth of large and small towns. This corroborates the earlier mentioned view that since endogenous forces are weak, the entire hierarchy/order of towns is not well developed; and exogenous forces are responsible in formation of lower level of hierarchy *i.e.*, small towns. Had urbanisation been really from within (endogenous) and hierarchy of settlements would have been complete and balanced. Even most of the large towns owe their origin and sustenance to exogenous forces. Otherwise, had their origin been endogenous, a proportionate development of descending order of towns would have taken place naturally and vice versa as well in the beginning.

Time has come to evaluate potentaility of an area for urbanisation. This will certainly help in 'town planning' and 'forcasting of towns'. Several parameters can be selected to assess supporting capacity of an area for number, size, order, nature, function and role of towns. In other words, it has to be calculated that what number, order and size of towns an area can support. Such evaluation will include assessment of potentiality of an area for rural and urban centres both, *i.e.*, for rural economy (including agriculture) and urban economy (secondary and tertiary activities including industries0 and other avenues of economy leading to formation of towns. Potentiality of an area can be assessed for urban centres by taking into account following parameters. (*i*) Inventory and appraisal of resources (both human and natural) and their economic potentiality in generating endogenous process of unbanisation. (*ii*) Evaluation of existing technology, strategy, and level of ultilisation of the potentiality. (*iii*) Future technology, strategy and level of resource utilisation, (*iv*) Existing and future growth centres, nodal points and transport network, and (*v*) Future needs of towns, their location and role in spatio-temporal-functional organisation and hierarchy of settlements. This appears to be stupendous task since it encompasses all possible evaluation of entire area for every coneivable economic activity and other purposes. Certainly it will require lot of efforts from scientists of different disciplines. There is scope to develope further this idea in future. Some other ways and means can be employed to do it, not necessarily comprehending entire gamut of the problem. Just for 'forcasting towns', W. Syiem's paper in this book can be cited. She has pin-pointed places and nature of future towns of Meghalaya.

PROBLEMS

In the second step a thorough indentification, understanding and analysis of problems of hill towns have to be made before embarking on 'hill town planning'. So that solutions to existing problems and precautions against occurrence of such problems in new hill towns can be presented. Several types, nature, magnitude and dimension of problems occur in hill towns. These are primarily related with the process of unbanisation, site, location, size, structure and functions of hill towns.

Humans settlements in the hills are located usually on the slopes, but of late in the flat valleys also, for example Ziro, Along, Seppa, Williamnagar etc. Location in both the sites pose specific problems. However problems connected with construction, maintenance and supply of basic urban infrastructure and amenities are common to both. Unplanned growth and over-population are major problems in the hill towns, and other problems are mostly related with these two.

Construction of houses and localities is rather difficult in hilly rugged surface. Very few suitable sites are available for it. That's why hill towns suffer either from congestion or scattering of houses. Pollution of space is evident from haphazardly constructed and congested houses and localities, which destroys beauty of landscape also. In want of suitable land, the places of residence and work are located at uneasy distances. Construction of houses and buildings becomes more difficult with the increase in degree of slope. These problems are witnessed in hill towns like Bomdi La, Tawang, Khonsa, Kohima, Tura, Changlang, Aizawl etc. The scattered housing/locality pattern creates problem of transport, communication and supply of amenities. Moreover, the cement, concrete and iron rod buildings of these towns are dangerous in high seismic zone, because most of these 'concrete jungles' are constructed disregarding measures against earthquakes, fire accidents, landslides, and building norms. Gross ignorance is shown to principles of availing sunlight for a house/building and aesthetics of the townscape also. Of course, high buildings (vertical growth) are answer to critical limit of horizontal expansion of a town. But on all accounts this has to be avoided in small towns of hilly region for the sake of safety, comfortability, cost and aesthetic value of the townscape as well. The concept of neighbourhood can not be materialised due to various reasons such as neither there is viable scope nor space to build all possible urban facilities in one locality.

Since flat lands are very few and limited in the hilly terrain, these are considered invaluable for agriculture, particularly for development of intensive settled cultivation. Therefore, establishment of townships on such precious lands is a great loss, for the flat fertile lands are put to unproductive use for ever. These flat lands should be exclusively reserved for agriculture purpose. But relative flatness of these small patches of land attracts man in modern times owing to comfort and increased accessibility they offer. In any case, the optimum and rational use of these lands is for rural (agriculture) instead of urban purpose.

Scarcity of water due to limited and scattered sources is another troublesome problem in hill towns, which is even present in towns situated in high rainfall zone. To make adequate supply of water springs, streams and rivulets are tapped in upper slopes to carry water to towns by gravitation force, or pumped from streams flowing below the height of the town. Both the techniques involve huge expenditure on construction and maintenance works for tanks, channels, pipes, pump sets, pumping station etc. Source of energy is required to run pump sets. Digging tube-wells is also a costly affair, and these are not successful always. Distribution of water in the uneven surface of town is another problem. Excess supply in the valleys (down the slope) and insufficient supply on upper slopes are inherent difficulties in water supply in human settlements located in hills leading to wastage at one place while scarcity at another place.

Apart from problems of housing and water supply, the residents of hill towns do encounter problems like—scarcity of energy resources, poor sanitary and sewerage system, landslides, seismic activities, violent winds, lack of space for recreation (parks, playgrounds etc.), inadequate communication links, shortage of essential facilities and commodities, relative isolation and distance from plains and centres of production, and disruption of communication links in the event of 'heavy rains', landslides, floods and snowfall. Acute shortage of essential commodities and high prices are noticed in such conditions. Supply of energy resources (firewood, coal, kerosene, L.P.G., electricity) is erratic and less than required. Energy resources are needed for cooking, lighting, heating and other domestic and industrial uses. The most easy and immediate source is fuel wood and charcoal from surrounding forests. This single most activity of man to meet energy requirements of the hill dwellers has taxed the forests to the extant of its complete elimination in the immediate vicinity. due to which denuded hills and barren rocks devoid of any respectable vegetation and soil cover are a common sight in and around almost all hill towns. Fuel wood is not available even at exorbitant rates. Thus demand for other resources of energy increases, which are not easily available.

In the hilly surfaces construction of a single

sewerage and solid waste disposal system is not feasible due to constraints of slope and scape. In absence of it, the sewage and garbage just find its place either into water bodies or spread on surface, thus polluting the aquatic and land systems affecting life of men, plants and animals. Heaps of solid waste and pools of sewerage create unhygienic conditions by polluting air, water and soil, producing foul odour, and spoiling beauty of the town also. Sanitation system remains non-operational or dysfunctional in such cases. Apart from the above mentioned problems there are many big and small problems experienced in the hill towns. Therefore, a proper planning is need of the hour not only to solve existing problems but to have 'problem free' towns in future.

PLANNING

After understanding the process of urbanisation, evaluation of potentiality and problems of hill towns, it is time now to attempt on 'hill town planning'. The following strategy can be adopted while planning for towns in hills of North-Eastern India.

(1) First of all the principle of 'small town' has to be followed for all urban settlements of hills. Because hill ecosystem can not support big towns on one hand, while on the other it is wise not to over burden the fragile hill ecosystem with big towns. The optimum small size will be determined on the basis of potentiality of the region. When further growth of a town leads to deterioration of environment, that can be considered an ideal small size. Therefore, it is suggested that two towns are better than one over-grown town. It means if size of a town is about to cross the critical limit, another settlement has to be built to accommodate ever increasing population of the existing town. So that its population and expansion remain within manageable

limit and environment does not face degradation. Undoubtedly, small town is governable, functional and practical in the hilly region, and it is beautiful too. However, population size limit of a small towns is relative, for it varies with potentiality of the area.

(2) As progress and development of rural economy is preceded to urbanisation in endogenous process, it is necessary to develop strong rural economy. This will have direct influce on the health and functioning of town by supplying it with the required goods and by checking migration of rural people to the 'mirage centres' of livelihood, dangerously more when rural economy-system is broken and weakened. Thus, development of 'modern strong villages' is part of 'town planning' to reduce burden and problems in big and small urban centres. This is more relevant when a 'reverse migration' trend has started in the world especially in sub-Sahara Africa and many parts of India, in which some urban people are now interested to have their residences located in the rural areas. This is due to many reasons, the polluted environment of towns is primary one, followed by high prices of land and congestion in towns.

(3) Concept of a balanced neighbourhood has to be followed for a better and comfortable life of the urbanites. In other words, maximum possible urban amenities and functions have to be provided within a locality to reduce pressure on Central Business District (CBD) and other important places where congestion and pollution of environment and space are present.

(4) Principle of 'urban renewal' has to be adopted in which those parts of city (generally confined to inner city and slums) are rebuilt which have fallen below desired level of standard. Such restoration works are necessary for good health of town and its citizen. Dilapidated structures deserve similar treatment.

(5) New administration headquarters should not be declared and created for the name sake, unless all urban amenities and functions are brought there. If at all it is necessary, then potentiality for such town must be seen in the area. Only difference in locating such towns will be that they will be 'premature' in birth.

(6) There should not be a township at the cost of environment, forest, fertile flat land, villages or rural areas and water resources. Because these factors have their own unique resource value and none of them can be sacrificed for a town to come up. Towns do have their importance, but at right time, at right place and at 'optimum size'.

(7) The townscape should be in harmony with the local environment and culture, even if it is result of exogenous process. It should not appear as an island of 'alien culture' in the local fabric. Further, while naming new townships local aspirations, history and language have to be given due consideration.

(8) If possible, efforts should be made to develop all functions of a town as required for its healthy functioning. So that it can act as a viable, vibrant and effective nodal/growth point in the network and hierarchy of settlements, land use, landscape and all three sectors of economy.

(9) Finally, an ecological equilibrium has to be achieved by maintaining harmonious relationship between 'small towns' and 'modern strong villages', and between urban centres and natural environment. It is only possible if rural and urban systems are considered two sides of a coin (*i.e.*, total economic activities of the region). Similarly, development of towns should not be detrimental to environmet, as the latter is base of resources on which rural and urban economy flourishes.

Chapter 7

SOCIO-TECHNOLOGICAL PROBLEMS IN THE GROWTH OF SMALL TOWNS IN THE NORTH-EAST INDIA

Jogamaya Saikia

A BRIEF DISCUSSION

North-East India is physically located in a backward and disadvantageous position.

Growth requires physical development of a place with its different facets towards recognition of scientific advancement. Advancement is forwarded along on the line of prospects of population, education, business-transaction, marketing, banking with well-connected communication system and transport feasibilities.

Any area whether rural or urban, if is situated on the National Highways and railway lines, are bound to get development. Places on the banks of river Brahmaputra and Barak which are connected with the network of transport system of roadways and railways are of exceptional importance for growth. Small arcas even in the remote places get importance for development if they are economically viable as in the case of Tuli (Nagaland), Panchgram (Cachar, Assam), Kapili Hydel Project (Meghalaya) etc. In the same way, religious relics, temples, holy places also give rise to township like Barpeta, Hajo, Batadroba, Majuli, Twang etc. Historical remains attract for development, tourism and interest. Educational

Institutions also give impetus for growth of township.

Society's growth in towns is faster than the rural areas. It is due to the reason mentioned as above.

With the development of these, men requires Socio-Technological upliftment. We are living in scientific age of development. We require technology. Technology has promoted audio-visual know hows to observe, realise, visualise the present trends of hi-fi activities around the world. Technology has minimised time, distance and remoteness. To achieve all these gadgets, our small towns still have to acquire many more requirements as preliminary essentials like rural sanitations, water-supply, low-cost housing, roads, electrification, education, motivation, awareness and on the top of it, participation of people concern. Non-coventional energy prevailed with local availabilities are yet to procure and requires understanding. Transport facilities with good road, river and railways, tele-communication facilities with banking, post office etc. are not adequate as per population growth. In small towns, Technical persons are less, people are new to new technologies lack of availability of spare parts for repairing and replacement of tools, machineries, agro-technology, supply of electricity, power for agra-industries and machineries, suitable environment, pre and pro demonstration facilities of new entries of technology, lack of training, markets, rigidity in entering the new area, proper efforts to motivate people etc. stands as problems in small towns.

Removal of these problems are though social and economic yet government and non-government organisations can pursue for eradication. These organisations can illustrate the needs of technological development and prospects and help for eradication of poverty, ignorance and make people aware of present day's needs and upliftment that effects the growth of small towns in proper perspectives.

Chapter 8

URBANIZATION IN MEGHALAYA: GROWTH AND PROSPECTS OF SMALL TOWNS

Amaresh C. Dubey

INTRODUCTION

The main objective of this paper is to analyze the urbanization process in Meghalaya with special reference to growth of small towns. Meghalaya became autonomous sate in January 1972 with two administrative districts from the then Assam, United Khasi and Jaintia Hills and Garo Hills. Subsequently these two districts were reorganized into five and in 1992 further reorganized into seven districts, viz; Jaintia Hills (JH), East Khasi Hills (EKH), West Khasi Hills (WKH), East Garo Hills (EGH), West Garo Hills (WGH), South Garo Hills (SGH) and Ri Bhoi (RB). However, due to unavailability of comparable data on two newly created districts viz., South Garo Hills (SGH) and Ri Bhoi (RB), the analysis at disaggregated level is limited to five districts only.

Urbanization pattern in India in the recent decades has been like in many developing countries and reported to be consistent with her level of economic development (1). But contrary to this some water balanced macro level scenario, there appears to be large inter-state vaiation (2). Urbanization level (UL, hereafter) in Meghalaya when looked upon from this consideration presents a very interesting picture. It has one town in existence for long. But since 1901, it has been lagging behind the national average. And in recent decades, it has gone further away from the average. For example, in 1961, it ranked 12th in terms of UL which has gone down to 15th position in 1971 to 17th in 1981 and further down to 18th in 1991 out of the 25 States in India for which comparable data is available (3).

In this paper we shall investigate urbanization in Meghalaya, its distribution over space and reasons behind the apparent movement away from the average in terms of Urbanization level. The rest of the paper is organized as follows. In Section II, we trace urbanization in Meghalaya since 1901. This is followed by disaggregated analysis at district level in section III. In section IV, factors affecting urbanization are identified. Finally, conclusions are reported in section V.

URBANIZATION IN MEGHALAYA: AN OVERVIEW

In Table 1, urban population, UL, decadal variation in urban population and tempo of urbanization is reported along with number of towns in Meghalaya in Columns 6 through 10 since 1901. As can be seen from the Table, with very low level of urbanization of 2.83 per cent in 1901, it has gone up to 18.69 per cent in 1991. It remained below the national UL throughout as can be compared with Column 3 of the same Table. During 1901 to 1991, urban popultion rose thirty four times and during 1951-91 period by five and half times (Col. 6 of Table 1). This is well above the variation in urban population at national level of eight and half times and nearly

Table 1: Urbanization Trend in Meghalaya

Year	U. Pop. Trends-All India					U. Pop. Trends-Meghalaya			
	Urban Population	U. Level	Decadal Variation	Urbanization Tempo	Urban Population	U. Level	Decadal Variation	Urbanization Tempo	Number of Towns
1	2	3	4	5	6	7	8	9	10
1901	2.55	10.70	—	—	9621	2.83	—	—	1
1911	2.59	10.27	0.35	- 4.02	13639	3.45	41.76	22.52	1
1921	2.81	11.18	8.27	8.86	17203	4.07	26.13	17.65	1
1931	3.55	12.01	19.12	7.42	26536	5.52	54.25	35.51	1
1941	4.42	13.87	31.97	15.49	38192	6.88	43.93	24.62	1
1951	6.04	16.73	41.42	20.62	58512	9.66	53.20	40.47	1
1961	7.89	17.96	26.41	7.35	117483	15.27	100.78	58.06	3(6)*
1971	10.91	19.91	37.96	10.86	147170	14.55	25.27	-4.73	3(6)*
1981	15.97	23.31	46.24	17.08	241333	18.07	63.98	24.19	7(12)*
1991	21.72	25.72	35.97	10.34	329079	18.69	36.36	3.46	7(12)*

Note: * Numbers reported in parenthesis are the number of towns as per Census Reports. However in 1961 and 1971 3 towns and 1981 and 1991 5 towns are outgrowth towns around Shillong. Hence these have been included as part of Shillong UA in the size-class comparision.

** Urban Population in Column 2 is in Crores.

Source: (*i*) Census of India-1991, Series-1, Government of India, (Various issues)

(*ii*) Basic Statistics of North-East Region, NEC, Shillong (Various issues).

three and half times during the same periods (Col. 2 of Table 1). The decadal variation too has been higher in Meghalaya during 1901-1991, it changed by above 100 per cent once during 1951-61 period and second highest variation is seen in 1971-81.

Despite higher growth of population in absolute terms and also in terms of decadal variation, ranking of Meghalaya in terms of UL has consistently gone down as reported earlier. Infact, if we compare Columns 4 with 8 of Table 1, we notice that decadal variation in Meghalaya has been consistently higher than that of the national level except during 1961-71. Similar observation can be made in case of tempo of urbanization which remained above the national level till 1961 and stagnated thereafter (Col. 5 and 9 of Table 1). This presents a paradoxical situation in terms of deteriorating ranking of Meghalaya in terms of level of urbanization. One possible explanation for this could be the lower popultion base at which we compare the absolute and decadal variations. Therefore, this situation appears to be more of statistical in nature.

In addition to poor urban population base, other factors which may have contributed for poor UL as well as deterioration in the ranking of Meghalaya in terms of UL could be poor rural population base, slower economic development and poor infrastructural facilities in the state as a whole. In fact from 1901 to 1951 there was only one urban centre Shillong which grew as the regional centre of governance. From 1901 to 1951 what ever additional urban growth took place, it was in and around Shillong. During the post independence period, Shillong became Capital of erstwhile Assam. This perhaps explains the very high variation of about 101 per cent of urban population during 1951-61. During this period two new urban centres were added viz; Tura and Jowai as class IV and V towns with three othr towns as outgrowth of Shillong. Similar explanation can be put forward to explain the variation during 1971-81 when Meghalaya as a state was carved out as an autonomous state from Assam which resulted in reorganization of districts and emergence of new towns.

URBANIZATION AT THE DISTRICT LEVEL

As pointed out in Section 1, after formation of autonomous Meghalaya state, there has been several reorganization of administrative units, the latest one being the addition of two new districts SGH and RB. Due to non-availability of comparable data on these two districts, our analysis is confined to remaining five districts only. Further, during pre-1961 period, only one town Shillong existed which falls in EKH district. Therefore, for pre-1961 period other features are not reported.

Table 2: Total and Urban Population of Meghalaya (District-wise)

Year		J. Hills	E.K. Hills	W.K. Hills	E.G. Hills	W.G. Hills	Meghalaya
1901	(T)	35950	127130	39170	35227	103047	340524
	(U)	—	9621	—	—	—	9621
1911	(T)	41783	147760	45526	40491	118445	394005
	(U)	—	13639	—	—	--	13639
1921	(T)	43240	152910	47113	45638	133502	422403
	(U)	—	17203	—	—	—	17203
1931	(T)	51534	182242	56150	48637	142274	480837
	(U)	—	26536	—	—	—	26536
1941	(T)	59057	208847	64347	56957	166112	555320
	(U)	—	38192	—	—	—	38192
1951	(T)	64629	228552	70418	61672	180403	605674
	(U)	—	58512	—	—	—	58512
1961	(T)	82147	290500	89505	78270	228958	769380
	(U)	6197	102398	—	—	8888	117483
1971	(T)	113562	380650	110872	102698	303917	1011699
	(U)	8929	122752	—	—	15489	147170
1981	(T)	156402	511414	161576	136550	369877	1335819
	(U)	12923	180800	3880	4290	39440	241333
1991	(T)	219186	657160	217462	189043	477775	1760626
	(U)	20713	230106	14378	11985	51897	329079

Notes: (*i*) Letters T and U in paranthesis are Total and Urban Population respectively.

(*ii*) — denotes does not exit or data not available.

Source: As in Table 1 above.

In Table 2, total and urban population of five districts and along with Meghalaya since 1901 is reported. In Table 3, urbanization at district level is reported from 1961. As can be seen from Tables 2 and 3, EKH district has the highest UL at 35.25 per cent which has increased only margnially in 1981 to 35.35 and gone down to 35.02 per cent in 1991. Other two districts which has town in 1961 are JH and WGH with rather low level of urbanization at 7.54 and 3.88 respectively. From 1961 to 1991 census, UL in these two districts has reached to 9.45 and 10.86 per cent respectively. As reported earlier between 1971 and 1981 census three new districts were and in 1981 census they had very low level of urbanization at 2.40 and 3.14 respectively which in 1991 stands at 6.61 and 6.34 respectively.

Looking at the decadal variation of urban population at the district level in Table 4, it ranges

Table 3: Urbanization at District Level

Distt.	1961	1971	1981	1991
JH	7.54	7.86	8.26	9.45
EKH	35.25	35.25	35.35	35.02
WKH	—	—	2.40	6.61
EGH	—	—	3.14	6.34
WGh	3.88	5.10	10.66	10.86
MEGH	15.27	14.55	18.07	18.69

Note: (*i*) JH, EKH, WKH, EGH, WGH and MEGh are districts of Jaintia Hills, East Khasi Hills, West Khasi Hills, Eats Garo Hills, West Garo Hills and State of Meghalaya, respectively.
(*ii*) Two newly created districts are not included in the analysis. For details refer to the text.
(*iii*) — denotes no urbanization of data not available.
Source: As in Table No. 1.

Table 4: Decadal Variation of Urban Population (District Wise)

Distt.	1951-61	1961-71	1971-81	1981-91
JH	—	44.09	44.73	60.28
EKH	100.78	19.88	47.29	27.27
WKH	—	—	—	270.57
EGH	—	—	—	179.37
WGH	—	74.27	157.63	31.58
MEGH	100.78	25.27	63.98	36.36

Note: As in Table 2.
Source: As in Table No. 1.

from 27.27 per cent in EKH to over 270 per cent for WKH in 1991. Similar variation may also be observed for other districts at their initial stages. As pointed out earlier, this exorbitantly high decadal variation reflects poor urban population base at which decadal variation is computed.

Another important characteristics of urbanization in Meghalaya is size class distribution of towns reported in Table 5. From 1901 to 1951 there was only one town which increased to 3 in 1951. In fact, two new class V towns emerged with three other recognized as town were part of Shillong UA. Number of towns as well as its population has stagnated because of changes in the size-class of towns during 1961-91 period which is reflected in Tables 5 and 6.

Table 5: Size-class Distribution of Towns in Meghalaya

		Size-Class of Towns					
Year	No. of Towns	I	II	III	IV	V	Vi
1961	3(6)	1	—	—	—	2	—
1971	3(6)	1	—		1	1	—
1981	7(12)	1	—	1	1	1	3
1991	7(12)	1	—	2	2	2	—

Note: As in Tables 1 and 2 above.
Source: As in Table No. 1 above.

Table 6: Population of Towns by Size-class in Meghalaya

	Size-Class					
Year	I	II	III	IV	V	VI
1961	102398	—	—	—	15085	—
1971	122752	—	—	15489	8929	—
1981	174703	—	35257	12923	6097	12353
1991	222273	—	66390	26363	14025	

Note: — denotes no town exits
Source: As in Table No. 1 above.

The decadal growth of towns in various size class could be computed only for 1971-81 and 1981-91 periods which is reported in Table 7. Somewhat peculiar picture emerges from Table 7 which again reflects changes in size class of towns. Finally, percentage distribution of total urban population as per the size class of the towns is given in Table 8. This shows continuous decline in share of Shillong UA. In 1961, its share was 87.20 which declined to 66.35 in 1991. In other size class, only class III town has

Table 7: Decadal Growth of Population of Towns by their Size-class

	Size class of Towns					
Year	I	II	III	IV	V	VI
1961	—	—	—	—	—	—
1971	—	—	—	—	—	—
1981	42.32		—	– 16.57	– 31.72	—
1991	27.23	—	88.30	104.00	130.49	—

Note: — denotes no town exits
Source: As in Table No. 1 above.

Table 8: Percentage Distribution of Total Urban Population by Size-class

	Size-class of Towns					
Year	I	II	III	IV	V	VI
1961	87.20	—	—	—	—	—
1971	83.41	—	—	10.52	6.07	—
1981	72.39	—	14.61	5.35	2.53	—
1991	66.35	—	20.92	8.30	4.43	—

Note: — denotes no town exits
Source: As in Table No. 1 above.

recorded increase in its share. Class IV and V towns have recorded sharp decline in 1981 and then moderate increase in their share in 1991.

Now, three observations stand out clearly from these tables. Firstly, UL in EKH the most urbanized district has stagnated over the period 1961-91. Secondly, despite very high decadal variation, urbanization in other districts has been rather low. And, thirdly, share of class I city Shillong in total urban population in very high making it a primate city in Meghalaya.

FACTORS AFFECTING URBANIZATION

In previous sections, various facets of urbanization in Meghalaya at aggregated as well as disaggregated level is reported. As pointed out above, at the aggregate level, despite high decadal variation, UL has been moving away from the national average. This observation is supported by rather erratic tempo of urbanization during 1961-91 period.

This may be attributed to components of urban growth where nearly 60 per cent of urban population growth is accounted for by reclassification (rural area to urban area) in 1961 and 1981. Contrary to this observation, in 1971 and 1991 around 80 per cent urban population growth came from residual category and only about 20 per cent from migration (3, 4). This seems to apply not only for the state as a whole but for various districts also. For exmaple, in EKH three new towns were reported in 1961 as out growth of Shillong and once again in 1981 three more towns were included.

Another possible reason for stagnation in urbanization may be found in the poor rural population base which might have weaker 'rural push'. In addition to these, 'urban pull factor does not appear to be very strong either. For, the functional characteristics of all most all the towns in Meghalaya is such that nearly 60 per cent of the work force is engaged in tertiary sector activities (3, 5). In the absence of significant manufacturing sector activities, job prospects for rural migrants appear to be limited. Thus, weak rural push and still weaker urban pull factor might have slackened the tempo of urbanization in Meghalaya.

CONCLUSIONS

In this paper we have looked at urbanization and growth of small towns in Meghalaya. The main observations which emerge are: (*i*) at the aggregate level, despite high decadal variation, ranking of Meghalaya has deteriorated, (*ii*) there is large inter-district variation both in urbaniation level and decadal urban population growth, (*iii*) despite presence of a class I city, functional characteristics of the town is similar, (*iv*) urbanization in Meghalaya has been mono centric with share of class I city being about 67 per cent in toral urban population.

These observation have far reaching consequences on both urbanization and economic development of Meghalaya. It is argued that urbanization and economic development have close association (1, 6). If we look at the urbanization in Meghalaya in this context, it appears to explain not only present level of under development but also hints at the shape of the things to come. In general, share of migration in urban population growth is reported to be around 40 percent which is rather low at around 20 per cent in Meghalaya (3). It is argued that migration takes place for better job opportunities in urban area which is dominated by manufacturing activities. As share of jobs in trade and commerce, transport and services is extremely high in Meghalaya accounting for about 60 to 70 per cent, expecting a sustained growth in urban population is rather remote.

Historically, role of human settlement has undergone revolutionary chages. In the post-industrial revolution period, urban centers are regarded center of non-primary activity, growing mainly due to substitution of capital and labour for land thereby creating positive externalities which is believed to be reason behind the growth of factor productivity (1, 7). As opposed to these functions, in pre-industrial revolution growth of urban centers became a pre-requisite from where polity could govern efficiently (8). It may be argued here that despite presence of big urban center, Shillong, positive externalities and scale of economy generated is not fully exploited here. Rather, the available data points towards the later use of urban centres in Meghalaya.

REFERENCES

1. Mohan, R.: *Urbanization in India's Future*. Paper presented at the UGC National Seminar on the future of Indian Economy, NIPF&P, New Delhi, July 3-5, 1984.
2. Jain, M.: Inter-state variation in the trend of Urbanization in India, IIPS, Bombay, (Mimeo.), 1977.
3. Government of India, Report of the National Commission on Urbanization, Vol. 2, New Delhi, 1988.
4. North East Council, Basic Statistics of NER, Shillong (Various issues).
5. Government of India, Census of India, Occassional paper-1 of 1986, New Delhi, 1986.
6. Kuznets, S.: Population Redistribution and economic Growth: United States (1870-1950, American Philosophical Society, Philadelphia, 1960.
7. A survey of Cities, The Economist, Vol. 336, July 29, 1995.
8. Mutulu, S.: *Urban Concentration and Primacy Revisited: An Analysis and Some Policy Conclusions*. Economic Development and Cultural Change, Vol. 34, 1986.

Chapter 9

PLANNING AND DEVELOPMENT FOR SMALL AND MEDIUM TOWNS IN MEGHALAYA

W. Syiem

Meghalaya has an Urbanization rate of approximately 18.6% as compared to the national rate of 25.72%. It is much higher than the average rate of the North East which is around 13.90%. Barring Mizoram and Manipur which have higher rates of urbanization, the other states of the North East have lower rates of Urbanization in the Region. The total population of the state if 17,74,778 and the total Urban population is 3,30,047 as per 1991 census.

As per 1991 census, it appears that the density of population both in urban as well as in the rural areas has increased in the last decade. The density in the rural areas rose up from 49 in 1981 to 65 per sq. km in 1991. The density in the urban areas increased from 2846 to 3883 per sq. km. The population growth for rural and urban areas in absolute terms has been to the extent of 3,50,245 and 88,714. Table No. 1 gives the density of population, sex ratio, growth of population during the last decade.

There are twelve settlements which have been classified as Urban areas. Shillong being the predominant Urban centre has six towns within its agglomeration with the total population of 2,23,366.

Table 1: Density of Population, Sex Ratio and Growth of Population in Meghalaya by Districts

District	Total/ Rural/ Urban	Density per sq.km.	Sex Ratio (Females per 1000 Males)	growth		Population during
		1981	1991	1981	1991	1981-91
1	2	3	4	5	6	7
1. Jaintia Hills	Total	41	58	978	973	64071
	Rural	38	52	978	973	56393
	Urban	1657	2575	994	975	7678
2. East Khasi Hills	Total	98	128	945	947	153804
	Rural	64	84	966	970	103461
	Urban	5446	7004	907	906	50343
3. West Khasi Hills	Total	31	42	949	951	58581
	Roral	30	39	953	951	48122
	Urban	318	1195	795	940	10459
4. East Garo Hills	Total	52	73	941	958	52280
	Rural	51	68	947	964	44566
	Urban	953	2401	772	875	7714
5. West Garo Hills	Total	66	86	963	960	110223
	Rural	60	77	972	967	97703
	Urban	1455	1924	888	903	12520
6. Meghalaya	Total	60	79	954	955	438959
	Rural	49	65	965	966	350245
	Urban	2846	3883	904	910	88714

Source: Census of India.

The other towns are all District Head Quarters except for Cherra Punjee which is a Sub-Divisional Head Quarter. The Shillong agglomeration with six towns has nearly 68% of Urban population and is the only class I city in the State followed by Shillong Municipality, Tura with the population 46,066 is a class III town, its population being less than fifty thousand. There is only one more District Head Quarter which falls in the category of class III town namely Jowai which has population of 20,601. The rest of the towns are all either class IV or class V towns. Nongstoin and Williamnagar are class IV towns, while Cherra Punjee and Baghmara are class V towns.

It is thus apparent that urbanization is

concentrated in Shillong Agglomeration as the remaining six towns only contribute a small percentage of Urban population. These Urban areas are basically administrative/commercial centres sub-serving the interest of agriculture economy in the hinterland. A close examination of the population in the urban centres reveals that the growth has been an induced one due to establishment of Administrative machinery and not because of the inherent strength in the economy of these towns and their hinterland.

What has been then the impact of urban growth in the State and in the small towns? Due to higher concentration of urban population in Shillong Agglomeration, the urban infrastructure has considerably been adversely affected. The civic services have been strained to the limit and unable to cope with the present requirement. On the other hand, the remaining six towns with low levels of population are not in a position to sustain various urban services.

These small towns are basically over grown Villages and got converted into urban centres through the setting up of various Govt. machinery changing the economy of these areas from agriculture to non-agriculture. These towns do not have much scope for growth except that if Govt. Machinery expand, these towns may also grow in the near future. There is no such scope of the Govt. Machinery getting expanded and thereby increasing the employment opportunity and strengthening the economic base. If this does not happen the growth of these towns may remain more or less static. Hence, if these urban centres have to develop as vibrating centres and as engines of growth, the potentaility of the district and the region needs to be exploited for *e.g.* In Jaintia Hills, Jowai is the only Urban centre which has 33,110 ha. of land under crops, only one registered factory & 238 small scale Industries. It has substantial mineral deposits including coal, relatively more enterprising people and friendly environment for setting up of enterprises and business. The coal deposits of Jaintia Hills are being exploited for export to Bangladesh as well as different parts of the country but all the services including finance & banking are largely done in Shillong and not at Jowai which has some infrastructure though not adequate. Jowai has a potential for development as a marketing centre/a Mandi town. If it has such potential then why so far not much has happened in this direction. It may be attributed mainly to proximity of Jowai to shillong where better level of services are available. This has affected the growth of Jowai. A conscious effort has to be made in this direction by adopting the following strategy.

1. Techno economic survey of the entire Jaintia Hills District.

2. Preparation of a project profile based on the above survey for economic exploitation of natural resources.

3. Providing such services at Jowai which are required.and necessary for exploitation of resources. This will not only improve the economy of the District but will also generate employment opportunity for the people of this area. It will also reduce considerably the cost of services which is required for business/ industrial activities and reduce the load on the National Highway.

Tura which is a class III town as per 1991 census is by now estimated to cross the fifty thousand mark hence no longer in the category of small towns. The small towns needed to be considered for proper development are Cherra Punjee and Nongpoh in the East Khasi Hills and Nongstoin in West Khasi Hills.

Cherra Punjee, though one of the oldest urban centres and the seat of Administration during the

British rule has remained more or less as a little urban area inspite of the fact that it has enormous tourist potential; well known through out the World as a place of one of the heaviest rainfall area. The Net Work of waterfalls are the main attraction to the Tourists besides its beautiful landscape including interesting places of cultural, religious or historical importance. If due attention is focussed on this aspect and appropriate actions are taken to tap its potential keeping social conditions in mind, Cherra Punjee can be developed as a tourist centre. However, talking about tourism leads us to the natural corollary it involves *i.e.*, infrastructure. Hence, adequate investment should be made in providing infrastructure to attract tourist inflow.

Nongpoh do not classify as an urban area as per census 1991. A Town Committee has been set up only recently. As per census 1991 any town having a Town Committee, a Municipal Board or a Notified Committee may be classified as an Urban Area. Hence, Nongpoh is a recent addition to the list of towns in the State. Nongpoh is a small settlement on the National Highway and can develop as a Transport Centre with adequate facilities for both goods and passenger traffic. Due to transportation activity, trade and commerce can also be developed. Hence Nongpoh can be developed as Commercial centre in East Khasi Hills. In West Khasi Hills Nongstoin has a population of 14,339 in 1991 and is a class IV town. It is mainly an Administrative headquarters, a rural area now out-grown into an Administrative Centre. The West Khasi Hills with rich deposit of silimanite and large tracts of forest area can support the town of Nongstoin to serve as Administrative cum Trading centre mainly in forest allied activities. It may also be the headquarters of small mining and related activities. The other urban area in West Khasi Hills is Mairang which has been declared as an urban area for the same reason as Nongpoh. Mairang Town Committee was set up three years ago after the census operation and was not included in the list of Urban Areas. Mairang has potential of being developed as a Mandi town due to its proximity with Agricultural land and State Highways passing through it-one leading to Nongstoin and Garo Hills and the other leading to Nongkhlaw both areas of which are rich in agriculture and forest land. Mairang may thus be developed as Mandi town with all the facilities as required so that it may facilitate Agricultural activities in the area.

In the Garo Hills the two small towns are the headquarters of East Garo Hills and South Garo Hills, Williamnagar having 12,004 populatin and Baghmara with 5894 population. Williamnagar is also an Administrative Centre. Commercial activity had not yet developed though it has a big hinterland including some of the areas in Assam. This town started in 1972 as a Sub-Divisional Head Quarter and its growth is mainly attributed to the development of Govt. machinery during the past twenty years. Although it has the potential of being developed as a Mandi Town as well as a commercial and Administrative Centre, this aspect has not been fully exploited due to its weak economic base and hence could not keep pace with the increased administrative activities. The fertile agricultural land and the forest is the vicinity provide ample opportunity for taping its potential.

Baghmara, the headquarters of the Sourth Garo Hills District, is close to the Inter-National Border and can serve as an International Trade Centre. Its coal is exported to Bangladesh from the vicinity of the town and plenty of trade between the two countries also take place. There is potential to develop this town as a trade centre for export of mineral, agricultural and forest produce. This, of course, requires heavy investment.

In the above paragraphs, an attempt has been made to examine the various towns in the State and their probable roles as centres of economic growth and to broadly classify these towns with respect to their potentiality of grow. In order to make more realistic assessment, it is necessary that further studies are carried out by the Govt. and non-Government Agencies to identify such activity which have potential and take necessary steps for their promotion.

Chapter 10

GROWTH OF TOWNS IN GARO HILLS

Kshirode Marak

The composite district of Garo Hills is situated in between 25°9' and 26°1' N and 89°49' and 91°2' E at the western most part of Meghalaya bounded on the north and the west by the districts of Goalpara and Dhubri of Assam, on the east by the district of Khasi Hills and on the south by the district of Mymensigh of Bangladesh covering an area of 8,160.86 sq. Km. with an international border of 171.2 Km. with Bangladesh. During the Mughal rule the plain tracts lying at the foothills of Garo Hills were under the occupation and control of powerful Zamindars of the estates of Mechpara, Bijni, Ghurla, Kalumalupara, Karaibari, Sherpur and Susang Durgapur (Sherpur and Susang Durgapur are now in Bangladesh). The Zamindars imposed tributes and cesses on the Garos and were encroaching upon the territories of the independent Garos. This led to the continual conflicts between those two peoples. The Garos used to make frequent murderous raids and head hunting into the Zamindary villages. This coupled with the internal quarrels among the Zamindars brought chaos and confusion in the area. On receipt of numerous complaints the Culcutta Fort William authorities in 1815 asked David Scott, Magistrate of Rangpur, to inquire and report on the prevailing situation in the area. David Scott after making extensive tour and meeting Garo chiefs submitted his report in 1816. On the basis of his recommendation Regulation X of 1822 was enacted by the Governor General-in-Council. Under this Regulation the control of Zamindars over the Garos was removed and also the General Regulation was not made applicable to the Garos. A special system of administration was introduced in the area under the direct control of the Commissioner of Cooch Behar.

The British were finding great difficulties to administer Garo Hills from their station at Goalpara because of lack of communication and infrastructure. Unrest in the frontier tracts was increasing due to continued head hunting and murderous raids being perpetrated by the turbulent mounteneer Garos. For the convenience of subjugating and bringing the turbulent Garos under the British rule, it was decided to set up a permanent administrative centre well inside Garo Hills and post a British Officer there. With this end in view, Lieutenant W.J. Williamson (later Capt Williamson) was appointed Asstt. Commissioner-in-Charge of Garo Hills. He entered Garo Hills via Singimari and established a station at Tura in 1867. Tura is derivative of 'Dura'. According to the Garo legend, 'Dura Abri' or 'Tura Hill' was the abode of an exceptionally beautiful and commanding Garo deity called "Durama". After her name the two villages in the Tura Range are called Duragiri and Durabanda. Even now many Garos living especially in Tura Ranges call Tura as Dura. Tura with the elevation of 1300 ft. above the sea level grew into a nerve centre of administration surrounded by the panorama of flora and fauna encompassed by the chirping of birds, chattering of monkeys and hullocks, murmuring of Gudumi, Rongkhon, Ringre and Gandrake streams as if a crazy beat displaying a musical concert. It occupied some portions of three Akhing Nokma lands, viz. Danakgre, Alotgre and

Megonggre Akhing lands. Population of Tura was around 300 only in 1868. It became accessible to the people after the construction of Tura-Damalgre-Mankachar road joining the Roumari steamer ghat, Tura-Goalpara road via Singimari, Tura-Dalu road and it attracted people after opening the Tura weekly hat in 1876. The establishment of American Baptist Mission in 1876 added more charm to Tura as it opened normal school in 1878, girl school in 1882 by Miss Miriam Russel. It was closed down in 1884 when Russel was transferred to Gauhati with her husband Rev. Edwin Charles Burdette. It was reopened by Miss Ella Cecillia Bond in 1886. One 15 bedded hospital was established by the Missionary named Dr. Galen Greenfield Crozier in 1908. The administrative complex started posing dignified and commanding centre as police barracks, jails, treasury, small hospital, court building, other office buildings, Deputy Commissioner's and other officiers' residential buildings and the residential houses of the office workers around it came up during the period 1868-1890. Population and size of the locality started increasing by new settlement, migration and opening of shops etc. Yet it did not come up to the status required for notifying it as town.

With the purpose of taking up social welfare works in the district the Government of Assam constituted a district committee called "The Garo Hills District Fund Committee" in 1915 by a Notification No. 4600 M dated 2nd October, 1915 with the Deputy Commissioner as the Chairman under the provision of the Assam Local Rates Regulation, 1879 (Regulation No. 3 of 1879) and within the ambit of the District Fund Committee, a separate fund called the Tura Fund Committee was constututed with the Deputy Commissioner as the Chairman vide Government Notification No. 1993-R dated 30th July, 1925. The District Fund was abolished by the Garo Hills Autonomous District Council when it came into existence on 14th, April, 1952 by an Act called the Garo Hills (Abolition of the Garo Hills District Fund Committee) Act, 1952 (Garo Hills Act No. 1 of 1952) for the purpose of constituting town committees under paragraph 3 of the Sixth Schedule to the Constitution of India. The first town committee came into the picture when a provisional Tura Town Committee was constituted by the Garo Hills Autonomous District Council vide Notification No. GDC-T/1/53/10 dated 30th July, 1953 which was validated by an Act called "The Garo Hills District (Administration of Town Committees) Act, 1956" (Act. No. 1 of 1957). The Rules called "The Garo Hills District (Constitution of Town Committees) Rules, 1957 were framed to carry out the purposes of the said Act. Under the said Rules a town committee shall be composed of six members of whom four shall be elected on the basis of adult suffrage and two nominated by the District Council. The term of the town committee shall be three years.

With the emergence of the Garo Hills Autonomous District Council with its headquarters at Tura the face of Tura started changing from wild looking into smooth and its stature from a sleepy looking hills into a buzzing urbanity. The District Council provided an avenue for availing of opportunity for an intercourse between the hill people and the plain people by starting operation of up and Down transport Bus Services from Tura to Goalpara, Tura-Mankachar, Tura-Dalu and Tura-Baghmara in 1953. It rose from a humble begining to a great height with booming countenance when the first President of India Dr. Rajendra Prasad visited Tura and Dalu in January, 1954. It was followed by a most attractive District Fair held at Tura with, among other things, pageantry performance when Miss Urmilla Ch. Momin and Shri

Prasad D. Sangma were adjudged Miss Garo Hills and Mr. Garo Hills respectively. Tura town stepped into a brighter arena when 50 KV Diesel Operated Power House was established at Hawakhana, a constituent of Tura town, in 1956. The town looked so beautiful at night from a distance as if a new planet with the wave of the twinkling stars dropped from the space and smiling at the darkness around it.

As per population norm for classification of towns as provided in the Census of India, Tura town came under the category of Class VI in 1941 Census when its population was 4,587. It was upgraded to Class V when its population exceeded 5,000 in 1951 census and Class IV in 1961 census as it exceeded 10,000. According to 1971 census, its population recorded was 15,489 and placed it under catagory of Class IV as the population norm for Class IV catagory is 10,000 to 19,999. It qualified to be rated as Class III when its population rose to 35,257 in 1981 census. It retained the same Class III status with 45,980 in 1991 census as the norm for that category ranges from 20,000 to 49,999 population. As empowered by the aforesaid Acts and Rules The Town Committee collected latrine tax at the rate of .50 p and light tax .50 p per household per month. It employed scavengers for clearance of night soils from the service latrines. This system was later done away with. The Tura dwellers were asked to go either for pit latrine or sanitary latrine. The garbages collected from the bazar areas and the roads in the truck were dumped at the dumping place outside the town area. it raised its fund by leasing out Tura bazar including Chandmari, Araimile and Najing bazars. Najing bazar was inaugurated on 14th October, 1974. Its fund also consisted of rents from the buildings and the Town Hall naming it Chhabighar for showing films every day. It also received grant-in-aid from the Garo Hills Autonomous District Council from time to time. But the fund was not sufficient for carrying out development and other works of civic amenities and town beautification scheme. The election to the town committee held only four times under the management of the District Council. The last election was held in July, 1974.

As moved by the District Council and demand made by the people of Tura the State Government established a Municipality constituting Tura Municipal Board consisting of 11 members including Chairman vide its NBotification No. MUN 67/74/130 dated 13th August, 1979 replacing the Tura Town Committee. Officially it came into existence on 12th Sept. 79. With the financial assistance from the State Government the Board has taken up measures for providing certain facilities and basic amenities of the people under NRY Schemes. It is implementing schemes of town beautification including street lighting, cleaning of bazars and roads etc. The construction of Tura Super Market of Rs. 4.70 crore estimate is also being done through the Board. it is observed that for want of sufficient fund the Board could not implement many welfare schemes to the dismay of general public.

The Municipal fund consists of own resources and the Government grant. The income and expenditure for 1994-95 and 1995-96 as estimated by the Board are shown below—

INCOME

	Item	1994-95	1995-96
1.	Development Fund from the State Govt.	15,00,000	3,00,000
2.	Income from own resources	5,12,000	(It will be known after the end of the financial year)
		Total = 20,12,000	

Income from the auction-sale of Tura bazar including Najing bazar, Araimilex and Chandmari	1994-95 = 1,72,000 1995-96 = 3,03,500

EXPENDITURE

Head	1994-95	1995-96
A. Pay and allowances	12,39,467	13,19,231
B. Office equipment & Stationaries	3,53,904	4,06,000
C. Other miscellaneous contingencies	20,500	45,000
D. Town Conservation	3,83,777	4,03,800
E. Public Safety	6,88,000	11,80,487
F. New Proposal	—	2,75,000
Total =	26,85,648	36,29,518

Works being undertaken—

1. General Scheme.

2. Re-construction of Tura bazar—

(1) Estimate 4.70 crores.

(2) Fund released by the State Govt. till the writting of this paper 243.19 lakhs.

3. Central Govt. Sponsored Schemes—

(1) NRY—Administrative and operational expenses.

(2) SUWE—Scheme for Urban Works Enterprises: Under this Scheme 60% is spend for materials and 40% for labour.

(3) SUME—Scheme for Urban Micro Enterprise. It is a loan-cum-subsidy scheme for taking up small scale industries such as weaving and black-smithy etc. Out of the total amount sanctioned three-fourth percent loan will be given by the State Bank of India and one-fourth per cent subsidy by the Tura Municipality.

(4) MEDICAL PROGRAMME—It is called Urban Basic Service Programme under which the following programmes are being implemented since 1991-92.

Supplementary Nutrition Programme (SNP) for the poor children of the age group 0-6 years, deworming and immunization and also nutritional programme for pregnant and the lactatic women for breast feeding upto the age of 6 months.

Apart from the development works taken up by

the Municipal Board the District Council has constructed two parks one of which has been beautifully developed by the Coal India Ltd. and installed a full-size statue of late Capt. Williamson A. Sangma, first Chief Minister of Meghalaya and named the place William Point. The State Forest Department has also constructed D.C. Park near Deputy Commissioners' Office and Nehru Park at Danakgre Near MBOSE. It is constructing another Park at Araimile near Home Guards' Office complex.

No election has been held till now though there is a demand from the Tura dwellers and though delimitation of 11 ward-constituencies had already been done in May, 1985 by the Delimitation Committee constituted by the State Govt. vide its Notification No. MUN. 91/83/18 dt. 5th March 1984. It is learnt that the present Municipal Board had moved the Government for increasing the number of wards from 11 to 15.

To meet the demand of the time two Town Committees were constituted by the District Council, one is Baghmara Town Committee is 1975 with population of 4,128 (1981 census) another William Nagar Town Committee in 1987 with population of 4,290 (1981 census). These Town Committees did not have own resources. The fund released by the District Council from time to time was not sufficient for carrying out development works. Very recently these two own committees had been upgraded to Municipality by the State Government. It is yet to be seen the performance of these new Municipalities. Two more town Committees viz. Dalu Town Committee and Resubelpara Town Committee each having less than 5000 population had been constituted and Notifications in this regard had been issued vide No. GDC-RA/DTC/180/85-86/142 dated 20-9-94 for Dalu and No. GDC-RA/RTC/210/92-93/200 dated 29-9-

94 in respect of Resubelpara but both these towns are still having rural outlook. It will take considerable time for them to assume the urban character unless the State Government and the District Council take keen interest in their development.

CONCLUSION

Tura Town has registered tremendeous development during the last three decades. It is expanding in demension with increasing population year after year with the establishment of more Government offices, schools, colleges, small scale industries and business enterprises. But the sufficient basic amenities are yet to be provided by the Municipal Board. A proper line of action should be taken by the Board for removal of garbages regularly not only from Tura main bazar but also from other connected bazars and households. Action should also be taken for utilising the garbages for production of bio-gas for public use.

A town committee or municipality pre-supposes local self-government based on the doctrine of democracy. It losses its democractic character if the people cannot send their representatives to the town committees or municipalities through election. Tura Municipality has not yet comtemplated for holding election. At present the Municipal Boards and the town committees are composed of ad-hoc Boards and the committees consisting of members appointed by the State Government. The Town Committees are under the control of the District Council which confers powers and functions as deemed necessary on the committee. Therefore, in order to realise the goal of the local self-government and make them economically viable the District Council should arrange for holding elections to these Committees after the expiry of each term and entrust them with the power for mobilising resources. The municipality is controlled by the State Government. So, the State Government should see that it functions properly in the interest of the public and also see that election is held regularly to build up strong democratic local self-government institution in the interest of the general public of the town.

Chapter 11

URBAN SOLID WASTE MANAGEMENT IN A SMALL TOWNS

1. With the rapid increase in Urbanization, the Civic services such as water supply, sanitation and sewerage, are under considerable strain. One of the most neglected services in towns and cities is the solid waste collection and disposal. Even the large cities with relatively higher resources are not in a position to collect and dispose of the solid waste properly. It is more so in small and medium towns where solid waste disposal system get the least priority. In the following an attempt is made to suggest a machanism for proper solid waste system in small towns of Meghalaya.

2. Solid wastes consist of—

(a) Domestic waste—Such waste are generated from the residential and commercial areas of the town.

(b) Industrial waste—Small towns in Meghalaya barring Cherra Punjee does not have any medium or large scale industries; industries wastes are generated from the auto repair workshops saw mills and other service Industries.

(c) Waste from Hospitals, Clinics etc—Except for Govt. hospital and one or two private hospital, there are not many such units in small towns in the state, unlike Shillong where private nursing home, and private hospitals and clinics are on increase. Wastes from hospitals is hazardous and need to be separated from the domestic waste. This is hardly done. The hospital waste and domestic waste are collected together in the same vehicles. The incineration units installed in Govt. and private hospitals invariably do not function.

3. For proper solid waste management in small towns, the need for stream lining the process of collection, transportation, is imperative. The present system of collection is through dustbins which is not efficient and are provided only in Jowai & William Nagar. The numbers of dustbins are ar from satisfactory and generally household waste is disposed of within the compound of the individual houses. Such disposal system now perhaps is not workable. At present even in the small towns such as William Nagar and Baghmara and Jowai there is a need for collection of garbage from the individual houses as there is enormous pressure on land and open space within the residential area is getting reduced.

3.1. There are two methods of garbage collection one is that dustbins/containers are installed at convenient distances from houses to dispose of the garbage which is collected by the conservancy staff of Municipal Board/Town Committee. The other system to collect garbage from door to door and dump into the garbage vehicles. Both system of collection has shortcoming. In the first case, since the responsibility of disposing of the garbage is with the individual household there is a tendency to throw the garbage in the road side instead of disposing the same within the dustbins and containers. Even if the householder throws the garbage in the dustbins while doing so the garbage spills around the dustbins, there by making the area filthy and unapproachable. The Municipal staff also while taking out garbage leave behind small pieces of waste materials which become a breeding ground for bacteria to grow and become potential health hazard.

3.2. The system of collection of garbage from door to door is expensive as man power and vehicles have to move through out the town. This system of collection is generally not adopted by Municipal Board on consideration of cost. Cost of collection of garbage either in the plastic bags or some other containers are generally not affordable by the inhabitants of small towns.

3.3. The Municipal waste are generally transported by trucks/tractors and such other vehicles; except for Jowai where there is a truck available; in the other small towns there is no vehicle available for the purpose. There is an urgent need for purchase of at least two vehicles for each of the small towns so that garbage is collected and disposed of regularly.

3.4. As regard the final disposal, in none of the small towns there is any scientific disposal system. The garbage is just thrown in the dumping yard at Jowai and Willian Nagar; Baghmara and Nongstoin do not have a regular dumping ground. Hence there is no proper disposal system. It may not be desirable to wait and watch the situation to get aggravated and then think of a system for efficient collection and disposal of garbage; right from now an attempt should be made in this direction as outlined below.

3.5. Proper collection of Waste from Household—This may be done from door to door once a day, as house holder in the small towns may not like to keep the garbage within the house. This may be acceptable in the long run and perhaps we may reduce frequency of collection to the thrice or twice a week. Since bio-non degredable materials cause enormous difficulity in disposal and are intermixed with degredable material in the domestic waste, its disposal become difficult. Hence it is necessary that in-organic and recycleable materials are segregated at the household level itself and collection may be made every day for which services of ragpickers and NGOs may be utilized for collection of garbage from door to door. Such arrangement may be more economical as Municipal Boards may not deploy their own staff. Small towns in the State do not have large number of cleaning staff. NGOS and unemployed may be encoraged to form groups/ societies to take up such works. Financial assistance may be provided to such groups of people for procurement of small vehicles such as motor cycle, with a small trailer or attachment (similar to auto rickshaws) with suitable body for collection of solid waste from individual house holds. These vehicles may be used from house-hold up to the main road where garbage can be transported to the Municipal trucks. This will mean that from every house-hold two packet is to be collected one containing non-degredable material like plastic and recycleable like paper and the other having organic waste. In the small towns, the daily markets are not many, it is desirable that garbage is collected every day directly by the Municipal trucks.

3.6. The common disposal system of land filling is not practical. In our context, land in depressions and valleys are normally used for Agriculture purposes even in the Urban areas, for *e.g.* in Baghmara and Nongstoin vast stretches of the land in the town areas even now are used for growing paddy. Even if such land is available, the system is not scientific as through the leaching action, ground water gets contaminated. The compact garbage in the land fill under pressure under goes slow-de-composition and methane and other gases find its way to the surface and pollute to the atmosphere. There is a chance of flash fire when methane comes out of the surface. Incineration if adopted for disposal of waste, may lead to environmental pollution. Humidity content in the garbage in the small towns is in the range of 60-80%

system of collection is generally not adopted by Municipal Board on consideration of cost. Cost of collection of garbage either in the plastic bags or some other containers are generally not affordable by the inhabitants of small towns.

3.3. The Municipal waste are generally transported by trucks-tractors and such other vehicles; except for Jowai where there is a truck available; in the other small towns there is no vehicle available for the purpose. There is an urgent need for purchase of at least two vehicles for each of the small towns so that garbage is collected and disposed of regularly.

3.4. As regard the final disposal, in none of the small towns there is all cities perhaps such units may be sustainable at the State/Regional level.

4. In other to make operation successfull and to sustain the above collection and disposal system, it is imperative that services of N.G.O.s are availed for iniating an awareness programme about the new system of waste management. The palletisation plant may be installed by the State Govt./Urban local bodies and may be managed by N.G.O. Group of unemployed youth or other private parties.

REFERENCES

1. Planning for solid waste management at Shillong National Environment Engineering Research Institute Nagpur, 1991.
2. Community based solid waste Management, Project Preparation, Panaji care Study.
3. Proposal for Shillong, UCAL, Power Systems ltd. Madras.

Chapter 12

SPATIO-TEMPORAL PATTERN AND CHARACTERISTICS OF SMALL TOWNS IN ASSAM

B.K. Kar and M.M. Das

The urban centres, small or large, play a significant role in the overall socio-economic functioning of any region. As a matter of fact, urbanisation is the result of economic changes that take place as the region develops. A place, being influenced by locational advantages, resource base, population, functional activities and infrastructural facilities, etc., may emerge as a centre of agglomeration. Such a centre definitely exerts a great impact on the socio-economic life of people of its surrounding rural area. The process of urbanisation has been altogether very alwo in Assam. It gained momentum only after the Independence of the country, as a result of which the percentage of urban population in the state rose from 4.30 in 1951 to 11.10 in 1991 as against the corresponding national averages of 17.30 and 26.10. With the urban population size of 2,487,795 Assam constitutes only 1.14 percent of the total urban population of the country (1991 census). Again, depending on the potential resource base, socio-economic transformation and locational factors, the level of urbanisation and its trend spatially vary

---

Mr. B.K. Kar is Lecturer in Geography, Gauhati Univeristy and Dr. M.M. Das is Professor of Geography, Gauhati University.

across the state.

In this paper, an attempt is made to examine the spatio-temporal patterns of urbanisation with special reference to the small urban centres (the urban centres whose population size is below 20,000 as per census of India) in the state and understand the underlying characteristics of the urban centres, especially the small ones, based on the data from census of India for the periods 1901-1991 in general and 1971-1991 in particular.

Out of the six categories of urban centres as per the Census of India, such as Class I with a population of 1 lakh and above, Class II with 50,000-99,999, Class III with 20,000-49,999, Class IV with 10,000-19,999, Class V with 5,000-9,999 and Class VI with below 5,000, the lowest three categories (*i.e.*, IV, V and VI) have been clubbed together to designate as small town, whereas the class I as City, Class II as large town and Class III as medium town for meaningful comparative analysis of the urban centres in the country.

SPATIO TEMPORAL PATTERN

Temporal pattern—As per the 1991 Census, Assam has a total of 87 urban centres including 6 urban agglomerations, such as Jorhat U.A., Dibrugarh U.S., Digboi U.A., Lumding U.A., Badarpur U.A. and Bongaigaon U.A. Out of these urban centres there are 59 small towns which comprise 32 class IV towns, 15 class V towns and 12 Class VI towns and constitute 25.05 per cent of the total urban population of the state. On the other hand, only 4 cities (Guwahati, Dibrugarh, Jorhat and Silchar) constitute as high as 37.69 per cent, 4 large towns (Nagaon, Tinsukia, Dhubri, and Tezpur) 11.60 per cent and 20 medium towns 25.66 per cent. Although in respect of total urban population, the small towns seem to be not very significant, they are expected to play a greater role in acting as growth centres for development in the rural areas in comparison to the big urban centres (medium, large and city).

Upto 1921 there was not a single big urban centre in the state. But 1931 onward with the increase in the number of medium and large towns as a consequence of conversion of the small towns, the percentage of urban population constituted by the small towns started falling from 86.55 in 1931 to 25.05 in 1991. However, the population size of the small towns increased from 1,40,369 in 1931 to 6,23,232 in 1991 witnessing an average annual growth rate of 2.51 per cent as against 4.65 per cent for all the urban centres. In addition to this, it is observed that the small towns in the state have always recorded a lower decadal growth rate from 1931 onward compared to the big urban centres and for that matter all the urban centres. It may be mentioned that during 1971-1991 the population growth in the small towns was 23.23 per cent as against 137.98 per cent in the big urban centres indicating a glaring gap between the two categories (Table 1).

As regards the growth in the number of small and big urban centres, it is observed that upto 1921 all the 22 urban centres in Assam were small towns. Only in 1931 one small town (Guwahati) was upgraded to medium category town. Whereas it emerged as only city in the year 1961. On the other hand, the number of small towns has been gradually increasing since 1901 to 1991 except in the year 1951 when it decreased to 18 only from 22 in 1941. This is because of the fact that during 1941-1951 four small towns were upgraded to big towns, but there was no addition of small towns. From 1961 to 1991 there was rapid growth in the number of small towns from 31 to 59. In spite of the fact that some of the small towns were

Table 1 : Trend of Urban Population in Assam, 1901-1991.

Year	Number of Towns		Urban Population		% of popula- tion total urban popula- tion in small	Population Growth (in per- centage)		
	All Towns	Small Towns	All Towns	Small Towns	Towns	All Towns	Big Towns	Small Towns
1901	12	12	77,074	77,074	100	—	—	—
1911	14	14	92,916	92,916	100	20.55	—	20.55
1921	22	22	1,27,107	1,27,107	100	36.80	—	36.80
1931	22	21	1,62,166	1,40,369	86.55	27.58	—	10.43
1941	24	22	2,08,067	1,55,278	74.83	28.30	142.18	10.62
1951	24	18	3,44,831	1,56,985	45.52	65.73	255.84	1.10
1961	53	41	7,81,288	3,31,255	42,40	126.57	139.57	111.01
1971	69	54	1,289,222	5,05,731	39,23	65.01	74.10	52.67
1991	87	59	2,487,795	6,23,232	25.05	92.97	137.97	23.23

* Small Towns are those whose population size is below 20.000

** Big Towns are those whose population size is above 20.000.

Source: Census of India. Assam. Provisional. 1991 and Final. 1991.

upgraded to big towns, the number of small towns had increased as a result of the emergence of new small towns. It may be mentioned that as high as 53 new small towns emerged during the period 1951-1991 (Table 1 and Fig. 1).

Spatial Pattern—The urban centres including the small ones are distributed unevenly in the state. While Dhubri, Barpeta and Kamrup districts have the highest number of urban centres each accouting for 7, followed by Nagaon and Karbi Anglong each having 6 urban centres, Dhemaji has the lowest number of urban centre accounting for only 1. It is found that the districts like Dhubri, Barpeta, Kamrup and Karbi Anglong each contains 5 small towns, highest among the districts, whereas Jorhat district does not contian a single small town. In respect of population size, these 20 small towns together comprise 31.47 per cent of total population of all the 59 small towns in the state. Among the small towns again, there are 10 towns whose population size is below 5000. The

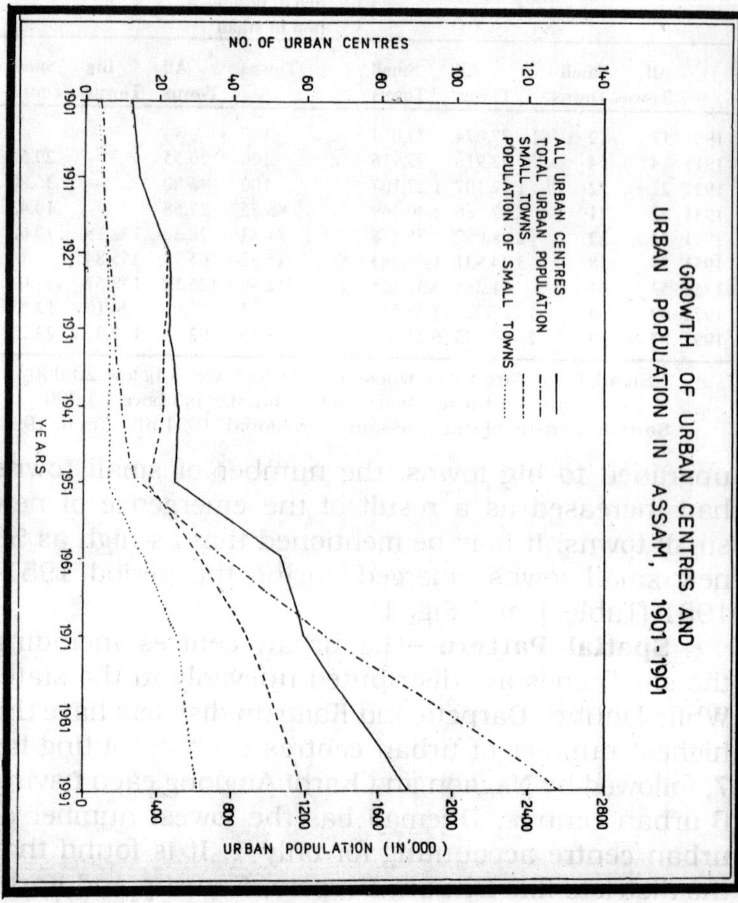
GROWTH OF URBAN CENTRES AND
URBAN POPULATION IN ASSAM, 1901-1991
ALL URBAN CENTRES
TOTAL URBAN POPULATION
SMALL TOWNS
POPULATION OF SMALL TOWNS
NO. OF URBAN CENTRES
0
20
40
60
80
100
120
140
URBAN POPULATION (IN'000)
0
400
800
1200
1600
2000
2400
2800
1901
1911
1921
1931
1941
1951
1961
1971
1981
1991
YEARS

FIG-1

number of small towns in each of the districts of Goalpara, Lakhimpur, Dhemaji, Karimganj, Hailakandi and Cachar is only 1. It may further be mentioned that each of the districts of Kamrup, Jorhat, Dibrugarth and Cachar has 1 city. It is interesting to note that the districts of Jorhat and Cachar have shown the tendency of concentrated urbanisation, whereas urbanisation in the districts of Nagaon and Tinsukia seems to be balanced one (Table 2 and Fig. 2).

Table 2: Catagorywise Distribution of Urban Centres in Assam, 1991.

District	City (Population Size 1 Lakh & above)	Large Town (Population 50,000 - 1 Lakh)	Medium Towns (Population 20,000 - 50,000)	Small Town (Population below - 20,000)	Total
1. Dhubri	—	1	1	5	7
2. Kokrajhar	—	—	1	2	3
3. Bongaigaon	—	—	1	3	4
4. Goalpara	—	—	1	1	2
5. Barpeta	—	—	2	5	7
6. Nalbari	—	—	—	2	2
7. Kamrup	1	—	1	5	7
8. Darrang	—	—	1	3	4
9. Sonitpur	—	1	—	3	4
10. Lakhimpur	—	—	1	1	2
11. Dhemaji	—	—	—	1	1
12. Marigaon	—	—	—	3	3
13. Nagaon	—	1	2	3	6
14. Golaghat	—	—	1	2	3
15. Jorhat	1	—	1	—	2
16. Sibsagar	—	—	1	4	5
17. Dibrugarh	1	—	—	4	5
18. Tinsukia	—	1	2	2	5
19. Karbi Anglong	—	—	1	5	6
20. N.C. Hills	—	—	1	2	3
21. Karimganj	—	—	1	1	2
22. Hailakandi	—	—	1	1	2
23. Cachar	1	—	—	1	2
Assam	4	4	20	59	87

Source: Census of India, Assam, 1991, Final.

Like the uneven distribution of urban centres, there is spatial variation in the levels of urbanisation

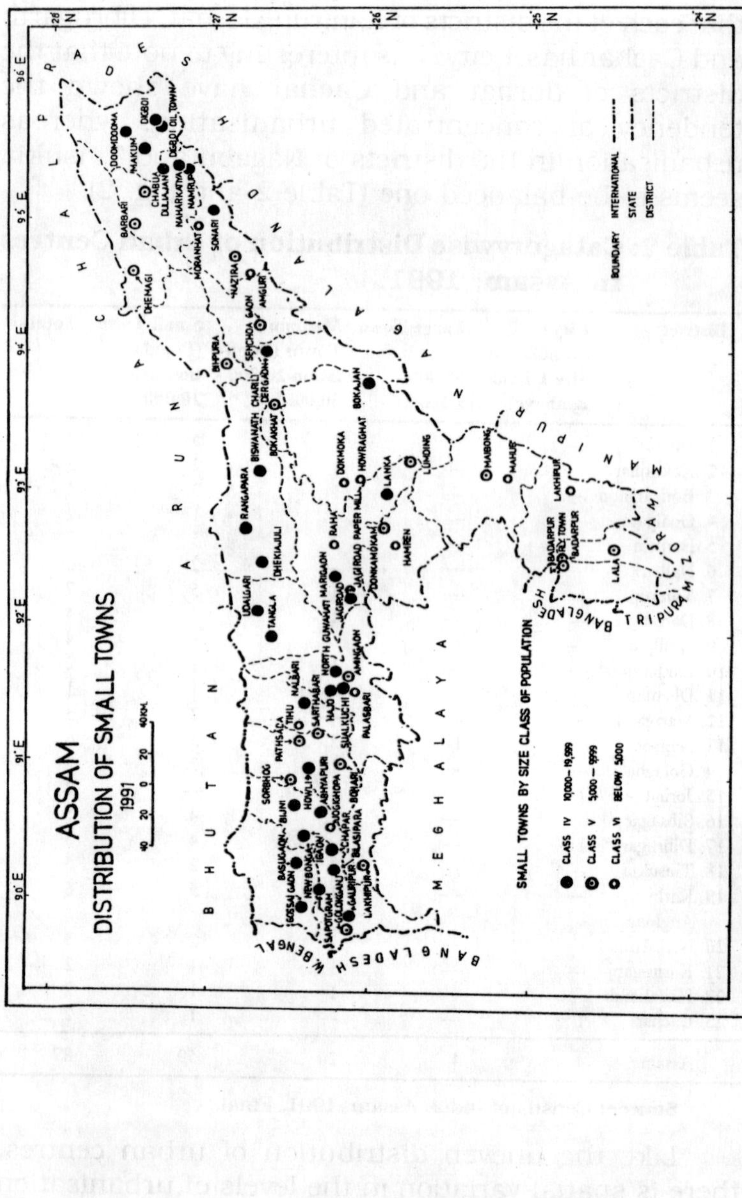
ASSAM
DISTRIBUTION OF SMALL TOWNS
1991
SMALL TOWNS BY SIZE CLASS OF POPULATION
CLASS IV 10,000 – 19,999
CLASS V 5000 – 9999
CLASS VI BELOW 5000
BOUNDARY INTERNATIONAL
STATE
DISTRICT
BHUTAN
ARUNACHAL PRADESH
NAGALAND
MANIPUR
MEGHALAYA
MIZORAM
TRIPURA
BANGLADESH
W. BENGAL

FIG- 2

indicated by percentage of urban population to total population in different districts of the state. It is observed that among the districts Kamrup has recorded the highest level of urbanisation (32.76 per cent) on the one hand, and the lowest level of urbanisation (1.86 per cent) is found in Dhemaji on the other (Figure 3). Although, N.C. Hills district shows the second highest level of urbanisation (22.87 per cent) in the state, the percentage of urban population to total urban population is very low (1.38 per cent). While taking into consideration the three indicators of urbanisation number of urban centres, percentage of urban population to total population and percentage of urban popultion to total urban population in the state it is found that the districts of Dhubri, Kamrup, Dibrugarh and Tinsukia exhibit a higher level of urbanisation compared to other districts.

The population growth of individual urban centres also significantly varies across the state. Depending upon the varying nature of population growth during 1971-1991, the urban centres in the state may be boradly categorised as having explosive growth (200 per cent and above), rapid growth (100-200 per cent), moderate growth (60-100 per cent), slow growth (30-60 per cent), stagnating growth (0-30 per cent) and declining growth (below 0 per cent) (Table 3). Accordingly, while three urban centres viz., Sonari, Haflong and Diphu witness the explosive growth, two urban centres, viz. Barpeta and Badarpur exhibit declining growth. Among the small towns in 1971, Sonari recorded the highest percentage growth during 1971-1991 (408.53), followed by Haflong (407.41) and Diphu (287.71). The highest percentage growth in Sonari is accounted for by the declaration of Sub-divisional headquarters of Charaideo sub-division of Sibsagar district accompanied by extension of urban area covering several adjacent villages. The explosive

Table 3: Distribution of Small and other Urban Centres in respect of Population Growth Categories during 1971-1991 in Assam.

Population Growth	Number of Urban Centres	Small Towns (As per 1971)	Other Towns (Medium & Large Towns and Cities)
Above 200 (Explosive Growth)	3	Sonari, Diphu, Haflong	—
100-200 (Rapid Growth)	10	Goalpara, Gosaigaon, Rangia Dhemaji, Namrup, Margherita Makum	Guwahati, North Lakhimpur, Silchar
60-100 (Moderate Growth)	12	Abhayapuri, Lakhimpur, Man-Kachar, Kokrajhar, North Guwahati, Barpeta Road, Mangaldoi, Tangla, Marigaon, Bihpuria.	Bongaingaon, Nagaon
30-60 (Slow Growth)	33	Bilashipara, Gouripur, Bijni, Tihu, Nalbari, pathsala, Howli, Kharupetia, Dhekiajuli, Rangapara, Biswanatha Chariali, Mariani, Amguri, Nazira, Moranhat, Golaghat, Dergaon, Bokakhat, Chabua, Duliajan, Oil Town, Naharkatia, Doom Dooma, Hailakandi, Lala.	Dhubri, Tezpur, Lumding, Hojai, Jorhat, Sibsagar, Dibrugarh, Tinsukia, Karimganj.
0-30 (Stagnating Growth)	11	Sapatgram, Basugaon, Sualkuchi, Niz-Hajo, Amingaon, Palasbari, Sarbhog, Sarthebari, Dhing, Digboi, Lakhimpur.	—
Below 0 (Declining Growth)	2	Badarpur	Barpeta

Source: Census of India, Assam, 1971 and 1991.

growth of urban population in Haflong and Diphu is the result of the growth of tertiary activities in the recent years pulling large number of people from other part of the state. In the case of Diphu there has also been expansion of urban boundary covering some adjacent villages. In consequence of such an explosive growth of population, the small towns like Haflong and Diphu have been upgraded to medium category towns. On the other hand, Badarpur is the most declining small town (– 16.25 per cent growth during 1971-1991) as a result of reduction of the area

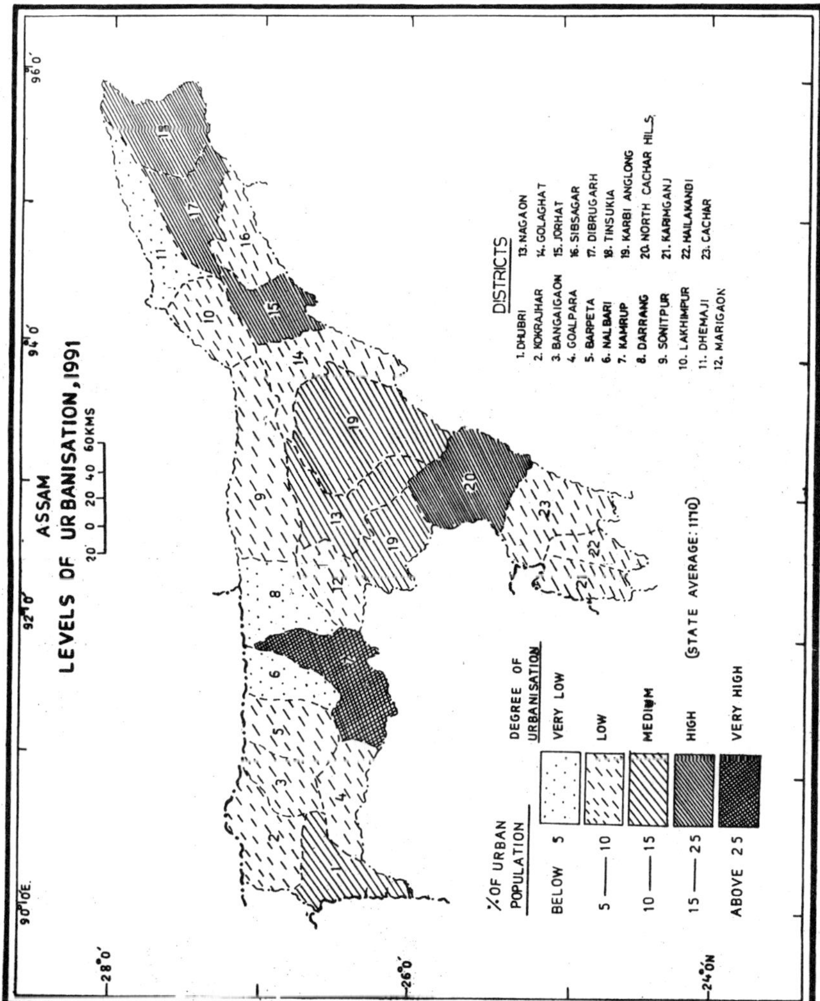
ASSAM
LEVELS OF URBANISATION, 1991
20 0 20 40 60KMS
% OF URBAN POPULATION
DEGREE OF URBANISATION
BELOW 5 VERY LOW
5 — 10 LOW
10 — 15 MEDIUM
15 — 25 HIGH
ABOVE 25 VERY HIGH
(STATE AVERAGE: 11.10)
DISTRICTS
1. DHUBRI
2. KOKRAJHAR
3. BANGAIGAON
4. GOALPARA
5. BARPETA
6. NALBARI
7. KAMRUP
8. DARRANG
9. SONITPUR
10. LAKHIMPUR
11. DHEMAJI
12. MARIGAON
13. NAGAON
14. GOLAGHAT
15. JORHAT
16. SIBSAGAR
17. DIBRUGARH
18. TINSUKIA
19. KARBI ANGLONG
20. NORTH CACHAR HILLS
21. KARIMGANJ
22. HAILAKANDI
23. CACHAR
90°0'E
92°0'
94°0'
96°0'
28°0'
26°0'
24°0'N

FIG. 3

of Badarpur Town Committee by government notification in 1979. Another town which shows a declining growth of – 4.12 per cent during 1971-91 is Barpeta, the head-quarters of Barpeta district. Being surrounded by low-lying areas, the town has little scope for horizontal expansion and development of transport communication and industrial activities. As a consequence of such a repulsive situation the town dwellers have been compelled to outmigrate in large number in search of economic opportunities elsewhere. Besides, there are 11 small towns in the state which have stagnating growth. This is because of the fact that there has neither been expansion of urban areas nor expansion of secondary and tertiary activities in all these towns during the referred period. Among all these towns, Sualkuchi is the most stagnating one (growth during 1971-91 was 3.90 per cent). Based solely on traditional silk industry at household level, Sualkuchi two does not have any other kinds of economic activities. Due to non-availability of other economic opportunities and limited absorption capacity of the silk industry, large number of people are compelled to outmigrate in search of various tertiary occupations in other urban centres leading to the stagnating growth of population in the town. like Barpeta town, transport bottleneck is also one of the repulsive factors for the growth of the town.

CHARACTERISTICS

The urban characteristics in the small towns of the state can be understood from the study of occupational behaviour of their people. It is found that the overall work participation rate was 29.38 per cent in the small towns in 1991 census as against 29.69 per cent in medium and large towns and 33.21 per cent in the cities. There had been marginal growth of work participation rate during 1971-1991 in the small towns of the state (Table 4). This is indicative of the fact that there had been little expansion of employment opportunities in these towns. Moreoer, during this period the high dependency ratio indicated by higher percentage of non-workers is the result of their slow progress of economic development.

Table 4 : Occupational Pattern of Urban Centres in Assam, 1971 and 1991.

Category of Urban Centres	% of workers to Total Population		% of workers in Primary Sector		% of workers in Secondary Sector		% of workers in Tertiary Sector	
	1971	1991	1971	1991	1971	1991	1971	1991
1. Small Town	28.67	29.38	13.88	12.97	22.72	19.98	63.30	66.55
2. Medium and Large Town	30.25	29.69	4.67	11.05	20.25	19.39	73.36	71.10
3. City	32.92	33.21	2.22	5.32	18.25	17.21	79.52	77.44
All Urban Centres	29.81	30.40	8.82	8.84	21.35	19.22	68.63	71.19

Source: Census of India, 1971 and 1991, Assam.

So far occupational structure is concerned, the small towns still engage 12.97 per cent workers in primary occupation as against 11.05 per cent in medium and large towns and 5.32 per cent in the cities, while almost all the urban centres are primarily based on tertiary occupation (trade and commerce and services). Industry-based secondary sector also engages less than 20 per cent of the total urban workers in the state. It is interesting to note that although the small towns have relatively low percentage of workers in tertiary sector, they have experienced a higher rate in this sector than the medium and large towns and cities during 1971-1991. But on the whole, the urban centres including the small ones have not witnessed any significant change in their functional characteristics.

Little functional diversification in most of the

small towns is due to the fact that they are nothing but service centres with limited adiministrative, transporation and educational functions serving the surrounding rural areas leading to slow population growth. However, some towns like Digboi, Naharkatia, Duliajan and Nazira which are basically industrial centres also have not experienced a significant functional diversification and higher population growth because of the absence of locational advantage, administrative functions and trade and commerce in all these towns. For such a situation the small towns have not been playing a key role in the balanced dispersal of economic growth and development in the state.

CONCLUSION

The above analysis reveals that with slow growth of population the small towns of Assam witness little functional diversity. Being merely the aggregates of few advanced villages with some urban services including transport facilities, the small towns in the state are nothing but some service centres or market centres or important transport nodes. That is why the small towns have little scope for rapid expansion. Morever, the pattern of urbanisation in the state is somewhat concentrated or accumulative in nature which gives little opportuntieis to the small towns to expand both in population size and functional behaviour. The predominatly agro-based economy of the hinterland and absence of industrialisation also hinder the process of sound urban development. On the whole, at the present situation, the small towns play a less significant role in the overall socio-economic development of the state and bring a little change in the social life of the people.

Thus in order to bring about a balanced development and to solve the growing probelms of congestion and other associated problems in the large towns and cities, there is an urgent need for proper urban development planning. Planned decentralisation of dispersal of certain activities or functions and services from the large towns and cities to the small towns also needs to be emphasised and executed. This would no doubt help the urban centres to function as growth poles for diffusing the process of development both in the urban and rural areas.

REFERENCES

Census of India, 1991: Primary Census Abstract of Assam, (Comptuer Print out).

Census of India, 1991: Provisional Population Totals: Rural-Urban Distribution, Series 4, Assam.

Census of India, 1991: Aspects of Population Profile of Assam, Series 4.

Census of India, 1991: Final Population, Series I, India, Paper 1 & 2.

Directorate of Statistics and Economics, 1980 & 1994: Statistical Hand Book, Assam.

Jain, M.K., Ghose, M. and Kin, W.B., 1993: *Emerging Trends of Urbanisation in India: An Analysis of 1991 Census Results*, Census of India, 1991.

Chapter 13

MUNICIPAL MANAGEMENT IN SMALL TOWNS

S.K. Agnihotri

The broader definition of "municipal" encompasses all the functions within the municipality viz. delineation of specific goals, sustainable use of environmental resources, "enabling" (as against top down) approach involving participation of all important actors including women; change in planning paradigm conceived as a process and supported by realistic strategies, identification of key areas and options for improved municipal management (incluidng land management, infrastructure and services, transport, financial management and organisational performance), institutional partnership including government support. In the present paper an attempt has been made to consider improvement in some of these areas.

The municipal governments at all levels find it hard to cope with their statutory functions, let alone undertaking innovative management programmes because of lack of resources, both financial and organisational. Therefore, urban management is not yet generally practised beyond the frame of traditional urban administration except for some innovative approaches adopted in selected cities. Urban management has yet to be given the attention it deserves as a specialisation in the field. This is inspite of the fact that some institutions have been offering academic courses in city and regional planning, housing, transport etc. In addition, there have been sporadic efforts in improvement of management practices under the World Bank projects in the urban sector. Of late, there has been a conscious support to strengthen the institutional capacity of urban local bodies.

DECENTRALISATION OF POWERS

The current official policy in India recognises the need for decentralised approach to development by strengthening the municipal bodies along with steps to mobilise community and private resources. In different states, initiatives have been taken in this regard. For example, the state municipal fiscal relations have been rationalised in Gujarat, West Bengal, Kerela and Madhya Pradesh. The system of Mayor in-Council has been introduced in the municipal bodies in Calcutta and Howrah.

The passing of the Constitution (74th Amendment) Act, 1992 is a landmark development which would allow the Constitutional frame work and permit urban local bodies to function as effective units of democratic self government at the town/city level. The main innovative provisions of the Act are—

Constitutional recognition of urban local bodies as a tier of government.

Ensure regular and fair elections to these municipal bodies.

Representation for women (not less than 1/3rd of members) and for the weaker sections like SC/ST (in proportion to their population in the municipal bodies).

Constitution of committees at ward levels in larger municipal bodies to bring the municipal government closer to the people.

Enlargement of functional responsibilities

including planning for economic and social development, urban poverty alleviation programmes, urban environment, etc.

The law of the state should specify proper devolution of taxation powers, sharing mechanisms of state taxes and grants-in-aid system.

The setting up by each state (every five years) of a finance commission to review the finances of municipalities and to recommend principles for determining the taxes to be assigned to municipalities, state taxes to be shared with municipalities and grants-in-aid from the state to these bodies.

The establishment of district planning committees in each district of a state consisting of elected representatives from the urban local bodies and rural local bodies (panchayats) for consolidating the plans of the panchayats and the municipalities and preparation of a development plan for the district.

In the case of metropolitan areas with a population of about 2 million the setting up of a metropolitan planning committee. This would consist of both elected members of both panchayats and municipalities in the metropolitan area of official members for preparation of a development plan for the metropolitan area as a whole.

The municipal and urban development legislation in the states is being modified as per the broad framework given in the Constitution Amendment Act. It is expected that these reforms would go a long way in ensuring effective local self government for economic and social development particularly of small and medium towns.

PLANNING FOR BALANCED URBAN DEVELOPMENT

The present physical planning process in the municipal bodies is not appropriate and there is a need to change over to planning as a participatory process. However, very little has so far been done in evolving innovative frameworks in this regard and re-orientation of planners through suitable training programmes.

The Government of India has placed considerable emphasis on the development of small and medium towns in order to bring about balanced urban development. A special scheme called Integrated Development of Small and Medium Towns is being implemented since 1979-80. Under this scheme assistance is being given for infrastructure development on a matching basis to state governments for development of towns having a population of below 3 lakhs. More than 600 towns have been assisted under the scheme. There has been a slight modification during the current plan (1992-1997) by dovetailing of institutional finance with budgetary support. There has an additional emphasis on improvement of infrastructure for generating increased employment opportunities in small and medium towns. It is expected that investment of the order of Rs. 600 crores would be made in 200 small and medium towns during the 8th plan period.

URBAN POVERTY

Another important problem in small and medium towns is urban poverty, the Government of India has sanctioned a package of programmes for handling the problems of urban poverty. The details are as follows:

(a) The programme for Environmental Improvement of Urban Slums (EIUS) operated by the state governments to provide for *insitu* physical improvements in slums and provision of certain basic minimum physical amenities—roads, water supply, drainage, street lighting, low cost sanitation, community latrines, etc. The average cost incurred under these programmes is Rs. 525 per capita. In carrying out these improvements low cost appropriate solutions are given emphasis.

(b) Nehru Rojgar Yojana—A programme for generating employment opportunities for the urban poor living below the poverty line with an annual household income of less than Rs. 11850. The programme consists of 3 schemes:

(*i*) Scheme of Urban Micro Enterpriser which aims at skill upgradation and provision for subsidy and loan to beneficiaries to enable them to set up micro enterprises in the sphere of industry, services and business.

(*ii*) The Scheme of Urban Wage Employment for employment to the urban poor by utilising their labour for construction of socially and economically useful public assets in low income neighbourhoods.

(*iii*) Scheme of Housing and Shelter upgradation to provide training in construction trades as well as loan and subsidy for upgrading the existing dwelling units of beneficiaries belonging to economically weaker sections.

(c) Urban Basic Services for the Poor—The objective of this scheme is to foster community groups in urban slums for effectively participating in development efforts and to coordinate the convergent provisions of various social services and physical amenities through the programmes of different departments such as Education, Health, Women's Development, etc. This process is expected to improve the quality of life in the slums and to strengthen grass roots democracy. About 500 towns are expected to be covered under this programme in the 8th Plan period.

All these programmes for urban poor are being implemented through the municipalities. It is expected that this process would result in greater interaction with municipal government and the urban poor. This may also lead to improved municipal management because of the involvement of community groups and non-governmental organisations in the provision of various services.

LAND MANAGEMENT

Another problem in this sphere is land market assessment in the India context. There is no specialised agency which is engaged in studying the operation of land markets. Maps in urban areas and land records are generally stroed manually and their retrival is a lengthy process. Most of the time land records are not updated regularly and very often these do not truly reflect land transactions. The Government of India have been implementing a scheme for preparation of urban maps using satellite imageries and aerial surveys. In due course this would serve different uses in the municipalities including utility planning, tax-information system, land use changes, etc.

The Government of India have also initiated a number of changes in the regulatory and legislative framework covering land assembly and disposal. These changes include modification in the Rest Control Laws, Urban Land Ceiling Act, Apartment ownership Act. In addition, it is proposed to enact a legislation to regulate the activities of private developers and pass a special legislation for execution of assembly of land for urban development. These measures would increase the supply of developed land and also improve municipal management.

The country does not have sufficient experience in direct public intervention by state in urban land markets. Even though plot reconstitution has been used in Gujarat and Maharashtra and recently in Kerala, this has been done mainly on the urban fringes. In Andhra Pradesh, the municipal administration have used land sharing as a part of up-gradation of squatter settlements in Hyderabad.

This is one of the areas which need encouragement as a measure of effective land management.

PRIVATISATION OF MUNICIPAL SERVICES

Of late, private sector has been associated in provision of housing, education, health and solid waste management in India. Most of these functions come within the purview of the municipal functions. It may be necessary to formulate detailed guidelines so that private sector is in a position to supplement municipal efforts.

The existing municipal laws governing the urban local bodies do not envisage involvement of private sector participation in the provision of infrastructure and delivery of municipal services. This is one of the areas which needs to be encouraged. The delivery of urban services even now is privarily a basic function of the urban local bodies except in few cases. The only services offered to the private sector include grabage disposal, street lighting, beautification of traffic islands etc. This association with the private sector will reduce the burden on municipalities, and at the same time allow them to give attention to other fields of activities of equal importance.

FISCAL SYSTEM

Property-taxation is one of the important sources of revenue for municipal bodies. Much headway could not be made in improving the resources from property-tax due to various reasons particularly rent control laws. There is a need to identify alternative tax sources in view of abolition of octroi in many cases. The constitution of municipal finance commissions as proposed in the Constitution Amendment Act would also facilitate formulation of investment plans at the local level.

HUMAN RESOURCE DEVELOPMENT

There is also a genuine need to take measures for human resources development in order to improve municipal management. One of the first steps in this direction was taken in 1963 by the Union Government by way of appointment of a committee on the training of municipal employees. Centrally aided institutions were set up to train municipal employees at Delhi, Bombay, Lucknow and Hyderabad. These institutions generally cater to the senior and middle level functionaries and councillors and broadly cover similar areas of training. These institutions have also started interacting with the foreign and UN agencies in order to build up infrastructure and training inputs. However, it is necessary to have an evaluation of these inputs to find out the impact of training activities and the directions in which these need to be improved in view of the Constitution Amendment Act.

Most of the efforts in improving human resource in the municipalities have been sporadic and reflect lack of any conscious policy or direction. There is a need to develop appropriate content and methodology of training in municipal management. It is also necessary to organise training of trainers, designing and implementing cost effective programmes, development of case studies and training materials, strengthening of research capacity and mechanism for impact assessment. It would be necessary to make an assessment of training needs and take steps to strengthen existing training institutes and programmes in view of the increased role of municipal government.

Chapter 14

OPEN SCHOOLING A VIABLE SOLUTION FOR SMALL TOWNS OF THE NORTH-EASTERN STATES

Neelam Sinha

INTRODUCTION

The seven sister States of the North-east comprise a geographical area of 25,508 sq. km in total and constitute 8.74% of the total geographical area of India. The total population inhabiting these seven states of the North-East India is 3,138,6911 as per the 1991 census. The total population of the seven states in North-East constitutes only 3.88 per cent of the total population of the country. This indicates the low density of population, *i.e.,* 123 sq. km as against 265 per sq. kms for India as a whole. Arunachal has the lowest density, that is, 10 persons per sq. km, while Assam has the highest density of 284 persons sq. km.

Between 1981 to 1991, there has been a continuous growth in the number of townships *i.e.,* from 153 to 195; while the percentage of urban population is ranges between 11 to 28 per cent the highest being in Mizoram, *i.e.,* 46.20 percent. These cities are the centers for learning for many. People from rural areas come here for education and employment. Statistics reveal that out of 195 towns in the north-east, only 49 towns have a population more than 20,000. Rest of the towns referred as small towns have a less percentage of population, vast geographical area, and a thin density per sq. Km. These areas have the potential for growth and development.

ROLE OF EDUCATION

The crucial role of education in society and its development is well-established. As Prof. B. Sarveswara Rao emphasised, "Education provides strength and resilience to people to respond to the changing situations and enables them to cause and contribute to societal development through development of attitudes, values, and capacities, "both of knowledge and skills and development of human resources is the main function of Education." 2.

EDUCATIONAL SCENARIO

The States of Arunachal Pradesh, Assam, Meghalaya, Nagaland and Tripura (where more than 80 per cent population is in rural areas) have 29.41, 39.96, 32.60, 47.60 and 45.63 per cent literacy rate, respectively which is much below their counterparts in the urban areas.

Continuous planned efforts of these State Governments have substantially improved the accessibility position at the elementary stage, but when we look at the figures of the population between 6 to 14 years of age we find that there are still 10,62,413 children out of the school boundaries. Beside this we have adult illiterates and drop—out children to bring within the purview of Education for all. [Table]

Table I: Literacy rates in Decending Order 1991

States	Literacy rate	States	Male Literacy rate	States	Female Literacy rate
Mizoram	82.27	Mizoram	**90.18**	Mizoram	78.60
Nagaland	61.65	Manipur	**71.63**	Nagaland	54.75
Tripura	60.44	Tripura	**70.58**	Tripura	49.65
Manipur	59.89	Nagaland	**67.62**	Manipur	47.60
Assam	52.89	India	**64.13**	Meghalaya	44.85
India	52.21	Assam	**61.87**	Assam	43.03
Meghalaya	49.10	Meghalaya	**53.12**	India	39.29
Arunachal Pradesh	41.59	Arunachal Pradesh	**51.45**	Arunachal Pradesh	29.69

Source: Annual Report, Ministry of Human Resource Development, Govt. of India, Department of Education, 1994-95. Statement No. 5.

Table II: Dropout rates 1994-95

S. No.	States	Classes I to V B	G	T	Classes I - X B	G	T
1.	Arunachal Pradesh	60.09	61.09	**60.52**	77.99	80.11	78.82
2.	Assam	38.65	39.55	**39.05**	78.37	75.80	77.26
3.	Manipur	68.02	68.53	**68.26**	75.17	79.84	77.32
4.	Meghalaya	29.96	34.43	**32.06**	67.28	67.57	67.42
5.	Mizoram	56.73	58.54	**57.58**	73.45	71.12	72.33
6.	Nagaland	37.56	24.13	**31.65**	75.01	78.92	76.87
7.	Tripura	60.57	66.95	**63.49**	79.12	78.49	78.84
8.	India	35.05	38.57	**36.32**	68.41	74.74	70.90

Source: Annual Report, Ministry of Human Resource Development, Govt. of India, Department of Education, 1994-95. Statement No. 19 (*i*), 19 (*iii*).

The problem gets more complicated as the drop-out rates continue to be high in these states. The number of drop-outs from class I to VIII in Arunachal Pradesh, Assam, Tripura and Manipur is more than 70 lakhs students. The position of Meghalaya (64.22), Mizoram (43.9), and Nagaland (56.90) is slightly better but is still quite high. In Arunachal Pradesh, primary schools are within walking distances. The number of schools are as high as 1122, but all of a sudden the number of high schools fell to 68 and to 45 at the secondary stage. How are we then going to accommodate 58,99,866 (1992) children of the north-eastern states in 4491 high schools? Majority of these schools are concentrated in bigger towns. Similar positions are existing in the States of Manipur, Mighalaya, Mizoram and Nagaland. The wide disparity in the provision of educational institutions at the middle, high and higher secondary school level is a matter of concern. Passout students from primary schools have to migrate to the towns for higher education.

ARUNACHAL PRADESH

Arunachal Pradesh is spread over 83,743 sq. kms of land with the lowest density of population being 10 persons per sq. km. There are about about 1,43,163 children between the age group of 6 to 14 years whcreas enrolment between class I to V (primary) is about 1,12,197 in the 1,122 primary schools of the state. It indicates about 30,966 children still out of school. Beside this, we have a very high rate of dropout, *i.e.,* 78.82 between the classes I to X. The enrolment and institutions fall sharply at the high and higher secondary levels. All the towns including Itanagar have less than 20,000 population with only 113 high and Higher Secondary School. It is an expensive preposition to construct new schools and appoint full time teachers for them.

ASSAM

Being one of the largest State, the number of towns (93) and villages (21,995) are also in high number. Density of popultion is 284 which is higher than the All India figure of 265 persons per sq. kms. Out of 93 towns. 56 may be termed Small towns with a population less than 20,000: Accessibility in primary education is well achieved but high and higher educational institutions are less than it is required. It is interesting to find that dropout rate at the primary stage (classes I to V) is only 39 but by the time they reach class X, the dropout rate happens to be as high as 77.26. (1993-94).*

Source: Annual Report, Ministry of Human Resource Development, Govt. of India, Dept of Education, 1994-95. Statement No. 19 (*iii*), P. 221.

MANIPUR

Manipur represents the second largest number of towns (31) among the north-eastern States. Only four towns, *i.e.*, Imphal. Churachandpur. Thoubal and Katching have a population above 20,000. In about 3226 primary schools, the enrolment is about 2,64,589; whereas children population is about 305521. There is a back-log of about 40932 children at the age group of 6-14 age who are out of schools. To add the complexity, the dropout rate of this stage (classes I to V) is 68.26. (Table II), and it increases upto 77.32 between classes I to X. Out of the total number of 2937 educational institutions in Manipur 779 are located only at Imphal. Next is Churachandpur with a total population growth rate which is higher for Thoubal 76.27 and Mayang Imphal (125.74) between the year 1981-91.

Statement No. 19 (1).

MEGHALAYA

A population of nearly 1774778 is spread over 4.874 villages and 12 towns is seven (7) districts of Meghalaya. Except for Shillong, Jawai and Tura, rest of the towns have less than 20,000 people with 356675 children between the age group of one of fourteen years, the State has managed to enrol 2,42,570 children (I-V) in about 4163 primary schools. But there are still about 114105 children out of school. The dropout rate at the primary is indicated to be only 32.06 at the primary stage, but goes upto 67.42 at the secondary-stage. The quality of text books, lack of qualified and trained teachers at the secondary level some of the reasons for the number of dropouts being so high. Availability of white collar jobs may also be one of the reason for the high rate of dropouts at the secondary-stage.

Although there has been an increase in the number of schools during 1990's (primary and middle schools having risen from 4,163 and 693 respectively in 1990-91 to 4,175 and 725 in 1993-94, and high schools from 303 to 305 with additional 6 Higher Secondary Schools over this period), the pace of growth of schools to cope up with the demand for schooling is rather slow. This will be inadequate to accomplish the goal of universalization of elementary education in the state.

The high growth of unemployment and underemployment high lights the need for vocationalisation of education at the secondary-stage.

MIZORAM

The population of Mizoram according to 1991 census is 6,86,217 of which 46.10 percent live in the urban areas and the remaining 53.90 percent are spread over 700 villages in three districts of the State. There are 22 towns, under the five categories of population with a low density rate of about 33 persons per sq. kms. Out of 22 towns only three towns (3) have a population more than 20,000. Though educational status of Mizoram in terms of literacy level is much higher (82.27 per cent) than the national average (52 per cent), the dropout rate is high. More than 56.73 percent of all enrolled children leave the educational system without completing elementary level of education and more than 73 percent of all enrolled children dropout before completing the secondary stage of education. A positive aspect of this state is the female literacy rate which is the second bigest (78.60) at the all India level. In Aizwal alone, out of 392000 population there are still 48000 illiterates. Bigger towns indicate more illiterates. Another interesting aspect of education in this state is having a very high ratio of enrolment of about 135.6 at the primary classes.

NAGALAND

The total population of 1209546 is divided between nine big towns and 963 villages with a density of 73 persons per sq. km. The present literacy rate of 61.65 in due to adequate member of 1287 primary schools. The ratio of enrolment and number of institutions at all levels are quite high; 106 at the elementary stage and about 70 at the high and higher secondary stage. The dropout rate is comparatively lower. *i.e.*, 31.65 between classes I to V and goes high (76.87) between classes I to X. Except for four towns of Nagaland *i.e.* Dimapur, Kohima, Mokokchung and Tuensang, other towns have less than 20,000 population.

TRIPURA

Tripura is the second largest state in terms of population (27,44,827) with the smallest geographical area. That is the reason for high density 262 per sq. km. Large number of villages 4724 and 13 small towns have tremendous scope for development. It has about 60.44 percent literacy ráte with 70.58 percent literacy rate among male and about 50 percent among females. A good number of institutions are there even at the high and higher Secondary levels. But the dropout rates (63.49) between classes I to V, and 66.17 between classes I to X (66.17) indicate low standard of education and high number of working children.

The number of high schools (146) are more in West Tripura than in North (82) and South Tripura (79). Accordingly, Khowai (West Tripura) indicates highest literacy rate of 69.84 of the State while Chandachhera (South Tripura) reflects its lowest literacy-rate of 25.68 (1991 census). It is generally due to inadequacy of educational institutions in the small towns.

VIABLE SOLUTION

As analysed earlier, socio, economic demographic and educational profile of the north-east states provide an adequate justification for open schooling system to reach the remote and small pockets of habitations in smaller towns.

Are we in position to construct schools and appoint teachers in these towns? Even if the resources are available, the qualified teachers and quality production of text books will pose a big problem before us.

We have to look for another viable solution to achieve education for all by the year 2000. National Open School has the potential for providing alternative schooling to neo-literates, early school dropout, dropout from non-formal education system in a cost effective approach. The prioritised client group will include dropout students from formal schools, adult illiterates who are eager to enhance their status, girls or females who are shy to go out for schooling, working children who are unable to attend formal schooling and handicapped who wants to take his own time to finish a lesson may go for distance mode of education. Over and above, there is no pressure of examination-which is being conducted twice in a year with credit accumulation system.

OPERATIONAL MECHANISM OF OPEN LEARNING

In the distance mode of teaching-learning, the practice all over India is to accredit the already established schools for the implementation of its academic and vocational programmes.

Levelwise Scheme of Open Schooling at NOS

Level	Course-Programs	Equivalence with Formal School grades
Open Basic Education	1. Preparatory	(*iii*)
	2. Primary	(*v*)
	3. Foundation (Elementary)	(*viii*)
Open Secondary Education	4. Secondary	(*x*)
Open Higher Secondary Education	5. Senior Secondary	(*xii*)
Open Vocational Education	Optional component at all levels	
Life Enrichment Programs	Cources offered to teachers, principals, executives in Private/Public Sector enterprises.	
Dual Enrollment and formal Part Credit Programme.	Dual or more subjects additional to school subjects at Secondary/ Senior Secondary stage.	

Students come to the study-centres for registering themselves, and appearing for the examination which is held twice in a year a given date. To deal with the learners difficulties, personal Contact Programmes are held at the study-centres on the holidays. Subject tutors drawn from formal schools come to on their spare time to provide academic guidance to a learner. Principal of the school who is known as implementing the various programmes of NOS. On the basis of the number of students admitted, the study-centres are give financial assistance. Coordinator, Asst. Coordinators, Tutors and Chowkidars are paid regularily for facilitating functions.

Since its inception, the National Open School has been designing, developing and offering flexible self-instructional materials with an opportunity to integrate academic courses with vocational courses. Distance learners can persue their studies in their own convenient time, at his own place and pace, in their own languages and subjects to their liking. Once a student is admitted, he/she is registered for five years and may even appear in one or two subjects at a time. Examinations are held twice in an academic year so that a learner may appear at the examination whenever he is ready for it.

FUNCTIONS OF A STUDY-CENTRE

(A) Main Functions of the Study Centres—

1. Sale of the Prospectus of NOS for admission.

2. Accept application forms alongwith the fees for admission and send the application and the fees to NOS.

3. To receive the study material sent by NOS and distribute the same to the students.

4. To prepare a time table and conduct classes as per time table usually in the weekend and holidays for students. They are expected to send a copy of the time-table to NOS.

5. To assign and assess requisite number of assessments to the students under the scheme of Tutor Marked Assessment (TMA). (Necessary guidelines in this regard are under issue by the Academic Department).

6. To provide necessary laboratory facilities for holding practicals in the concerned subjects and ensure that the requisite number of practicals are

held.

7. To use audio-video materials supplied by NOS.

8. To accept applications from the students for change of subjects(s) and/or offer of additional subjects (s) upto the prescribed date and forward the same to NOS in a consolidated form for confirmation.

9. To provide counselling services to the students.

10. To receive the applications alongwith the fees for examination from the students and forward the same to NOS.

11. To issue Identity Cards, Marksheet and Certificates etc. to the students.

12. On demand, to act as Examination Centre.

13. To maintain necessary records for receipt of admission fees, examination fees, attendance to teachers and students, pay ment to tutors and other staff stock register for receipt and distribution of study material, stock register for audio video material etc.

FINANCIAL IMPLICATIONS

The resources are crucial for development and they include both quantitative and qualitative assets, Quantitatively it includes local and govt. aids, physical facilities and educational technology (hard ware). Qualitatively resources like human skill, leadership, qualified teachers, communications technologies (software) are difficult to find in a small town.

In such a situation, the first consideation is the maximum utilization of available resources. Constraints like shortage of human and financial resources in small towns is a widespread phenomena in any developing society. The case for north-east is much more focused in the lack of sources for revenue. This leads us to look for an alternative strategies for more effective goals oriented programmes for education.

Table III (a)

Table III (a)

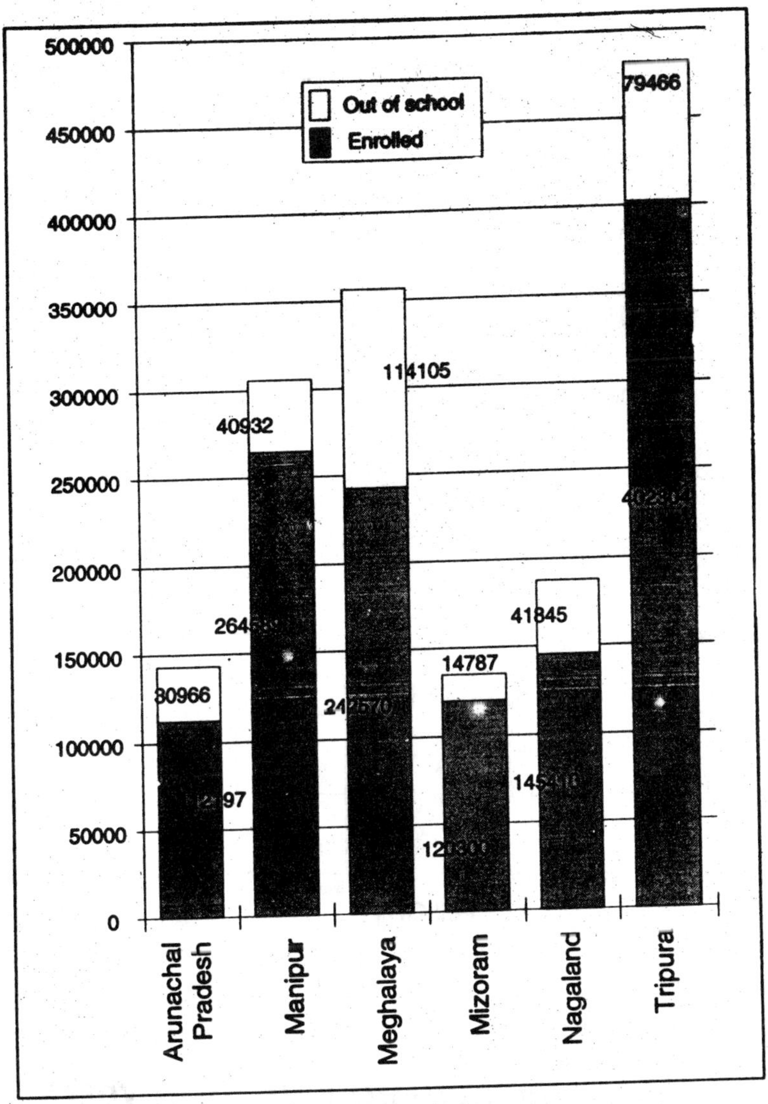

School-going age-group (6 to 14 years) in North-Eastern States

Table III (b)

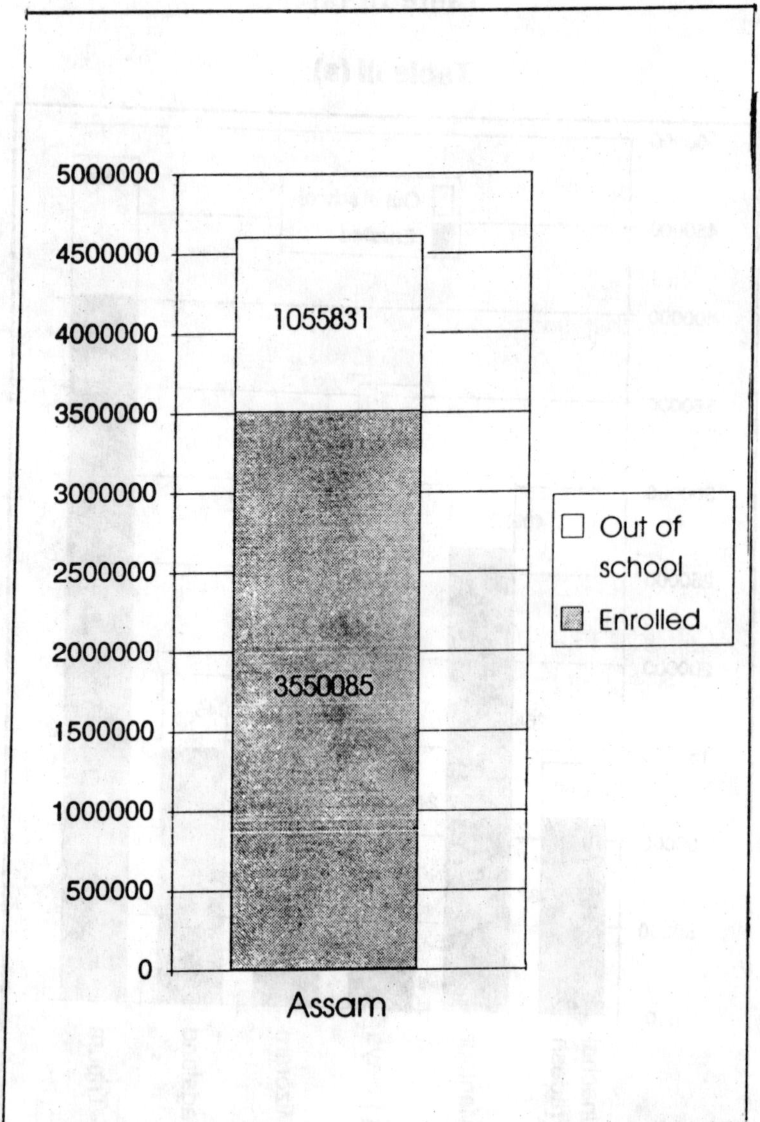

School-going age-group (6 to 14 years) in Assam

The annual unit cost of education at the elementary level is estimated to be ranging between Rs. 700 to 1000/- per year. The open learning mode of education provides a cost effective alternative. With the increase number of enrolment, the developmental cost of open learning is shared and spread over the learners and within four-five years it will be almost negligible.

CONCLUSION

North-east region with its cultural and linguistic heritage as well as its educational needs, call for an open learning system to expedite education for all in shortest possible time and in cost effective approach. This will not only enable to draw the deprived section in the fold of learning but will break the isolation of being alienated from the main stream of the nation.

Chapter 15

SMALL TOWNS AND SOCIO-CULTURAL CHANGE IN ASSAM: THE NECESSITY OF ORAL HISTORICAL APPROACH

Kishore Bhattacharjee

In Assam, as many other places, small towns are the centres through which rural people directly come in contact with various aspects of modern life ranging from market commodities, opportunities for higher education, bureaucracy and politics. Modern activities find a base in small towns which evolve in the midst of rural areas. This is still now an on-going process as in the last 20 years 17 small towns have emerged, of them 8 are in the tribal areas. Most of the small towns have developed from a market to a centre of trade, commerce and service. They find their convenient location near a railroad, national highway or motorable road. At this state, two interrelated hypotheses can be suggested for discussion. There are: small towns emerge when modernisation of rural society takes place and small towns filter down an alternative model of life to rural society. Villagers find a reference group at their doorstep. It is also observed that small towns can be regarded as more important arena of interactions between traditional/rural culture and modern/urban culture than a village or city.

SMALL TOWNS AND SOCIO-CULTURAL CHANGE

The process of development of small towns can be observed in different stages. In the initial phase, a value for modern life is created with the penetration of market network, economic relations and education. The modern culture and value created by education system, health service, print media and art forms spread out in parallel with social, political and economic relations. Each reinforces the other. These processes create small towns and make them inevitable. In this process, agrarian class situation also plays a role and mobility of the individuals in the secondary sector is important. There are various market like urban agglomerations, rural in character with certain modern amenities, like Kuwaritol or Chaygaon. These cnetres in some cases grow as an incipient town. This will be illustrated with the example of Goreswar.

In the early part of this century the current of modern life was felt in Goreswar centering round a weekly market which was established with the effort of local freedom fighters and reformers. Marwari traders also came to settle down in the place in the 1920s. The market was started near the railway station, thus agricultural produces of the locality found a market in outside. Goreswar became a place for transhipment of agricultural produces, like rice and mustard seeds, by railway or motor links. Marwari traders first took the lead in this respect. The market was taken over by the Gaon Panchayat in 1957 but it came under a Bazar Commttee in 1964. Meanwhile, Guwahati-Shukla Road constructed in 1951-52 had increased the importance of the market. Various types of shops were established and a daily market was spontenous development. The heterogenity of population increased when Bengali Hindus followed the Marawaris in the 1940s. The migrants began to purchase land and a section of the local peopld also became involved in the process and settled near the market. Certain local elities started further developmental activities centering round the place. The local leaders wanted expansion of education and other modern facilities in the areas. The established Betna Siksha Aru Krisi Unnayan Sangha in 1958. The mouzadar, some educated persons and freedom fighters were actively involved. They were mainly from higher and middle ranking castes. This organisation took initiative to construct at auditorium, Kalaguru Bishnu Rabha Bhavan in 1967, which is the only public hall in the area and presently also being used as a cinema hall, and sestablished Goreswar College in 1974. Growth of Goreswar was further accelerated with the establishment of a number of government offices since the '70s'. Now there is a Telephone Exchange, Sub-Deputy Collector's office, Block Development Office and Eri Seed Farm. Now there are more than hundred persons working in these offices. Total population of five constituent villages of this emerging town is 7841 which includes the Assamese, Bodo-Kacharies, Saraunia Kacharis, Marwaries, Bengalis and a few Nepalis. The entry of the salaried persons have introduced a different quality of life which according to rural people is more luxurious. Such incipient urban life-ways have developed new tate, outlook and life style (Kalita, 1995).

The case illustrates how an incipient town grows in a rural area. The process is the creation of the necessity of a local market, growth of an area as a transhipment centre of the local products with the intermediation of the trading communities and finally emergence of a local businessmen and entrepreneur class and expansion of government offices. It is noticed that a section of the rural traders, teachers, college students keep regular contact with their nearby town and many of them are regular visitors. Some pass their leisure hours if the place is within their reach. These activities make an impact on surrounding villages which can be noticed at various levels from the speech pattern to religious activities.

In the process of emergence and development social differentiations and alignments come into relief where family, caste, class and community background of individuals are important when their roles are considered. Therefore, it is also possible to develop deep insight into the social structure of contemporary Assamese society and its organisation from the study of this process.

The initial phase of the development of towns can be observed in Lala in Cachar or Dhing in Nagaon or Donkamokam of Karbi Anglong. At the second phase of development, a place start to stabilise as a township and its town like activities increase in scale as observed in Dheiajuli, Rangapara or Lanka. At the next stage towns develop further as seen in Diphu, Haflong, Hojai and Mongaldai. Then the transition to a larger town can be the subject of further research for which substantial records are also available. This typology is some what arbitary and not strictly developed from empirical observations. The idea is to suggest a logical scheme and emphasise the importance of socio-economic process of this development and its impact on culture.

A brief outline of culture change has been already presented. Further, it is to be recognised that modern entertainment is also introduced in towns. It is a common scene in Assam to notice that touring theatre groups perform in small towns or market areas. Cinema halls are also located in those areas. Moreover, interactions between village institutions and modern institutions or outlook mainly take place in small towns. For example, at the religious level, in towns, certain organisations develop to establish a temple or a common namghar, in an organised manner, often as an identity maker. In Assam, religious reform movements of Sankar Sangha has its bases in small towns. New role of religion, activities of the political parties, education, entertainments, literary activities, book shops and other modern elements bring an alternative life style.

In Assam, there are places where these phases of development are either visible or in the memory of the aged persons and therefore, can be subject of ethnographic and oral historical research. At least 25 towns are still in the initial phase of growth and two-third of the towns have less than 25,000 population. In this situation, application of the methods of oral history will not be difficult. Increase in heterogenity in population, commercial activities, salaried employment and entertainment activities induce socio-cultural change. These factors change social relation, quality of life and personality types. The details of this process and its impact on family, kinship, attitudes and values and other spheres of society can be assessed after a series of ethnographic and oral historical research are undertaken. This type of study may help to develop a model of emergence of towns in Assam.

ORAL HISTORICAL RESEARCH: AN AGENDA AND BRIEF NOTE ON METHODOLOGY

It has been stressed that a study of socio-cultural history of small towns is very important for understanding socio-cultural change, because small towns emerge and function in such context. As recorded materials in this regard is insufficient, ethnographic and oral historical methods can be fruitfully applied. It has been discussed above that data on history of immigration; local intitiative and interest for development in the background of family, caste, class and community relations, newly formed socio-economic relations; history of commercial activities; history of local market, growth of an area as a business and transhipment centre of local products; emergence of new power relations, may be consideraed useful. Moreover, the direction of socio-cultural change in towns and their impact on surrounding areas are also important. Understanding of this process will help to recognise how modern economic and power relations as well as corresponding taste and outlook filter down to rural areas through small towns. These types of data cannot be generated easily as for small towns very little records exist and usually thick descriptions of personal lives are not preserved. In this situation, qualitative methods of ethnography and oral history can be applied.

REFERENCES

Cohn, B.S. 1990. *An Anthropologist among the Historians and other Essays*, New Delhi: OUP.

Dorson, R.M. (Ed.), 1973. *Folklore and Traditional History*. The Hague: Mouton Publishers.

Kalita, N. 1995. Socio Cultural History of Goreswar Area, Unpublished M. Phill. Dissertation.

Lummis, T. 1990. 'Oral History', In Bauman, R. (Ed). *Follare, Cultural Performances and Popular Entertainment*, New York, OUP.

Chapter 16

HAFLONG : PAST AND PRESENT

S.K. Barpujari

In the wake of the great Naga uprising of 1879-80, the revolt of the Dimasa hero Sambhudhan Phonglo in 1882 resulted in the burning and destruction of Gunjung, the sub-divisional headquarters of North Cachar Hills. Haflong was established in 1896 in its place considering it to be the most suitable place near the plains of Cachar.[1] However, the progress of railway construction works connecting Badarpur and Lumding through the hill section was the most deciding factor which influenced the shifting of the headquarters from Gunjung to Haflong. Sonaram Thaosen, a Dimasa scholar has rightly said:

Haflong town was built by the foreign rulers of both civil and Railway administrations, a hundred years ago. Whoever, the planners might have been, they represented a brilliant galaxy of talents. Their intention was that Haflong town should not only be the administrative headquarters of the North-Cachar Hills subdivision or Railways, but a beautiful hill resort too.[2]

Geographically also, Haflong nestling on the spur of the Barail range of hills at a height of 3,117 feet above the sea level appeared like a 'natural fortress' surrounded as it were almost by rock walls, beyond which the river Diyung and its tributary Ravi flows towards the north, east and west of Haflong. The climate of the place is also moderate neither too hot nor too cold.

The history of the origin, growth and development of hill towns like Haflong is difficult to be told due either to the total dearth, or very limited nature of source materials. prof. J.B. Bhattacharjee, an eminent historian and scholar, while presenting a paper on the 'Urban History of North East India' in connection with Mokokchung Town's Centenary Celebrations in 1990 says:

'Data on the pre-colonial urban centres are extremely scanty...Even for the colonial period, we have to depend by and large on the British archival records. This category of data consists mostly of administrative reports and political correspondences.... There are no doubt some survey and census reports, but they fell far short of what is required for projecting a comprehensive view of a total social situation.[3]

The above observations of Prof. Bhattacharjee, may aptly be applied in respect of the history and growth of Hill stations like Haflong. Haflong must have had a history of its own, but due to the absence of any historical record, we are in the dark about its hoary past. Haflong and North Cachar Hills as a whole is inhabited by numerous hill tribes, such as the Dimasas, Zemis, Kukis, Hmars, karbis, Jayantias (Syntengs), Bietes, Hrangkhols, Khelmas, Vaipheis, etc. Local tradition and folk tales of some of these tirbes may give us the required informations.

Stray references about Haflong spelt as 'Haplung' in connection with Angami Naga raids on the Dimasa and other Naga villages (probably Zemis) living in the territory of Tularam Senapati and the Raja of Manipur are available in the early official records of the colonial period.[4] In this connection, it may be pointed out that immediately after the British annexation of Cachar (1832), a detachment of the Sylhet Light Infantry was posted at Haflong (spelt as Haplung in the official records), but was withdrawn due to the unhealthiness of the place.[5] Again, in an official map prepared in the Surveyor General's Office (copied from the original map of Kachar, signed by T. Fisher, dated 6 Nov. 1836) 'Haplung' was shown near Jatinga. In several other correspondences of the period from 1836 onward upto 1851 one comes very frequently with the word 'Haplung' (Haflong), mentioned sometimes either as a 'village' or 'thana' or 'pargana'. It is interesting to note that in one of such records, the Nagas effected by the Angami inroads were designated as 'Haflong Nagas', these were without doubt the Zemi Nagas.[6]

Mr. E.R. Grange, Sub-Assistant Commissioner of Nowgong who led the first exploratory expedition against the Angamis in January 1839, who was also the first European to reach Haflong accompanied by Tularam. Grange's expedition may not be successful from military point of view but his report on the Angami Nagas is a mine of information. For our purpose it is very important that for the first time, he mentions in his report that the *'thana* of Haflong is the hill called by the Cacharees and the Nagas 'Honglong' which our corruption has beocme Haflong'.[7] According to Sonaram Thaoson and some other Dimasa scholars, the word has come out from the word 'Halong' (hollow earth) or 'Haflow' (raised earth or Ant Hill). However, the Dimasas in their folk-songs call Haflong as Hang Kolong (repository of life) almost a nearer approximation to 'Hon klong' as stated by Grange.[8] In this connection, it may be pointed out that Haflong bar is a very old patriclan (Samphong) of the Dimasas.[9]

Whatever the nomenclature of the place, in our opinion it has emerged from the colonial base or outpost created by the then rulers for protecting the borders of their territories from raids of the neighbouring tribes. One scholar rightly says that such towns like Haflong functioned as colonial administrative outposts without much amenities of life.[10] Usually police officials were placed in charge of such administrative centres because their primary responsibility was to maintian law and order without the slightest possible interference in the internal affairs of the tribes. Haflong which was originally a very 'tiny spot' just below the present village of 'Boro Haflong' in the vicinity of Haflong Hill Railway station, was developed by the colonial masters of both the civil and railway administration and by the European tea-planters into a popular sanatorium. Fishing, hunting, golf and tennis were their favourite pastime. They established park, western style hotel, circuit house, Dak Bungalow and recreational clubs.

Till the fifties of the present century, according to Halflongites even now alive, Haflong was a 'sleepy town' having no motorable roads and railway was the only means of communication. The main roads in the town was stone-paved and clean. The town has lush green fields and two man-made lakes which added to the beauty of the town. There was no mosquito menace in the town. Haflong was variously described by visitors; while one described it as 'Switzerland of India' another as 'God's picture book'.[11] Thre was a mall market centrally located and also a weekly-market and tribal people from interior areas within a radius of 20 miles came on their foot with their hill products and procure their essentials.

Although with the formation of the Autonomous District Council in 1950, Haflong town was on the road towards development, the actual pace of development accelerated when the town was elevated from the status of a sub-divisional headquarters to district headquarters in 1970 with the formation of the separate district of North Cachar Hills District.[12] Till August 1965, Haflong town was managed by the Haflong Town Fund Committee when it was substituted by Haflong Town Committee by a notification of the District Council.[13]

In 1965 electrict posts were raised in the Haflong roads for the first time. It is now amazing to see the terrific changes which had been taking place in Haflong town. Till the seventies Haflong was really a clean and pollution free town. Most of the peripheries of the town were covered with forests with wild life. Peter James Bazeley of the IAS, in his paper 'Yester Years of Haflong' published in the Souvenir of Centenary Celebrations of Haflong town had observed:

Haflong was then an extremely clean, pollution free town. it was for all purposes a perfect sanatorium surrounded by tall elegant and graceful forests. Today's localities of the township such as Muolhoi, Sarkari Bagan, North Bagetar, Eiengpui, Lodi, Zion, Natun Gunjung, Dibarai, Digrik, South Bagetar, etc. all, were density forested areas, full of all orts of wild life including leopards and tigers. Wild fowl and pheasants would freely mix with domestic poultry in the back yards of settlements located in the periphery of the town, while barking deers and porcupines would graze on tenders garden plants, Leopards would frequently prowl around the outskirts of the town and birds abounded everywhere. Haflongites undoubtedly lived with pristine nature. There was total ecological harmony till things changed in the late fifties....[14]

The present area of Haflong town in 12.79 sq. km. with a population of 26,191 (1991 Census).[15] At present various state government and semi-government offices with residential quarters for office and staff have been set up and the town has been assuming the status of zonal headquarters of some departments. By now the town has more than 85 Government, semi-government and private offices and some with residential colonies and quarters, jail, several play grounds, three railway stations, civil hospital and health centres, schools from primary to

Higher Sectory levels, full fledged government college with arts, science and commerce sections, libraries, socio-cultural and religious institutions, Post & Telegrpah offices, Telephone Exchange, F.M. Radio Station, Low Power T.V. relay station, Convents, Churches, temples, mosques, cinema hall, hotels, restaurants, bus station and roadways and everygrowing market places all around Really Haflong has been representing an urban culture of its own.

Shri Binayak Choudhury, Assistant Director of District Town and Country Planning Officer, Haflong, in his paper 'Urbanisation: the Haflong Experience' published in the Centenary Commemorative Souvenir, describes the period 1971 to 1991 as the transition period of urbanisation of Haflong Town and says that the main force behind it is its conversion into an administrative centre.[16]

There is no doubt in our mind that elevation of Halflong's status since 1971 has been providing the necessary impetus for urbanisation of this town to pick up. However, Choudhury clearly states that the process of urbanisation has brought in its train, its inherent fall outs. He cites the following among others such as (*i*) poor economic base, (*ii*) acute housing problem, (*iii*) absence of zoning regulations, (*iv*) underdeveloped communication, (*v*) water supply, (*vi*) drainage, garbage disposal and street lighting, (*vii*) power scenario, etc.[17]

To manage the urbanisation of Haflong, Choudhury suggest the strengthening of the economic base of the town. For the same, he recommends the tapping of the vast forest, horticultural and plantation crops crops potentials of the district of North Cachar as a whole and also encouragement of tourism potential.

To combat acute shortage of housing, he suggests that instead of depending on governmental finance alone, encouragement be given to private investors in this regard. At the same time tenancy and rent control regulations be drawn up and enforced. While suggesting well planned intra town wass transit, he wants widening of roads and establishment of a number of parking place in proper places for motor vehicles, two-wheelers and other means of such transports. At the same time to check haphazard land use in the town Chudhury feels enactment of proper zoning regulations. To meet the water contingency during the lean season, he recommends encouragement of rain-water harvesting and to augment rain water supply, prevention of interception of rivers and denudation of forests. So far power supply is concerned Choudhury says that the power supply position has become satisfactory with the commissioning of the Kopili Hydel Project. Regarding drainage, garbage disposal, street lighting, etc. the Town Committee despite its limitations has taken up measures but it has yet to achieve the desired goal.[18]

B. Choudhury while discussing the fall outs of urbanisation of Halflong town, suggests for better management of the town, the Halflong Town Committee to be strengthened physically and financially. The Town Committee, may in its turn, also revise existing tax-structure of the town and impose a 'betterment tax' if necessary. But the most important thing in which he stresses is people's participation without which efficient management of the town is not possible.[19]

Early this year the centenary of the establishment of Halfong town was celebrated on the attainment of its hundred years of existence. In course of the century, the tiny sleeping town of Haflong developed enormously. Till late fifties, *i.e.*, just after independence when the town began to grow and develop there was 'ecological harmony'. But Haflongites now lament that along with this development many things have disappeared, the beauty and serenity of Haflong have gone. The rows of pine and tall trees of Haflong have given way to concrete buildings and paved roads. 'Kerosene lamps which used to flicker within well-cleaned jumbo-sized glass chimneys on lamp-post located at every corner' of the roads and given place to electric lights since 1965.[20]

The writer of the present paper has seen the change which has taken place in Halflong in course of the last three decades during the course of his stay and frequent visits to the town. He thinks it proper to highlight a few difficulties out of many faced by the people of Haflong based on media reports and personal experience. These are mainly hurdles of communication, shortage of housing facilities, inadequate water supply, congestion and lack of proper sanitation and drainage, adverse effects of ecology, encroachment of open space etc. The road and rail communication through the hills was always difficult. However, since the conversion of Guwahati-Lumding section of the N.E.F. Railway, from metre-gauge to broad-gauge transhipment at Lumding junction of both passenger and goods traffic has been causing unnecessary delay, expense and hardship to the people. These difficulties are accetuated during the rainy season when the traffic remain closed due to accident, land-slide, etc. The roads connecting Haflong with Silchar, karimganj, Lanka, Hojai and Lumding are in deplorable state. The people of Haflong who are mostly dependent on outside supplies are to remain at the mercy of the traders and middle men who charge exhorbitant prices.

Housing problem at Haflong has become very acute due to non-availability of rented houses and accommodation for staff and offices. Due to such difficulties, particularly low-salaried people who come on posting or transfer express eitehr their reluctance to come or even if they come, join, take leave and demand transfer. Haflong being a hill town, its water supply is mainly dependent on hill steams, nullas, springs and small water spots, but they dry up during the winter season. At the same time due to jhooming, erosion, constant felling of trees and destruction of forests, there is scantiness of water and rising of river beds. People living in the top of the hills mostly feel acute shortage of water which tell upon their health caused by disease and lack of proper sanitation.

As Haflong or North Cachar Hills district as a whole is industrially not advanced at present, we do not apprehend any envirnomental hazard like air-pollution, from wastes and affluents containing poisonous substances. However, felling of trees and burning of forests for jhooming will not only bring ecological and environmental disharmony, but rainfall, temperature and climate in the long run will be adversely effected. Even the flora and fauna which are in great danger will not escape. Again if there be ecological imbalance in the future, its repurcussions will have also social and political implications of great significance.

REFERENCES

1. Barpujari, S.K.: 'Haflong: A Historical Appraisal' in *100 Years of Haflong (Centenary Commemoration Souvenir)* 1995, pp. 18-21.
2. Thaosen, S.: 'Haflong and its Environs' in *Centenary Commemoration Souvenir*. p. 57.
3. Bhattacharjee, J.B.: 'The Urban History of North East India' in Hill Cities of North Eastern Himalayas (edited by Sinha, Chacko & Aier), New Delhi, 1993, p. 38.
4. Bengal Judicial Proceedings, 1835, 18 December, No. 44. Letters to the Court (J), 1837, 8 August, No. 26.
5. Ibid.
6. Bengal Judicial Proceedings, 1836, 22 November, No. 27, No. 37. Ibid, Ibid, 1851, 29 January, No. 643..
7. Foreign Political Proceedings, 1837, 8 May, No. 3.
8. Thaosen S.: Op. cit. p. 57.
   Thaosen, J.: 'Parvatan (Bengali) in *Centenary Commemoration Souvenir*, p. 211.

9. Bhattacharjee, T.: 'From Gunjung to Haflong—The Story of Head-quarters' See *Centenary Commemoration Souvenir*, p. 26.
   Barman, N.K.: *The Queens of Cachar or Hermabo and the History of the Kachchhari*, Barkkola, 1992, p. 57.
10. Sinha, A.C.: 'Urban Political Culture of the Hill Cities' in *Hill Cities of Eastern Himalayas*, New Delhi, 1993, p. 210.
11. Thaosen, S.: Op. cit. p. 58.
    Sadap, Mary John Basco: 'God's Picture Book' in *Centenary Commemoration Souvenir*, p. 29.
12. Zidung, P.: 'Evolution and Powers of N.C. Hills Autonomous District Council' in *Centenary Commemoration* Souvenir, pp. 53-54.
13. Nampui, T.: 'Evolution of Urban Institution of Haflong' in *Centenary Commemoration Souvenir*, p. 39.
14. Bazely, Peter James: 'yester Years of Haflong' in *Centenary Commemoration Souvenir*, p. 145.
15. *100 Years of Haflong Centenary Commemoration Souvenir*, see 'Haflong at A Glance', p. 145.
16. Choudhury, Binayak: 'Urbanisation: Haflong Experience' in *Centenary Commemoration Souvenir*, pp. 40-45.
17. Ibid.
18. Ibid.
19. Ibid.
20. Bazely, Peter James: Op. cit. p. 146.

Chapter 17

PROBLEMS OF SMALL TOWNS IN THE HILL AREAS OF ASSAM:

A CASE STUDY OF DIPHU TOWN

R.P. Athparia

INTRODUCTION

The Karbi Anglong district is bounded on the north by Nagaon and Galaghat districts, on the south by the North Cachar Hills district, on the east by Golaghat district and the State of Nagaland and on the west by the State of Meghalaya. It lies between latitutes 25°30' and 26°41' N and longitudes 92°7' and 93°52' E. The district has a total geographical area of 10,346 sq. km. The district was previously a subdivision of the United North Cachar Hills district which was inaugurated on 17 November, 1951. On 2nd February, 1970, Mikir Hills Sub-division was constituted into Mikir Hills district which was again renamed as Karbi Anglong in 1976.

The Mikir Hills Sub-division was created by means of curving out the areas with high concentration of the Karbis, *e.g.,* 4,421 sq. kms. from Nagaon district, 4,382 sq. kms. from eastwhile Sibsagar district and 1,543 sq. kms. from Khasi and Jaintia Hills district. The aeas taken from Nagaon and Sibsagar districts were partially excluded Areas of the two districts and were called Mikir Hills Tracts. On the other hand, those portions inhabited mainly by the Karbis in the United Khasi and Jaintia Hill district were known as Excluded Areas.

The Karbi Analong district is predominatly inhabited by the Karbis. According to 1971 census, the Scheduled Tribe population in the district was 2,10,039 which constituted 55.37 per cent of the total population of the district. Out of the total Scheduled Tribe population of 2,10,039, the Karbi population was 1,72,845. The density of population in the district was 37 persons per sq. km. as per 1971 Census while the overall density of population in Assam was 186 per sq. km. as per 1971 census. At present, Diphu, Hamren, Howraghat, Donkamokam, Bokajan and Dokmoka are the notified towns of the district. Before 1991 census, Diphu was the only town of the district. Diphu happens to be the oldest town in these hilly areas has its own typical problems.

Total population of Diphu town was 10,200 as per 1971 Census. In 1991 Census, population increased to 39,547 (24.78 per cent increase). Total working population in 1991 census is 31.29 per cent. Out of which, 27.29 percent are males and 4.00 per cent females. The census 1991 shows that the maximum workers engaged in the category of other services (37.54 per cent). It is followed by trade and commerce (18.21 per cent), manufacturing, processing, servicing and reparing of other household industry (11.40 per cent), construction works (10.17 per cent), livestock, forestry, fishing, hunting and plantation (6.12 per cent), cultivation (6.82 per cent), transport, storage and communication (5.0 per cent), agricultural labourer (2.65 per cent), marginal workers (1.13 per cent) and manufacturing, processing, servicing, repairing of other household industry (0.3 percent).

Maximum male workers engaged in the category

of other services (38.81 per cent) followed by trade and commerce (20.30 per cent), manufacturing, processing, servicing, repairing of other household industry (12.18 per cent), construction works (11.20 per cent), livestock, fishing, hunting plantation (7.30 per cent), cultivation (5.71 per cent) and transport and communication (5.62 per cent). In the occupational categories of agricultural labourer, marginal workers and manufacturing, processing, servicing of household industry, the male workers are negligible. On the other hand, the female workers are found maximum in the occupational category of other services (54.24 percent) followed by cultivation (13.51 per cent), trades and commerce (6.11 per cent) and agricultural labourer (4.21 per cent). Female workers are negligible in construction works (2.67 per cent), livestock, forestry, fishing, hunting and plantation (2.45 per cent), manufacturing, processing, servicing of household industry (1.71 per cent) and transport and communication (.33 per cent).

In this paper, on attempt has been made to highlight the problem of Diphu town in relation to the industiral growth, development of infra-structures, availability of civic amenities in the general background of the hill areas of Assam.

SMALL SCALE INDUSTRIAL FACILITIES

Industrial growth in the hilly areas like Diphu is still in embryonic stage. But there is tremendous scope for growth and development of various types of industrial provided the vast natural resources are utilised scientifically. At present, except rice mill, flour mill, saw mill and wood craft, there is no other major industry at Diphu. However, due to the initiative of the District Industry Centre, some units are coming up in the town like Hume Pipe Factory, Bakery, Stone Crushing, Lime Making and some miscellaneous industries like steel furniture making unit, printing press, spice grinding, candle making, tilex making, dry cleaner, knitting and embroidary, decorative textiles, laishimphe making, poultry, leather products and ice factory etc.

The office of the Assistance Director of Industries Diphu implements the entrusted schemes of the Karbi Anglong District Council. The schemes which are implemented so far are: (a) departmental training programmes on knitting, cutting, tailoring and embroidery, cane and bamboo etc; (b) study tour training programme; (c) common famility service centre; (d) production centre; (e) departmental cottage and small scale insutrial loom; (f) grants-in-aid in kind; (g) encouragement to master craftsman and (h) promotion of handicraft artisans.

It is observed that the common facility service centre was established at Dillaji to extend services of machinery and machinist to help the local consumers and artisans to obtain services of the machineship. As several such units have grown up in the heart of the Diphu town, the machinery installed at Dillaji becomes over looked and therefore, a step was taken to conduct training centre at Dillaji on both turning and fabrication.

In 1988, a mechanised carpentry unit was established at Diphu for production of wooden furniture and fitting while there was least of carpentry units. In absence of adequate saw mill in the town, the carpentry unit faced a lot of troubles for meet the departmental requirements. So, a saw-mill was also established as a component of the carpentry unit. As soon as the locality is developed with saw mill and carpentry units, Government has discontinued the function and converted the unit into a training centre.

Apart from all these merits and demerits of the industrial development in Diphu town, the Assam Hills Small Industries Development Corporation began to function at Diphu in the year 1974, under this corporation, five units have been established so far. These are: Khandsari Sugar Mill at Manja, Mustard and Castor Oil Mill at Manja, Citronella plant at Manja, Fruit processing unit at Deithor and ginger Dehydration unit at Lungnit.

Provision of financial help to the local enterpreneurs has also been undertaken by the corporation. Assistance in the form of seed money, working capital and loan, etc. is provided against sanction of the bank to the enterpreneurs with a view of creating a new dimension in the field of industrial development in Diphu town.

HANDLOOM AND TEXTILES

Handloom industry is one of the main cottage industries practised by the people of Diphu town. This industry has a vast potentiality in Diphu since it does not require huge amount of capital investment. The handloom and textile industry has fulfilled the unemployment problems of the girls and widows to a great extent. Under the weavers' extension service scheme, raw materials are supplied to the weavers on credit in order to carry out works on their looms at home. The products available from the looms are taken on payment of wages. The handloom training centre of Diphu imparts training to the unemployed girls for one year in modern methods of weaving and designing. There is also a provision of granting stipend of Rs. 80/- p.m. for each trainee. Moreover, on completion of the training period, each trainee is provided with a set of complete fly shuttle frame loom and accessories and yarns free of cost to undertake weaving for self employment.

Due to modernisation and high market competition, the weaver have failed to cope with the indigenous looms. As such district level co-operative socieites have been established at Diphu for providing financial assistance for common loomshed, working capital, managerial subsidy, etc. Members and office bearers of the handloom co-operative socieites are also provided with training to facilitate smooth functioning of the societies. Moreover, study tour in conducted for the members to have a fair knowledge about the working of the handloom industry outside the State.

EDUCATION

Education is the major problem in the hill areas of Assam. According to 1951 Census, the literacy rate in the United Mikir and North Cachar Hills was 5.9 percent as against 18.2 per cent for the state.

In 1961 Cenus, the literacy in the district increased to 17.4 per cent as against 27.4 per cent for Assam. Again, in 1971, the average literacy rate was 23.2 per cent (Karbi Anglong 19.2 per cent in North Cachar Hills 27.2 per cent) while it was 28.3 per cent for Assam.

In order to gear up developmental activities in the field of education, efforts are being made by the education department through various plans and programmes. For this purpose, the establishment of the Additional Director of Education (Hills) has been functioning with Headquarters at Haflong. The office of the Inspector of Schools, N.C. Hills, Haflong has come into being in the year 1975. Before that, there was only one Inspector of Schools with Headquarters at Diphu for the two hill districts and there was one Assistant Inspector of Schools with Headquarters at Haflong to look after the educational affairs. Presently, there are Assistant Inspector of Schools, Deputy Inspector of Schools, Sub-Inspector of Schools and Assistant Sub-Inspector of Schools working separately for the two hill districts. It may be mentioned here that the Primary education is under the control of the Karbi Anglong District Council with effect from 1st August 1961. Various Schemes such as supply of free text books to the students, supply of uniforms to the poor students, provision of attendance scholarship to the regular students and provision of mid-day meal are implemented by the District Council. Again, the management and control of the Secondary Education have also been entrusted to the District Council in the 1970.

Till 1971, there was only thirteen educational institutions at Diphu. Out of these, there were one Art College, one Polytechnic, one type-writing institute, two secondary schools, one junior secondary schools and seven primary schools. In addition to the above institutions, one Hindi Training Centre, one Law College and one Industrial Training Institute have been established so far. Science section has also been started in the Diphu College. It may be presumed that the percentage of literacy will increase over 1971 figure (19.7 per cent) on account of the measures taken in this regard by the Karbi Anglong District Council.

PUBLIC HEALTH ENGINEERING

Provision of Potable drinking water facilities to the people of the district is the basic objective of the Public Health Engineering Department. For this purpose, the department has been executing both urban and rural water supply schemes. In the district, there are 3 nos. of Rural Water Supply Divisions, namely, Diphu Rural Water Supply Division, Howraghat Rural Water Supply Division and Hamren Rural Water supply Division. In the year 1986, the Diphu Urban Water Supply Division with construction and maintenance subdivisions was created out of the Diphu PHE Division. The Diphu Rural Water Supply

Division has covered 36 Census and 39 non-Census villages during 1987-88.

With a view to providing safe drinking water to the people of the Diphu town, water is being brought from the river Lungi located 30 kms away from Diphu, through a pipe line. At first, the water is pumped from the river to the treatment plant constructed on the top of Silari hills. Later, on the water is gravitated to the R.C.C. storage reservoir at Diphu for distribution to the people. The Diphu water supply scheme which was executed in 1965 was completed in 1972.

Foundation stone for the Greater Diphu Water Supply Scheme was laid in the month of June, 1987. The water will be pumped from the Jamuna river at Manja to the in take point (Manja) which is only one km. away from the source. Afterwards, the water will be pumped out to the Reservoir having a capacity of 7 million litres per day (MLD) at the treatment plant near Binapani High School, located at a distance of 6 kms. from Manja for the distribution to the people of the town and adjoining areas.

It may be mentioned here that the drinking water is a problem at Diphu. There are hand tubewells and ringwells in the town. It the Greater Diphu Water Supply Scheme is completed then there will be less problem in the town.

ROAD TRANSPORT FACILITIES

Prior to Independence, the hill areas remained practically isolated from the rest of the state due to non-availability of suitable road communication facilities. People inhabiting therein had to depend mainly upon footpaths and bridle paths for purchase of essential commodities, sale of agricultural products and some other purposes etc. with the main commercial centres. It is true that the lack of proper road communication facility has hampered the socio-economic life of the people to a great extent.

After Independence, attempts have been made to improve the road communication system through the various Five year Plans in the Hill Areas. Even then, there are many areas which are not accessible today. During the 1st, 2nd and 3rd Five Year Plans, the total length of major motorable roads, fair weather motorable roads and village roads was 580 kms., 499 kms. and 578 kms. respectively in the Hill Areas of Assam. Upto the end of 4th Five Year Plan, the total road length was 2000 kms. It may be mentioned here that 117 km. of the National Highway No. 39 (Numaligar-Dimapur Road) and 53 kims. of the National Highway No. 36 (parakhowa-Bokulia-Manja-Dimapur) fall within the jurisdiction of Diphu town.

The Public Works Department (Road & Building) plays a vital role in the field of road communication by creating various infra-structures. The department could uptill now complete about 165 km. of surface/ black topped roads, 653 kms. of gravelled roads and 410 km of earthened roads in addition to bridges and culverts required for road communication. Diphu is now well connected with the important commercial towns of North East India.

HEALTH AND FAMILY WELFARE

In bygone days, the people of Diphu town had to depend on various sources, like offering worship/ sacrifice to the gods and goddesses, application of wild herbs and roots and chanting mantras by ojhas for treatment of diseases. With the advent of time and growth of medical facilities, the people are now more cautious and depend on scientific method of treatment. Even after Independence till 1960, there was no hospital in the town. Now, there are one Civil Hospital, one X-Ray Unit, one District Leprosy centre and one

Malaria Unit. In addition, there is one District Health Education Wing in the town. Besides these, the office of the Chief Medical and Health Officer, Karbi Anglong is functioning with headquarters at Diphu. All the national health programmes, such as, control of blindness, school health services, registration of birth and death, T.B. control, leprosy control, goiter, family welfare and mother-child health, integrated child development scheme, immunisation and malaria are directly run under the control of this office. Medical Officers are posted against each programme with other concerned staff duly trained. Still medical facility is inadequate in the town. Therefore, steps have to be taken for the establishment of better medical facilities to the people of Diphu township.

EMPLOYMENT SERVICES

With a view to providing assistance to the employers and job seekers, the District Employment Exchange at Diphu was established in the year 1959. Moreover, Employment Market Information, Vocational Guidance Unit, District manpower Planning and Employment Generation Council are located at Diphu. Over and above, Zonal Office of the Deputy Director of Employment has been functioning at Diphu. It is found from the records of the Employment Exchange that the job-seekers are increasing in the town. As in 1989, the total number of registration was 12,605, only 199 vacancies were notified and 53 employers used exchange. Till 1989, 8603 got employment in public sector and 521 in private sector.

BANKING FACILITIES

Till 1969, there was only one State Bank of India functioning in the town. Now, there are United Bank of India, Assam Co-operative Apex Bank and Central

Bank of India. Establishment of the commercial banks has helped in the improvement of banking facilities to a great extent. As on December, 1988, total deposits and credits of commercial banks in Diphu were Rs. 2587.89 lakhs and Rs. 1352.81 lakhs respectively. In 1989, the deposits and credits have increased to Rs. 2872.88 lakhs and 1613.58 lakhs respectively.

Apart from the nationalised banks, Langpi Depangi Rural Bank (LDRB) is functioning in the district. This rural bank was established on 27th January 1982 in collaboration with the Govt. of India and Govt. of Assam sponsored by the State Bank of India in pursuance of the Regional Rural Bank Act, 1976. It is the only Regional Rural Bank sponsored by the State Bank of India in the State of Assam. The bank has thus completed 13 years of dedicated service to fulfill the objectives of ensuring Integrated Rural Development and prosperity of the small and marginal farmers and labourers in the rural areas.

CONCLUSION

From the above discussion, it is clear that the Diphu town is expanding to a great extent. Some areas around the town have come up as urban areas. Such areas which are known as urban outgrowths deserve to tbe reckoned with the main town and the continuous spread including such urban growths would deserve to be treated as an integrated urban area.

Due to the urban outgrowth, civic and other amenities of the town have became diminishing day by day. Moreover, the Diphu town has its own problems due to its remoteness, lack of industrial growth, drinking water facility, road communication and so on and so forth.

Chapter 18

ECOLOGY OF A SMALL TOWN:

A CASE STUDY OF MARIANI TOWN OF ASSAM

H.C. Khaund, A.K. Borah, M. Hussain

INTRODUCTION

The term ecology broadly refers to the study of interrelations between the living species, their associations with various species and their physical and biotic surroundings. Hence it is mainly concerned with the concept of adaptation and with all properties having a direct measurable effect on the demography, development and behaviour of the human being. Within this orbit the contemporary ecology is also concerned with population dynamics, envirnomental degradation and conservation.

From 1900 onwards the term ecology however started linking the ecosystem in general. More recently work on ecology specifically focussed on maintaining environmental balance (Bennett, 1976). Again recent works are mainly directed to environmental problems viz., environmental hazards, perception of environmental resources, vivid portrayal of subsistence strategies etc. (Ellen, 1982).

From the above it could be seen that the term ecology harbours many things. However, in this paper an attempt is made to discuss about the environmental hazards of a small town named Mariani of the state of

Assam.

HISTORICAL BACKGROUND OF THE SETTING

The present Mariani town has a long history related to its name.

It has been informed by P. Bordoloi (1995) an elderly gentleman of Mariani Town that the name Mariani was derived from the word 'Morani'—a word of Ao Naga dialect—which referred to a place for taking rest a while or for halting overnight. Mariani is situated at foot hills of Nagaland, just 4 kms. away from immediate a high hills of present Mokokchung district of Nagaland. In Mokokchung district a major tribe named 'Ao' is inhabited. Before the advent of the British, during Ahom rule the people of 'Ao' tribe used to come down to the Brahmaputra valley from the high hills for barter trading with the plains people. They used to come down through the present Mariani-Mokokchung road which at that period was medre a foot path through dense jungles. They used to come from hills and take rest at the present place and while going back to the hills also they used to halt overnight. As such the place 'Morani' became widely known during Ahom rule.

With the advent of the British for catering the needs of trade and specially for meeting the various requirements of tea gardens, developed railway communication. In the year 1882 a survey was made for development of a railway main line through Assam and the whole line to Tinsukia was completed in 1903 (Banerjee, 1974: 104). When this metre gauge main line was completed one railway station was established in Mariani in the very first decade of 20th century and by mid of second decade of 20th century it was upgraded to junction for connecting narrow gauge line of Jorhat Provincial Railway from Jorhat town the then headquarter of Sibsagar district. This narrow gauge line however was converted to metre gauge in the year 1939. Thus Mariani became famous as a transport town in the early decades of 20th century and later on also, it continued as a transport town for providing vital railway link to different places of North-East India and to various parts of the country.

PRESENT SETTING OF MARIANI TOWN AND THE PATTERN OF URBAN GROWTH

The present Mariani town covers an area of 4.1 sq. mtrs. It is situated at a distance of 19 kms. from Jorha city and it is well connected to the city by Jorhat-Mariani road. 'Dhodar Ali' is passing through this town and connects Titabar on the western side and Nakachari on the eastern side. The town is bounded on east by river Bhogdoi, west by Hatipati creek, north by Katoni Bari T.E. and south by Hunuwal T.E. The present estimated population *i.e.*, upto 1995 was approximately 23,000 Nos. (M.T.C.O., 1995). However, as per 1991 Census the population of Mariani town was recorded only 20941 Nos. (Statistical Hand Book of Assam, 1991, Guwahati). As such populationwise it falls under category—III, town as per classification made by Census authority of India. The density of population based on 1991 Census figure was 5108 Nos. (approx.) per sq. km. The Mariani Town Committee was formed on 5th December, 1978 with 5 wards under it. Presently also there are only 5 wards in this town. This town is one of the key point of buiness of Nagaland with Assam as all sorts of commodities are available here.

From communication point of view the town is well connected with Jorhat, Titabar and Nakachari by train/bus/mini bus etc. As such there is no bottleneck of communication, Taxi and cycle rickshaw are available in this town for local transport communication. There is one college having all the three streams viz., Arts, Scince and Commerce in Mariani town. Besides this one Higher Secondary School, six High Schools, one M.E. School and seven primary schools are there in Mariani town. The town is surrounded by 12 tea gardens. As such 12 tea manufacturing factories are located in nearby areas of the town. Besides these plantation industries one plywood industry viz., Woodcraft is there is the town itself. There are eighteen Nos. of small industries and seven Nos. of cottage industries which are found available at the time of field study. Govt. offices both the central and the state government are there in the town. During field study, railway establishment, one post office, one telephone office, one telegraph office, one custom and central excise office of central government were found. Besides these, state government offices viz., one forest range office, one office of Assam State Electricity Board, one Assam State Transport station, one Police Station, one public health dispensary, one veterinery dispensary, one fire brigrade station are also there in Mariani town. One petrol pump is also there in Mariani town on the eastern side.

While tracing the sources of urbanization, it has been observed that the town Mariani for its spatial expansion followed a ribbon development pattern. In fact, Borah et. al., (1991), Contended that ribbon development was the source of urbanization in N.E. India. Ribbon development refers to be extension of a town or city along the main roads. It also forms as an agent of augmenting the process of urbanization along the roads in a linear fashion where some optimum facilities are there for sustenance of business centre, human habitation of mostly agglomeration of different cultural groups of people etc. **Further the definition of ribbon development is also includes**

the process of urban sprawl and also urban overspill. More concretely in the domain of sociology and geography ribbon development refers to an urban area which develops by adhereing the following criteria; however not all:

1. The urban area includes the communities which grow in size and power and in number also they become large and exercise area deninating group—termed as urban in the functional and cultural sphere in the society.

2. Secondly, the people are purely engaged in urban occupations.

3. Thirdly, transportation and communication facilities specially the transportation either in the form of road transport or in the form of railway transport are must for the growth of an urban centre.

4. Fourthly, industrialization paves the ways for the growth of urban centres. But there may be some exceptions as in some cases taking administraive or business centres as nuclei for growth of urban centre.

5. Lastly, the growth of urban centre should attract the inward flow of large numbers of people *i.e.*, urban sprawl, at the initial stage. **This is one of the earliest stage of ribbon development of an urban centre and later on urban overspill is also experenced in that process.** The former is *a priori* while the latter is *a posteriori* phase of the growth of urban centre (Borah et. at., 1991).

Now from the above stated criteria an attempt is made to portray the development of Mariani town over decades. Actually the criteria Nos. 3 and 4 are applicable to the growth of Mariani town with the construction of Mariani Railway station (which was later upgraded to junction) and building of the road connecting Mariani to Jorhat town from an east end point the town gradually grew over times. The foci of the urban growth in Mariani was a tri-junction of Mariani-Jorhat, Mariani—Titabor and Mariani—

Amguri Road. However the growth of Mariani town started by covering both sides of Mariani-Jorhat road in a linear fashion. A provision shop was established by a Muslim gentleman named Md. Nazmal Hussain near the above stated tri-junction in mid 20's where the then European Managers of the nearby tea gardens were coming for buying their provisions. Basing on that shop and relatively taking advantages of busy nature of Mariani-Jorhat road from traffic point of view, shops and other business establishments started growing along two sides of the road up to the railgate located at the extreme northern side of the town. During 30's of the present century Mariani-Jorhat road became metalled one and thus numbers of traffic in this road gradually increased till independence. After independence and more particularly during 1950-1980 *i.e.*, within a period of thirty years traffic increased exponentially. **This thirty year period was the peirod of urban sprawl process in case of Mariani town** when the business establishments, markets as stated earlier grew in a linear way. The length of this linear settlement from the earlier described tri-junction to rail gate is 1.5 kms. **But from the beginning years of 1980's urban over spill process took place.** At the time of field study it has been observed that the town extended towards north-eastern side from the main market point and the process was first started with the construction of a cinema hall just 200 metres away from the main market point on the north-eastern side. Gradually a few govt. office buildings were constructed in this area and finally residential buidling were constructed further away from the cinema hall followed by many more govt. offices. On the southern side no expansion could take place because of the existence of railway junction.

The process of urban overspill has already started as observed during field study because of

the absence of facilities for spatial expansion. Though it is a class III category town already spatial expansion is stopped and more actutely congestion in business areas and also in residential areas is noticed as these areas are already over crowded. Further a host of problems are cropping up in Mariani town area which are discussed below under the heading problems of Mariani town.

ENVIRONMENTAL PROBLEMS OF MARIANI TOWN

As stated earlier it is a transport town because there the railway junction is there from where one can go to any places of the country. Moreovêr, by 1996 March the existing metre gauge railway line wood be converted to broad gauge line and then it would become a more important centre for railway transport linking different parts of India. However, leaving the future scenario of the town during the field study it has been absерved that presently the town is facing acute environmental problems in certain spheres which are described as under.

(a) Problem of Potable Water—One of the acute problems of Mariani town is the non-availability of potable water. As informed by the office bearers of the Mariani Town Committee, 70% of the people living in Mariani town are using contaminated water of the river Bhogdoi for drinking and other purposes and the rest 30% perople are using water from shallow tubewells and ring wells for drinking and other purposes. The water of shallow tubewells and ring wells contained 5-8 p.p.m. soluble iron (as laboratory test has already been done by the office of the Mariani Town Committee) which are far above from permissible limit of soluble iron for human consumption. The permissible limit is only 0.3 p.p.m. of soluable iron in potable water. To tide over the situation the shallow tubewell and ring well owners as observed during our field study are using sand bed filters for removing the iron. It has been informed by the office bearers of Mariani Town Committee that very recently the Urban Sewerage Board with its branch office at Jorhat is taking plans to sink five deep tubewells in different areas of Mariani town to supply potable water to the inhabitants of the town and it is hoped that with the completion of the same a long felt need would be fulfilled.

(b) Management of Drainage System—The total length of the drainage system in Mariani town is 13 kms. Approximately 5 kms of the same was excavated by the railway authority for managing its drainage problem. That portion of the drain is still maintained by the railway authority. Of late the railway authority is replacing the 5 kms. kutcha drain with pucca drain in phased manner. The rest 8 kms. of the drain is presently maintained by the Town Committee. Out of 8 kms. only 500 metres of pucca drain is found along the northern side of Mariani-Jorhat road which is under Mariani Town Committee. The rest kutcha drains are periodically cleaned with the help of sweepers by the Mariani Town Committee on contract basis who are working under railway authority as there are no sweepers avaiable except the sweepers who are working under railway authority who are hired on contract basis. It is observed during field study that the management of drainage system of the town is very poor and in many places of kutcha drain water pools are formed which virtually become the breeding grouns of mosquitos. The ofifce bearers of the Town Committee informed that for maintaining the drainage system of the town through timely removing of the silt is becoming a problem due to non-availability of sufficient manpower and fund.

(c) Garbage Management—In Mariani town there are sixteen dustbins in different places of its jurisdiction and it is estimated that daily tonnes of garbages are produced. Earlier from the dustbins garbages were collected and dumped in a very low lying area just half kilometre away on the outskirt of north eastern side of Mariani town with two hand carts. However, at present it is being done with a tractor which has a trailer. However, with the increasing number of population not only in the main business, areas but also in the residential areas there is a steady increase of the amount.of garbage produced daily and the office bearers of the Town Committee informed that the earlier dumping ground for the garbages is already filled up and hence very recently another low lying area on the eastern side of the town is selected for dumping garbages. However, office bearers have informed that considering the amount of garbages produced daily in the town the new dumping area would be sufficient only for six months and after that there would be acute problem of dumping garbages due to non-availability of suitable garbage dumping sites. The members of the town committee are quite aware of the situation and they informed that the degradation of organic wastes through anerobic fermentation would be the long term answer for management of garbage problem in this town. They informed that for doing this at least four bio-gas plants with 15 cu.m. capacity to tackle the problem. Each bio-gas plant would have to be constructed somewhere in the outskirt of the town area and hence they are planning to contact the department of Non Conventional Energy Sources, Govt. of India and the Department of Science, Technology and Environment, Govt. of Assam for necessary funding and expertise. According to them this process would provide permanent solution to garbage problem and the bio-gas thus produced through this system could be used for running bio-gas powered engine to drive electric generator. The electricity thus produced could be supplied during load sheding period to important establishments/areas of the town. That way they even hope to get good economic return as they have already gone through the report of the working of bio-gas plant on garbages and producing of electricity by driving generators at Palta, Howrah, West Bengal.

The office bearers of the Town Committee informed during field study that for proper disposal/ management of human excreta, there is no well chalked out plant with them. In Mariani town as informed by the office bearers of the Town Committee there is no community latrine within town area. But as per the records available with the Town Committee office there are 462 sanitary latrines, 376 service latrines and 1100 pit latrines with in the town area. It has been informed that cleaning of sanitary latrines are done by the uses at their own cost and the excreta are generally dumped in a pit after putting sufficient bleaching powders and finally covered with earth. The service latrines are daily cleaned by the sweepers engaged by the Town Committee. But the dumping of the human excreta as observed are generally done in a particular area of the outskirts of the town and process is found quite faulty. Further, the pit latrines as observed during the field study are creating filthy atmosphere filled with obnoxous smells and this latrines are virtually becoming the breeding grounds of different water borne diseases like gastroenteritis, typhoid, and maleria etc. The office bearers of the Town Committee are very much alert to the situation and presentally contecting different departments of central as well as state governments for management of this environmentally hazardous problem. They informed that very recently the department of Municiapl Administration has written to the Chairman of the Town Committee for providing necessary data about the present human exereta management for providing fund to constract communicity latrines in the town under centrally sponsored scheme in which it is proposed at least 50 families would be able to use a community latrine in a particular locality. The composite unit of community toilet will consists of six water closets, 3 for male and 3 for female and 2 bath rooms alongwith a hand tube well of Indian Mark II model. The Mariani Town Committee is presently surveying the area where such community latrines could be built and for which active steps are also taken by the Committee to provide necessary land so that once for all, the environmental pollution creating by service latrine and pit latrine could be stopped.

Apart from that it is learnt from the office bearer of the Town Committee that they are contacting HUDCO, Regional Office, Guwahati for providing necessary financial assistance to provide low cost sanitary latrines to the needy ones in the town.

(d) Air pollution—Apart from the above mentioned water and garbage pollution problems it has been observed during the field study that the rate of air pollution is alarmingly increasing with the smoke of coal fired chimneys of the twelve tea garden factories which are situated in nearby areas of the town, eight coal fired brick kilns situated at the outskirt and the railway steam engines of the loco shed of the Mariani junction and running train engines and also of the smoking chemneys of Mariani Woodcraft Plywood Factory. All these smoke are filling the atmosphere with coal dust particles. This air pollution as already effected the whole atmophere of the town and nearby areas. These coals dust particles are falling on the leaves of different trees and thus preventing the processes of photosynthesis of the trees. As a result many trees became extinct and many more are on the verge of extinction. Trees like betalnut, orange etc. Are giving less fruit then before. It is feared that if such situation will continue unabated then time would come when the whole Mariani town area along with a large part of the surrounding areas would become barren and pose threat to human life also.

Now the need of the hour is that scientific study should be conducted on the vegetation in and around Mariani town to measure air pollution and suggest measures to stop the sources of such pollution. The present authors of the paper opine that a detail action plan should be prepared with research institutes, Assam Pollution Management Board and Universities with necessary financial support from the state as well as central government.

OTHER PROBLEMS

Apart from the environmentally hazardous problems faced by the inhabitants of Mariani town another problem is faced by them relating to their homestead land. The land are not under periodic lease settlement under the Department of Revenue, Govt. of Assam. These are the ceiling surplus land of the adjacent tea gardens viz. Katoni bari, Kathalguri and Hunuwal tea estates. Now because of the absence of periodic lease settlement system in case of the land of Mariani town the inhabitants are deprived from the facilities like bank loans or loans from other financial institution for productive purposes as they still do not possess myadi pattas (periodic settlement of land).

Further for spatial expansion of Mariani town in future no place is available in the fringe areas. As a result to harbour the growing population land would be very less and the situation would be griam one leading to forced over crowding human habitation almost like slums in no distant future.

CONCLUSION

To conclude, the town Mariani is facing some serious problems very recently though it was a sleepy town in the past. The ribbon development no doubt became the source of urbanization at a moderate rate for sometime and at a first rate in later years. The present urban settlement pattern can not be fitted to any urban growth model except ribbon development. Haphazard growth of Mariani town in a limited town landscape if not properly checked right now then within a few years many more problems of human habitation would raise their ugly heads like a hydra.

REFERENCE

Banerjee, D.K. (1974) The economic of Assam, Sharma Brothers & Co., Nalbari, Assam.

Bennett, J.W. (1976), The Ecological Transition: Cultural Anthropology and Human Adaptation, New York.

Borah, A.K. et. a. (1991) **Ribbon Development as a Source of Urbanization in North Eastern Region of India: a few case Studies.** Unpublished Paper presented is a seminar on Patterns, Problems and Prospect of Urbanisation in North East India, organised by NEICSSR, Shillong.

Bordoloi, P. (1995) Personal discussion with the authors.

Ellen, R.F. (1982), Envirnoment, Subsistence and System: The Ecology of Small Scale Formation, Cambridge.

ABBREVIATIONS USED

(a) MTCO—Mariani Town Committee Office
(b) P.P.M.—Parts per million
(c) cu.m.—Cubic metre.

Chapter 19

PROBLEMS OF COMMUNITY INTEGRATION IN SMALL TOWNS OF BARAK VALLEY DISTRICTS OF ASSAM:

A CASE STUDY OF LALA TOWN

P.C. Dutta and B.C. Pradhan

In the contemporary world, urbanisation is a vital problem along with others socio-economic and political problems in the last few decades. India, as a developing nation, is in no way an exception to it. There has been a shift in the population from rural to urban areas. The increasing urbanisation has led to a number of socio-economic problems like crime, alcoholism, drug abuse, housing shortage, over crowding, slums, unemployment & poverty, pollution & noise and communication & traffic control etc. At the same time, they are also centres of civilization and culture by helping a lot in the process of modernisation. They arę active innovative and alive. They provide opportunities to achieve citizen's aspirations. Hence the future of our country is linked with the development of urban areas because they play a major role in not only modernising our society but also give effect to the decentralisation of power in federal polity of India. Since the independence till now, Indian Govt., has been taking measures to remove the hindrences on the way of urbanization. Very recently, 74th Amengment Act to the constitution of India has added a new dimension to urban affairs and management. All these are sufficient proof of indication that urban areas or cities or towns are playing a major role not only in the preparation of plans for economic development but also to implement the constitutional provisions of social justice. However, a socio-economic study of the small towns reveals that the Governmental measures, since independence, is not adequate and proper, for which urbanization in India suffers from several sereious problems. To support our hypothesis, this study is confined to the problems of small towns in North-East India with a particular reference to the Lala small town of Barak Valley region of Assam.

North-Eastern Region is known as the land of seven sisters (Seven states like Arunachal Pradesh, Assam, Manipur, Meghalaya, Mizoram, Nagaland & Tripura). Geographically isolated, connected with the main body of the nation by a narrow strip of land and sharing four international borders; India's North-East has shot into limelight into recent decades owing to series of social movements, the more important being the stir over the foreigner's issue. Most probably, the movements in Assam are written in the history of India as mother of tension. Since independence, Assam is lagging behind in different spheres of development due to numerous factors. As urbanization is linked with the development and modernization, the problems of urbanization in Assam best deserves study. For our Convenient study, we have taken the problems of small towns of Assam as one of the causes for the backwardness of Asam in the Indian main stream. For all practical reasons, the small town of Lala in the district of Hailakandi of Barak Valley region of Assam has been taken as our field of study.

Before going to the topic it is wise on our part to define 'urban area' or 'a city' or 'a town'. This term is used in two senses like demographically and sociologically. In the demographic study emphasis is given to the size of popultion, density of population and nature of work of the majority of the adult males. Sociologically, the focus is on heterogeneity, in personality, inter dependence and the quality of life.

In India, census definition of "town" remains more or less the same for the period 1901-1951. But in 1961 a new definition was adopted. Till 1951, "town" included (*i*) collection of houses permanently inhabited by not less then 5000 persons, (*ii*) every municipality/corporation/notified area of what ever size, and (*iii*) all civil lines not included within the municipal units. Thus the primary focus in the definition of town was more on the administrative set up rather than the size of the population.

In 1961, certain tests were applied for defining a place as "town". These were—

(*i*) a minimum population of 5000.

(*ii*) a density of not less than 1000 persons per square miles.

(*iii*) ¾th of its working population should be engaged in non-agricultural activities, and

(*iv*) the place should have a few characteristics and civil amenities like transport and communication, hospitals, electricity and Banks, Schools, Markets, Recreation Centres etc.

As a result of this change in the definition, 1812 areas. As a result of this change in the definition, 1812 areas declares as towns in 1951 census were not so considered in 1961 census. The 1961 basis was adopted in the 1971, 1981 and 1991 Census too for defining the towns. Now demographically, areas with population between 5000-20,000 considered as small towns, those with population between 20,000-50,000 are considered as large towns, those with population between 50,000-1,00,000 are considered as big cities and areas with more than 1,00,000 people are considered as metropolitan areas.

From the above study of definitions we find that sociologists do not attach much importance to the size of the population in the definition of the cities because the minimum population standards vary greatly. As such, they give more importance to the Characteristics other than the population and size.

Theodorson (1969) has defined 'urban community' as "a community with high population density, a predominance of non-agricultural occupation, a high degree of specialisation resulting in a complex division of labour, and a formalised system of local Govt. it is also characterised by a prevelence of impersonal secondary relations and dependence on formal social controls".

According to Robert Redfield, urban society is characterised by a large heterogeneous population, closed contact with other societies, through trade, communication etc., a complex division of labour, a prevalence of secular over sacred concerns, and the desire to organise behaviour rationally toward given goals, as opposed to following traditional standards and norms.

Considering the above definitions into account and the result of the 1991 Census, it reveals that in the entire N.E. Region, there are 183 towns in total out of which 87 towns (*i.e.,* 47.54 per cent) are in Assam, 30 in Manipur, 22 in Mizoram, 18 in Tripura, 10 in Arunachal, Pradesh, 9 in Nagaland and 7 in Meghalaya. Out of 87 towns in Assam, 51 towns *i.e.,* 58'62 P.C. are small towns which we have taken as the purpose of our study. 'Lala town is coming under 5th class town so far as the recent definition of small towns of India are concerned.

Situated between longitude 92°–32' and 92°–33' East and Latitude 24°–34' and 24°-36' North covering an area of 4.1 Sq. Km. Lala town is 17 km away from Hailakandi town on the South.

According to Late Rajmohan Nath, son of Lala town, the word 'Lala' came from the Kuki language. In Kuki language 'La' means Giripath (narrow mountain pass). Thus according to this language the place where different Giripaths are connected may be called as Lala.

On 19th July, 1972, the Govt. of Assam announced 'Lala' as a town by passing a Legislation vide Govt. Notification No. MA. 299/66/91 dt. 19.07.72. On the 2nd October of the same year Lala Town Committee's door was opened by the then Congress M.L.A. Sri Santosh Kumar Roy and Sub-Divisional Officer, Hailakandi, Sri. P.C. Deori.

There are 4 wards under Lala Town Committee. Various statistical information regarding Lala Town are given in different tables.

Table 1

	1971			1991		
	Male	**Female**	**Total**	**Male**	**Female**	**Total**
Population	2867	2669	5536	4428	4231	8659
S.C.	349	321	670	676 (15.27%)	627 (14.28%)	1308 (15.05%)
S.T.	—	—	—	4	3	7
Literates	1596	1042	2638	3395	2869	6264
Literacy rate (in per cent)	55.66	39.42	47.65	89.41	78.22	83.91
Child of 0-6 age group	N.A.	N.A.	N.A.	631 (14.25%)	563 (13.31%)	1194 (13.79%)

	1971	1991
Area	0.68 Sq. Km.	4.1 Sq. Km.
Density	8141 Sq. Km.	2112 Sq. Km.
Sex Ratio	931 females per 1000 males.	955 females per thousand males.
No. of holdings	1207 Nos. (1972-73)	1479 Nos. (1995-96)
Length of the road.	9.1 Km. (1973-73)	11.72 Km. (1995-96)

Source: Annual Reports of Lala Town Committee. Statistical Hand Book, Hailakandi District. 1994.

Table 2: Lala Rural College

	1971	1995
Students on roll	191 (1971-72)	890 (1994-95)
Strength of teaching staff	12	26
No. of Streams	1 (Arts)	2 (Arts & Commerce)
Lala Rural College (Established in 1964)	Not under deficit system	Under deficit system (December' 1975)

Table 3: Educational Institution : 1995

	Students on roll	Teaching staff		
		Male	Female	Total
L.P. Schools	942	20	24	44
Middle Schools	1213	69	23	92
High/Higher Secondary Schools	1855	—	—	112
Degree College	890	—	—	26
Other Institutions	122	—	—	12

Table 4: Income Expenditure Statement of Lala Town Committee

Year	Opening Balance	Current Income	Total Income	Expenditure	Balance
	(in Rs.)	(in Rs.)	(in Rs.)	(in Rs.)	(in Rs.)
1992-93	65,879.83	7,27,423.85	7,93,303.68	5,39,821.02	2,53,482.66
1993-94	2,53,482.66	6,65,292.88	9,18,775.54	8,49,480.94	69,295.60
1994-95	69,295.60	27,28,719.28	27,98,014.88	21,59,040.75	6,38,974.13

It is observed that there is a general degree college in the town. Besides, twenty other educational institutions including one Madrassa and one Sangeet Vidyalaya are also established in the town. The offices located in the town are like two Nationalised Banks, Office of the Flood Control, Police Station, Electric supply, Water Supply (PHE), Office of the S.D.C., Office of the P.W.D., Railway Station, Office of the ASTC, Office of the Post and Telegraph, and Office of the Telephone Exchange. There is a 12-beded primary health centre, which is not sufficient to provide better facilities of health and sanitation of the town. However, the construction of 30 beded hospital has just started.

As per the statement given by the members of the Lala Town Committee, the Government's grants-in-aid to the Town Committee is not proportionate to the actual population and size of it. As a result the developmental works of the town has been suffering greatly since the last couple of decades. The members of the committee claimed that the population of the town should be more than 21,000 (Twenty one Thousand). Unfortunately, the cesus report shows that the population of the town stands at 8659 as some mouzas of the town have been excluded by the Census Authority.

However, within the limited grants and self fundings, the said committee had undertaken the responsibility of executing the developmental works such as—transfer of Gandhi Bhavan from Hailakandi to Lala Town Committee; allotment of R.C.C. rooms to intending Businessmen in ward Nos. 1 * 2; construction of culvert in ward No. 3 and market complex, water supply in the town; construction of low cost sanitary latrines. Besides, under NRY scheme, the committee provided facilities for house construction to the downtrodden, training facilities to the trainees for knitting, tailoring & T.V. Repairing; providing micro enterprise loan to the 56 persons living below poverty line. The committee also constructed 7 new roads and repaired 17 numbers of roads within its Jurisdiction.

PROBLEMS

From different studies of the problems of urbanisation in India we have accumulated the knowledge that urbanisation faces serious problems on the way of its progress. In small towns there is a serious problem of community integration too. The people belonging to all communities and caste live together and practically there are no separate localities for any community. Each community has full freedom to live in the way it likes. One community cannot stand in the way of living and the method of worshipping of any other community. However, the small towns are not free from the problem of integration. Though there are several problems of small towns in Assam, the most serious problem is the problem of community integration which is deliberately ignored by the different scholars who have studied on urbanization in Assam. In this study, attempts have been made to highlight the problem of community integration in the small towns of Assam and Lala, a small town has been taken as the purpose of our study.

In our study of Lala town the problem of community integration is clearly visible for several reasons. Although several factors are responsible for community disintegration, some of the important factors are like—

1. Political Patronage—In towns each inhabitant knows it very well that without political patronage no remarkable success in any walk of life is achieved. Each community tries to control political life. Those who succeed feel very happy while others get frustrated. The result is that they do not feel like integrating with the other communities and the political leaders try their best to take advantage of the situation and instead of helping in the integration of communities try to disintegrate them. During the AGP rule in Assam, a good number of people of Lala town showed their allegiance to the party in power due to different reasons.

A large number of Muslim population came in favour of the AG rule as they were feeling insecure because of their number in the town was very less in comparison to Hindu Population. Similarly, there is always political hustle and bustle between Metai Manipuris and Vishnupriya Manipuris. If Metais are supporting the politicies and programmes of Congress party, on the other hand, the Vishnupriyas are supporting the main rival of the Congress party *i.e.*, the AGP. As Lala Town is surrounded by the villages, which are completely dominated by Muslims, the Hindu population of the town, which is in majority *i.e.*, more than 80 per cent, support the Bharatiya Janata Party as their saviour. The political leaders of the above three dominant political parties of the town are taking advantage of the situation disintegrating the society for the furtherance of their own ends.

2. Economic Disparity—Another vital problem of community disintegration in Lala town is economic life.

Dutta (1992) observed that the pattern of household consumption is most unevely distributed in top 30 per cent groups of consumers. Further, after seventies, the richest section of the society has gained much at the cost of poorest section. The price differentials in the two sectors (rural and urban) result not only in the differences in the pattern of consumption and inequality in PCE (per capita expenditure) but also contribute substentially towards the inequality in standard of living between rural and urban region in one hand and among the groups of consumers on the other. The inequality is found to be maximum (0.275) among the states of NER. The income inequality is found to be 0.175 in the Barak Valley of Assam in 1989-90.

In the Lala town there is a mad race for earning money and wealth. Every community wants that the people belonging to its own community should become rich. As a result some communities go forward while others lag behind. For example, there is a common practice in Lala town is that a Mulim will buy essential commodities from the shop-keeper of his own community even if at a higher price. At the same time it is a practice too of the Hindus and others. As the Hindus are in majority in the town, the most of the big businessmen belong to this community and became eye sore in the eyes of the muslims and other communities. The Muslim feels disintegrated and instead of flowing in the main stream of the town life, it begins to keep away from it. This makes the whole process of communal integration difficult and hampers in the development of the town.

3. Conflict of Values—Communal integration is also effected by cultural outlook, approach and values. In Lala town, each community has its own culture. As Hindus are in majority it is quite keen that all other communities should follow what it believes. This creats a problem of cultural conflict and conflict of values. When the attempt is made by persuation, the situation remains under control but when efforts are made to accept a particular culture with the use of force, the sitaution takes an ugly turn in the form of communal riots.

4. Indifferent life Styles—Since in the society of the town there are various Communities, all have not similar approach towards life and its problems. Some Communities are peace loving and others are interested in the militant life. People of militant Communities wish to solve their problems by offensive means and methods. When approach towards life and method of solving social and economic problems is different obviously there can be problems on the way of Communal integration. As the Lala town comprised of two major sections like Hindus & Mulsims, it is quite obvious that their life styles will create obstacles on the way of Communal integration.

5. Immigration—Lala is a small town inhabited by the people migrated mostly from rural areas. There is also another form of migration to this town from the neighbouring towns of Lala like Hilakandi, Karimganj & Silchar. The latter type of migration is due to employment in different Govt. and non-Govt. offices and institutions. The population migrated from different rural areas have different backgrounds and believes. This mixture of people affects the working of informal controls—Mores and Institutions and reliance on formally designed mechanisms for regulating the behaviour of individuals and groups increases. People no longer share the common sentiments and being exposed to traditional ideas imported from rural cultures through contacts with migrants. Sometimes they challenged the ultra modern believes and practices of the town. Further, the common attitude, believes and economic status of the rural migrants in the town is not copying with the town civilization. As Lala is a small town, the dwellers of the town can be personally counted for which always there is a rural versus urban conflict of values that assumes the shape of intra-community dissention.

The second type of migration is of class-II officers of different offices and teachers and Lecturers of different institutions of Lala town, who are settled permanently in the bigger towns but they inhabited in the Lala town in the name only. Although people of Lala expecting much from these categories of population for modernization and different other forms of social development, they contribute nothing for this society on the contrary. They have alienated themselves as well as their family members far-off from this society on the ground of under development. Naturally, they are become eye sore in the eyes of the general citizens of Lala. They pay no heed to the general problems of this small town like, recreational centre, proper educational facilities, public library, reading room, Fire brigade, hospital, maintanance of Roads, streets, lighting, insufficiency of supply water, drainage system etc. because they are managing all these for themselves and for their family members in the bigger towns.

6. Multiplicity of Professions—A number of professional associations and trade guilds exists in

Lala town. These association and guilds are exclusive and have no connection with each other. Each professional association or trade guild is interested in protecting the rights and interests of its members. The union of Grade-IV employees and union of Grade-I employees, each tries to further the interest of its members. Many a time this leads to a bigger controversy and rivalry among various unions. As a result of which there is a bitterness and class struggle within the town community instead of integrity.

CONCLUSION & SUGGESTION

From the above study of the "problem of Community integration in small towns of Barak Valley Districts of Assam" we come to the conclusions that the definition of small towns by the leading authorities need a thorough revision.

In our opinion, census is not the sole criteria to categorise the towns into different classes of towns. It may be a vital factor but not the sole factor, Along with the factor of population, other factors like permanent town dwellers, better and swift means of communication, better facilities and higher academic institutions, a good health and sanitary measures, recreation centres and other instruments of modernization are to be taken into account to judge the standard of the towns. Further, our study reveals that the small tons are not only suffering from the traditional maladies like crime, alcoholism, drug abuse, housing shortage etc. but also a problem of community integration.

The first serious problem is political patronage of the town dwellers in which the so-called leaders of different political parties have a great role of play in solving the problem of communal disharmony. As it is observed that just before election there is a trend of communal tension in the town, hence our appeal to the political leaders that they should abstain from this type of activities. Further it is observed that due to lack of unity between two major communities *i.e.*, Hindus & Muslims, the integrity of the town is always in peril. A right education of the people in different aspects will sure to solve this vital problem. Again, our appeal to the nation-builders to pass legislations to solve the problems, as mentioned, by which small towns will not be suffered from the serious maladies. Instead of exploiting the communal situation for the furtherance of their selfish ends, the leaders should pay their attention for the development activities of the towns by which the town of Lala can be linked with the main stream of the State in the process of modernization and development. If "Small is Beautiful", the leaders should turn their attention towards Lala town (small town) instead of looking always to the neighbouring bigger towns like Silchar, Karimganj and Hailakandi as Pandit Nehru neglected North-East during his period. To conclude the topic our last appeal to the population of small towns is that they should not be persuaded by the "Loaves and Fishes" of the communal leaders.

REFERENCES

1. Bose Ashish, India's Urbanisation, 1979.
2. Dutta P.C., Certain Aspects of Consumer Behaviour in Assam—An Empirical Study, Unpublished Ph.D. Thesis, 1992.
3. Kolenda, Pauline, Caste in Contemporary India, Rawa Publications, Jaipur, 1984.
4. Theodorson, G.A. and Tehodorson. A.Q., A Modern Dictionary of Sociology, Thomas Y. Crowell Co. New York, 1969.
5. Statistical Hand Book, Hailakandi District 1994.
6. Purbayan, Weekly paper, Hailakandi.
7. Hailakandi Jela: Ek Sangkhipta Parichaya, Office of the publicity Deptt. Assam, 1990.
8. Sub-Divisional Statistical Hand Book, Hailakandi Sub-Division, 1973.

Chapter 20

POTENTIALITY AND PROBLEMS OF SMALL TOWNS IN ARUNACHAL PRADESH

A CASE STUDY OF BOMDILA TOWN

R.P. Bhattacharjee

URBANIZATION IN ARUNACHAL PRADESH

Urbanization process in Arunachal pradesh in just 2½ decades old. It started with 4 towns in 1971. The number of towns increased to 6 in 1981 and further to 10 in 1991. The first four towns are Pasighat, Bomdila, Along and Tezu (1971), while Naharlogun and Itanagar were added as Census Town in 1981. The new additions of towns as per 1991 census are Ziro, Khonsa, Namshai and Roing. There are 5 Class-IV towns and 5 Class-V towns in Arunachal Pradesh as per 1991 census. There were 5 Class-V towns and 1 Class VI towns in 1981. In 1971 there was only 1 class-V town and 3 Class-VI towns in this State.[1] These are shown in Table 1.

From the above table, it can be seen that Pasighat, Along and Tezu had better growth of urban population compared to Bomdila during 1971-81.[2] Similarly, the 5 towns of Pasighat, Along, Tezu, Naharlongun and Itanagar had better urban-growth compared to Bomdila during 1981-91.[3] Even the urban status of these towns increased to medium during the same period in 1991. Bomdila, one of the oldest town in the

State still remains a small town.

Table 1. Urban Population and Size-class in Arunachal Pradesh

Towns	1971	1981	1991
1	2	3	4
Bomdila	3172 (VI)	3860 (VI)	5655 (V)
Along	4818 (VI)	8074 (V)	13239 (IV)
Pasighat	5116 (V)	9139 (V)	14639 (IV)
Tezu	4182 (VI)	6239 (V)	15271 (IV)
Naharlogun	—	7710 (V)	14369 (IV)
Itanagar	—	6406 (V)	16545 (IV)
Zero	—	—	8862 (V)
Roing	—	—	6976 (V)
Namshai	—	—	7975 (V)
Khonsa	—	—	7097 (V)

Sources: Census of India (Arunachal Pradesh) 1971, 1981 & 1991.

The population of Bomdila town was 3172 persons in 1971 which increased to 3860 in 1981 and 5655 in 1991. It has lowest population growth of 21.7% and 46.5% during 1971-81 and 1981-91 respectively among all the town in the state. The newly declared Census Towns of Ziro, Khonsa, Namshai and Roing are also small-town but Bomdila, after over two decades of Urbanization in the State, is still a small-town. Due to this, it is thought to study the, potentiality and problems of this town here.

POTENTIALITY & PROBLEMS OF BOMDELA TOWN

Bomdila town is the head quarter of West Kameng District lies at an altitude varying from 8100' to 9000' above sea level.[4] It is one of the oldest administrative centre in the State opened in 1953.[5] it is an administrative town as like the other towns in the State except Namshai which has emerged as a town based on manufacturing sector.[6] But Bomdila town is not a planned town. Even the town's viability is questionable. The area of the town is only 1.27 sq.

km.[7] It has highest population density of 4452 persons/km^2 among all the towns of the State. Even the density of Bomdila town is higher than Naharlogun (4354).[8] In fact there is no flat land available in Bomdila where the town could have potentiality to expand. The town is on hill-slopes. Even it has no land to provide the newly created college. The villages of Sera and New Bomdila has come up at a distance of 2 km. in support of Bomdila town in its periphery as a hinterland with surplus produces of local vegetables, paddy, maize and apple. The next nearest villages are Wango and Singchung 8 km away each. Due to geographical insularity, these villages could not become an urban agglomeration of Bomdila. In fact, Rupa at a distance of 18 km. and Tenga Valley at a distance of 22 km. with population of 3444 and 2436 (1991) respectively are potential township in the district compared to Bomdila. This is due to the fact that the area of Bomdila town is situated on a hill slop with lack of expansion scope. The density of the town may increase in future but it is unlikely that there will be largescale expansion of population and area of the town.

One aspect of the town is encouraging that the indigenous people are increasingly taking part in urbanization process of the town. For example, in 1971, the percentage of indigenous people in Bomdila town was 15.76% which increased to 30.21% in 1981[10] and 34.38% in 1991.[11] The growth of indigenous people in Bomdila Town was 133.2% during 1971-81 but it was only 66.7% during 1981 91. This decline in the growth of the indigenous people can also be attributed to limited scope of expansion of the town. In consequence, the nearest villages of Sera, New Bomdila, Wango and Singchung has grown increasingly.

Beside geogrpahical insularity, the pattern of work-participation rate too shows the future potentiality of this town is not much favourable. The working population of the town is completely based on tertiary sector. This is shown in Table 2 below.

Table 2: Workers Classification of Bomdila Town in Borad Sectors (Percentage)

Year	Primary Sector	Secondary Sector	Tertiary Sector
1	2	3	4
1971	2.83	3.69	93.48
1981	2.95	0.58*	96.47
1991	5.29	19.78	74.93

Sources: 1. District Census Hand Book (DCHB), Kameng District, 1971, pp. 88-91;

2. DCHB, West Kameng District, 1981, p. 117;

3. DCHB, West Kameng District, 1991, pp. 83-85;

* It consists of Manufacturing sector only, since data for other sub-sector of Secondary sector not available.

From the above table, it can be seen that the tertiary sector is prominent in economic activity of urban dwellers in this town but it has decreased from 93.48% in 1971 to 74.93% in 1991. This can be attributed to lack of expansion scope of servicing-sector specially public administration and other services. The data for 1981 is not comparable due to non availability of 9 category workers-classification though it can be stated that service sector is the main contributory factor in the economic pursuits of urbanites. The percentage decrease in tertiary-sector is also due to percentage shift in Secondary-sector which can be attributed to manufacturing sector (other than house-hold).

In Secondary sector, the main economic activity of the town is woollen carpet manufacturing. The export of most important items of town is wooden-furniture, cane, wood, apple, and import of most important items of the town is food-grains, clothes, construction materials.[12]

The potentiality of a town cannot be gauged without Human Resource Development. In this respect, women are actively participating in the urbanization-process. The increasing sex-ratio is an indicator of women's participation. The sex-ratio in the town in increasing. In 1971, the sex ratio was only 396 which increased to 725 in 1981 and 743 in 1991. The increasing human resources in the town would have increased the size of the town if it had no geographical constraints. The literacy rate in the town is 69.75% in 1991 while it had 51.32% in 1971 and 48.73% in 1981. The table below shows the literacy rate of this town.

Table 3: Literacy-rate of Bomdila Town

Sex	1971	1981	1991
1	2	3	4
Person	51.32	48.73	69.75
Male	59.82	58.27	76.10
Female	29.89	35.57	60.79

Sources: 1. District Census Hand Book (DCHB). 1971. Kameng Distt. p. 65;
2. DCHB. West Kameng District. 1981. p. 23;
3. DCHB. West Kameng District. 1991. pp. 82-83.

It can be seen that female literacy rate substantially increased from 1971 to 1991 while male literacy rate decreased in 1981 compared to 1971 and again increased in 1991. In respect of medical facility, there is 1 District Hospital at Bomdila with authorised bed numbering 75 as on 31.3.93.[13] The estimated population of Bomdila Town in 6104 (31.3.93).[14] This shows that there is 1 bed for 81 persons in the town or 12.29 bed per 1000 persons. This indicates that future expansion of human resources too will be limited in this town.

The main problem of the town is water supply. The different sources of water are being dried up due to deforestation. The nearest river is Tenga-River at a distance of 22 km. down-stream from the town. Though there are a few streams near the Bomdila Town but these area not sufficient for continous water supply in the town. The scope of lifting water from the

Tenga river is perhaps difficult. If the water problem is not solved, it may be a deserted township in future. To solve the problem, afforestation is perhaps the only solution to maintain natural sources of water. The power-position is maintained from the Dirang, Rahung and Sessa mini-hydel stations and also with the help of Diesel-sets which are very costly. The consumers of power in the town are mainly domestic. In 1989, the total electric-connection was 1514 numbers and out of that, 952 numbers were for domestic purposes and 480 numbers for road-lighting points constituting 94.6% of total connection. The industrial connection was only 10 and commercial connection as 72.[15]

This clearly shows that the town is industrially backward. Prospect of tourism-industry is there. The important Trouist spots in the District are Rupa, Bomdila, Dirang and Sela Pass and Bomdila Town is at the centre of these places. But in the absence of basic-infruastructure, like bus-service and hotel, the prospect of Tourism is also unfavourable. It may be mentioned that the nearest Rail-head of the town is 100 kim away at Bhalukpong and nearest Air-port is at Salonibari near Tezpur 160 km. away from Bomdila. The transportation facility from these places to Bomdila is either absent or inadequate to facilitate Tourist-inflow. Due to locational problem top Bomdila has not developed like the other hill-stations in the country. Comparatively Rupa is a growing township and even some major administrative departments already established there. The growth of Tenga Valley is mainly due to army establishment, while Tenga Bazar is a ribbon-development's of the Tenga Valley township. Horticultural prospect is there specially the apple production at the periphery of the Bomdila town but due to lack of marketing facility, it could not flowerish as was expected even fruit-process-plant also could not be established till-date.

CONCLOUSION

Considering the different aspects discussed above, it can be concluded that Bomdila-as a Small-twon, will have little development in future specially due to its geographical-insularity notwithstanding administrative efforts.

REFERENCES

1. Bhattarcharje, R.P.: "Urbanization Trent it Arunachal Pradesh—A Brief Analysis" in J.B. Ganguly (Ed.) "Urbanization and Development in North-East India" (1995), Deep & Deep Publications, No. Delhi, p. 118.
2. The growth of Urban Population of Pasighat was 78.6%, Along 67.6% and Tezu 49.2% compared to Bomdila as 21.7% during 1971-81.
3. The growth rate of 5 towns were 60.2%, 64.0%, 144.8%, 86.4% and 158.3% respectively during 1981-91.
4. District Statistical Office (1993): "Statistical Hand Book of West Kameng District", Arunachal Pradesh, p. 2.
5. Headquarters of the Sela Sub-Agency was shifted from Charduar to Bomdila with effect from 28th February, 1953 (Vide Administrative Jurisdictions of North-East Frontier Agency), 1-11-1961, The Statistical Branch, North East Frontier Agency, Shillong, p. 86.
6. Bhattacharjee, R.P.: "Urbanization and Consumption Pattern of Urbanites in Arunachal Pradesh" Seminar Papper read at Arunachal University, Doimukh, on 24.11.95 (abstract, p. 2).
7. Census of India, 1991, Series-3, Arunachal Pradesh, Part-XII, A & B, DCHB, *ibid*, W. Kameng, p. 72;
8. Estimated by the author on the basis of Area = 3.30 sq. km. and population = 14,369 of Naharlogun, DCHB, Lower Subansiri, 1991, pp. 124-5.
9. Census, 1971, Series 24, Arunachal DCHB, Kameng, *ibid*, pp. 92-99, (percentage estimated).
10. DCHB, 1981, W. Kameng, *Ibid*. p. 144, (Percentage estimated).
11. Census of India, 1991, *ibid*, p. 76, (% estimated)
12. DCHB, 1991, W. Kameng, *ibid*, p. 25;
13. Statistical Hand Boo, 1993, *ibid*, p. 24.
14. Estimated by the author;
15. DCHB, 1991, W. Kameng, *ibid*, p. 73.

Chapter 21

LAMKA (CHURACHANDPUR) TOWN

H. Kamkhenthang

In India there are four types of urban administration or local bodies such as corporations, municipalities, town area committees and notified area committees whereas in Manipur there is no coporation and there is a three-tier system of local bodies. There are as many as seven municipal councils and 20 small town committees having a range of population of 5969 (Jiribam Municipality having the smallest number of 10 wards) to 1,97,097 (Impahal Municipality having as many as 26 wards). Criteria for treating a place as urban in the census of 1981 are all statutory towns like municipal corporation, municipal board, contonment board or notified town area etc. and other places having a minimum population of 5000 with 75% of the male wrking popultion engaged in non-agricultural and allied activities plus a density of population of at least 400 persons per sq. km. (1,000 per sq. km.). A town with a population of 1,00,000 and above is treated as a city. Imphal is a city having a municipal with its 2,14,991 population including the population of Scheduled Tribes of 16994.

The Manipur Municipalities Act, 1994 as passed by the Parliament in June, 1994 is not applicable to the hill areas of Manipur. The act states "It extends to the whole state of Manipur except the Hill Areas to which the Manipur (Hill Areas) District Council Act,

1971 extends or any area which is included in a cantonment under Cantonment Act, 1924".

In Manipur there are seven Municipal Councils which are formerly known as Municipalities and there are as many as 20 small towns. The only small towns in the District Council arcas of Manipur is Moreh Small Town at the Indo-Myanmar boundary in Tengnoupal District. This small town has an international importance for India as well as for Myanmar as it is one of the trade centres under the India-Myanmar Border Trade Agreement signed on the 21.1.1994.

There is town called locally Lamka. It is also known as Churachandpur by the non-local people. The official name of the town is Churachandpur in government transactions. It is the second town next to Imphal in size, population, bussiness and development in Manipur. It has a good potentiality for further development as well as problems. The name of the town poses a problem and this prblem gives raise to confusion on the local people. Initially Lamka and Churachandpur refer different places having different stories of origin. Lamka is the original name and place of the town. The name Churachandpur was superimposed through the governmental administrative machinaries on Lamka. The stories of their origin can be traced back to the establishment of Lamka and Churachadpur as different local places. Let us first see how Churachandpur and Lamka were established. A name Churachandpur was imposed as a name of the British Administrative unit on a native village. The condition prevalent during the British period in the Hills of Manipur may be briefly stated here as follows.

The political situation of the British Indian in Manipur Hills was turbulent as a result of the British policy of recruitment of the hill people into the British Labour Corps to serve the British soldiers in France in 1917. The Hill people of the Lushai Hills and the Chin Hills and Manipur Hills were recruited for the Labour corps. They did not like to oppose to the forced recruitments and most of the tribes unwillingly joined the labour crops as they could not and dared not oppose it. But the Kuki and Zou in Manipur objected to the recruitment. They did not like to go to a foreign land to die in the war, rather they preferred to die at their own places by fighting the British. This rebellion is known as Kuki Rebellion, 1916-17. In the meantime Jodonang and Gaidinliu, the leaders of the Kubui tribe made a dint in the Zeliangrong areas of Tamenglong against the British. The turbulent nature which existed then in the British Hill areas of Manipur compelled the British government to call back home these who joined the Labour Corps in France. It was required to open administrative centres in the hills of Manipur to contain the rebels. As such in 1919 the whole of Manipur hills was divided into three administrative units such as the South-West Sub-Divisional Unit with the headquarters at Suangpi, the west sub-divisional unit and the East Sub-divisional unit with the headquarter at Tamenglong and Ukhrul respectively. The headquarter of South-West-Sub-Divisional unit was located at Suangpi village which is on the hill top, 13 km. South-West from Lamka, the present Churachandpur town. It was this particular Suangpi that was renamed as Churachandpur at first. It was in 1921 Mr. B.C. Gasper, the S.D.O. of South-West Sub-Division at Suangpi threw a feast in honour of those France returness who were conscripted for Labour Corps. It was stated that the Meitei King, Churachand took part in the feast. It was on that occassion of the feast at Suangpi, the sub-divisional headquarters was renamed as Churachandpur after the name of Churachand. It was announced by the Lambus that the name of Suangpi was changed into Churachandpur from that day and that any boldy who called it Suangpi would be sent to Jail. In this way the local people were intimidated even they could not pronounce Churachandpur because of the absence of 'R' sound in the dialects of the local northern Chin Tribes, Zoumi. The new name did not penetrate much into the linguistic usage of the local people. They preferred to call and to refer to it as Suangpi in their local parlance whereas the educated persons used the new name also alternatively. But after about 10 years of the imposition of Churachandpur on Suangpi, the South-West Sub-division was abolished and the headquarters was abandoned and left behind by the government. The South-West Sub-Division was dismembered and the Western part of it was amalgamated to the Western Sub-Division with its headquarters at Tamenglong and the Eastern part of it was annexed to Sadar Hills Sub-Division with its headquarters at Imphal. In this way Churachandpur was abolished, abandoned and became *desuatude*. The abandoned Sub-Divisional headquarters was occupied by the North-East India General Mission inc. having its head office at Philadelphia, U.S.A. The NEIG Mission did not inherit the imposed name on Suangpi. But named it Mission Compound. However, both the names of Suangpi and Mission Compound went on side by side. However, the NEIG Mission never called its headquarters neigher Suangpi nor Old Charachandpur. The name of Churachandpur could not be perpetuated and disappeared. Later in 1934 an administrative outpost was created at Thanlon which was upgraded to a circle office in 1946 after the World War-II. In the same year after the World War-II a circle office was started at a new place called Lamka. The old seat of the government continued however, to be the main centre of activities as the NEIG Mission took possession of the site on payment to the village chief of Suangpi for the land and some payment to the SDO. for the abandoned houses. This

Mission Compound thrived on upto 1980s till the local churches under NEIG Mission became self supporting Indigeneous Churches. The place that assumed the name Churachandpur once now continues as a village in the name of Mission Compound and the people of the village rejected to call it Old Churachandpur even after a New Churachandpur was imposed on Lamka again. We said that the first administrative centre at Suangpi renamed as Churachandpur was abandoned. A seat of the S.D.O. was created at Lamka and the government imposed New Churachandpur on Lamka. Now let's give in brief how the indigeneous Lamka originated.

Just before the World War-II in 1929 one Paite named Zenhang established the present Lower Lamka and in 1930 another Paite named Phungkhothang also established the present upper Lamka with permission from the British officers. The two settlements divided by Tedim Road in between them grew in size, population and volume of trade into the present stage of Lamka town or Churachandpur town. At that time there were no settlements near by and the whole area was covered with thick forests about in wild animals and teemed with malarial mosquitoes. Then later Nghathal village was established in 1932, Rengkai village in 1938 and Gangpimual village in 1932 around Lamka. Lamka being a composite settlement became larger and larger. In became the main centre for all practical purposes. The Meiteis started knowing and calling Lamka 'Zelang' after the name of Zenhang who established Lower Lamka.

The World War-II was over. A new circle office was established about 10 years after the abolition of Churachandpur at the western outskirt at Suangpi, Mr. Pearson and Mr. Thangkhopao Kipgen were to select a site for the new circle office at the original administrative headquarters occupied by the NEIG Mission. But they found abandoned old houses and some structures at Lamka abandoned by the American troops after the War. Lamka happened to be a better place for the administrative centre. Lamka became the headquarters of the government. On becoming the headquarters of administrative centre New Churachandpur was superimposed again on Lamka in official parliance. In this way Lamka and Churachandpur go on side by side as the name of the same town as stated earlier. This is one of the problems faced by the local people.

The growth of Lamka town into Churachandpur town is due to urbanisation. People migrated not only from the interior hill areas but also from Mizoram and from the Imphal valley. It is a district headquarters and many government departments have their district offices. The expansion of the town was attributed at the first instance to the establishment of the second market place called New Bazar with the free contribution of land by Mr. late Thangzam in 1955. This led not only to the expansion of the marketing place but also residential areas. In 1962 the town became a notified area as Churachandpur Small Town. Migration from rural villages is a continuous process and the area of the town is expanding with the formation of New Lamka by new migrants. As such the small town was converted into Municipality under the Munipur Municipalities Act, 1976 which was amended in 1994.

The town developed into a notified area was converted into a municipality and the town is now without a municipal council by virtue of section-I proviso-I of the Manipur Municipalities Act, 1994. The area of the town is 6.50 sq. km. having as many as 16 wards. The total popultion of the town is 37334 persons with 6237 houses as per the latest census conducted by the town section of the Churachandpur District Council for the year, 1994-95. In terms of population the town is next to Imphal and followed by Thoubal Municipal having a population of 33011 population in the valley.

With the withdrawal of Municipality institution by the government of Manipur, the management of the town was handed over to the district council. The functions, liabilities and assets were taken by the District Council in March, 1988. Municipal Councils in the hill areas as that of Churachandpur town have the merits and demerits for the residents of the town in particular and general populace of the Scheduled Tribes of the district. During the terms of small town and municipal institutions from 1962 to 1988 for a period of 26 years the town had good experiences of development. The residents of the town enjoyed a good sanitary system. Sanitary services had been delivered to the residents regularly and smoothly. They could avail themselves of bank loan facilities, called 'Urban Poor Loan' for establishment of small shops in the town area. The amount of such a loan ranges from Rs. 5000/- to Rs. 10,000/-. A town having a municipality is more progressive than the one without a local body to look after it. The Ward Commssioners take interest in their wards and they like to take responsibilities for the development of their own wards every year in the implementation of development work. It is found that activities during municipal institution of the town were more intensive and extensive than before at least in the disposal of garbage and collection of revenues. The town was more neat and tidy. The Municipality Act provides clear cut provisions for enforcement of Law and order making market control easy and smooth. Now there is no proper maintenance of drainage in the town. Water floods in the rains. Sometimes garbages deposited in the drains are redeposited on the street by rain water and so on. Due to lack of provisions in the proviso of the District Council Act which is more or less constitutionally baseless, control of strayed cattle in the town, disposal of carcas on the road and traffic control and control of essential commodities are in free hands now. As it is a vast and fast developing town in Manipur. The District Administrative Officer, the Chairman or the Chief Executive Officer of the District Council could not pay adequate attention towards the smooth and proper functioning of the town at least from the sanitary and development points of view. The management of the town needs a separate entity as before. The provisions of the District Council Act which have no proper roots in the constitution of India are inadequate for nurturing the smooth growth and maintenance of a town. Manipur is neither under the Scheduled-V nor the Scheduled-VI of the Constitution of India. Tribal inhabited districts are neither Statutorily Tribal areas nor Scheduled Areas. They are simply Hill areas. The Jilla Parishads which are district Councils in the valley under the provision of the 73rd Amendment of the Constitution are more powerful than the District Councils under the 6th Schedule of the Constitution of India.

The Churachandpur town is the biggest district Headquarters in the hill areas. It has a vast potentiality for further growth and development in many spheres. It badly needs a good Master Plan for future development of the town. The pioneers of the town also had far-sightedness for the future expansion and development of the town. But their plans and proposals could not be implemented for want of public sanction and cooperation. Once Churachandpur Master Plan for a greater town had been prepared by the Chief Planner, Town Planning Development, Government of

Manipur. The proposal was submitted to the Secretary, Local Self Government, Government of Manipur vide letter No. 123/TP-69/CH-Plan dated 11.4.1969. The proposal was sent to the Deputy Commissioner of the District for implementation. However, the proposal could not be implemented due to lack of public co-operation etc. Special statutory provision for proper flow of fund for the maintenance of the town is the main requirement of this growing town. District Council Act should provide proper means of maintenance of a town. Town Planning Project failed to be implemented till now. The resultant effect was that there is no proper bus parking site, no proper and hygenic slaughter House, no childrens' park no super market etc. in the town. There was once a healthy sign while Mr. Vungzalian, elected to the Assembly from the town area as a Minister of State for Education. He was interested in establishing a super market. He along with members of the staff of the town office started for selection of site for a supper market in around 1974. However, the dream was aborted with the dissolution of the Manipur Assembly.

Application of Municipal Council in Churachandpur Town as in the cases of other seven municipalities of the valley of Manipur is Statutorily debarred by the Manipur Municipalities Act, 1994. The functions of municipalities were given to the Disctrict Council. But there are no proper provisions for maintenance of town administration in the present District Council Act without the backing of the 6th Schedule of the Constitution of India. Under these circumstances the town falls between two stools.

Different communities live in the town. The tribes, members of other backward classes and the non-tribe and non-castes are found in the town. Within the town the largest single community is the Paite followed by Hmar and then thirdly the Meitei. Other Indian communities are found in their hundreds mainly as businessmen. Apprehension of having a municipality in the District Council areas without sufficient statutory protection of the tribes will not only change the demographic situation of the town but also the control of the town will come in the hands of the non-tribals in a tribal area. Alienation of tribal land and other forms of exploitations of the tribals will be more evident in case a local body looks after the affairs of the town without proper protection with statutory provisions in the true spirit of the Constitution of India. The provisions of the Manipur Municipalities Act, 1994 even if it is permitted to be extended in the District Council areas will be repugnant and detrimental to the tribals without adding some more provisions for their safeguards. The town needs a separate entity as a municipal council but with statutory provisions for protecting the tribals either by amending the Manipur Municipalities Act or the District Council Act to suit the situation in a true spirit of the constitution of India. There should be proper flow of fund for the town in addition to the collection by the town office. The main problem of the town is lack of suitable statutory provision otherwise the town has a good potentiality for development and growth. The importance of the town lies in its situational location at the foot-hills only 60 km. away from Imphal, the state capital and only 56 km. away from the Indo-Myanmar boundary in the Southern end of Manipur. It is an important trade centre. Its commercial importance will increase all the more internationally in case a trade centre is opened at Chikha (Myanmar) Behiang (India) junction under the provision of the Indo-Myanmar Border Trade Agreement for which the local people had already approached the Indian authorities. The town is important for the State as well as the Centre

Government in having district offices of the State Government departments. The Central Government has important institutions like Training centre for Border Security Forces. All India Radio (to be commissioned). Educationally the town is an important place. It has two government degree colleges with teeming students.

The distribution of population among the wards of Churachandpur Town is very dispeoportionate. The New Lamka ward having a population of 5317 is nearly as big as seven times of the smallest Headquarter was having 766 population which is again bigger than the smallest ward in Nambol Municipality Council, Six wards in Bishnupur, eight wards in Jiribam and one ward in Thoubal Municipal Councils of the valley. The biggest population of municipality ward other than the Imphal Municipality wards, is 2909 in Kakching followed by 2865 in Thoubal. The average proporitionate distribution of population in Churachandpur town among the 16 wards in 2333. The smallest Jiribam Municipality having a total population of 6900 persons in 10 wards has an average population of 690 persons per ward is five times smaller than Churachandpur town. Imphal Municipal Council having an average population of 7580 persons per ward in 26 ward is five times larger than Churachandpur town. If the New Lamka ward is divided into three wards and the Phailian ward is split into two wards, each of the five new wards will be more populous than the other five smaller wards. As such Churachandpur town has a good potentiality to increase the number of wards from 16 wards to 19 wards.

As regards the name of the town it will be more judicious to name and call it officially as Lamka then Churachandpur on the grounds mentioned earlier at the beginning. Several organisations occasionally raised objections to the imposition of name on Lamka. Songs were composed and sung in lementation of the imposiion of a name Churachandpur on Lamka. Mr. H.K. Neitham, Executive Officer, Churachandpur Town is of the opinion that it will be more appropriate and correct to call and name Churachadpur Town by its original and indigenous name Lamka. Lamka is a name of a particular place and to name it and call it by the name of the Maharaja Churachand hurt the sentiment of the local people. It is not proper to impose any name on any local people or locality.

REFERENCES

1. *The Manipur Municipalities Act*, 1994 (passed by Parliament in June, 1994).
2. Thangzam G. *Churachandpur Chanchin* (History of Churachandpur): Jamkho-on Memorial Printing Prsss.
3. Gimsum H. *Lamka Vangkhua* (Lamka Town) Lamka, Convetion Press.
4. Neitham H.K.: A letter on Churachandpur town for which the author is indepted to him.

Chapter 22

SMALL TOWNS IN TRIPURA IN THE PAST AND PRESENT

Mahadev Chakravarti

There was virtually no town, properly so called, in princely Tripura during the nineteenth century. Although at the insistence of the British Political Agent, a Municipality was instituted at Agartala in 1871, still it was no better than a moderate village. In the contemporary records and documents, we have a vivid description about Agartala and the other two sub-divisional Headquarters, *e.g.* Kailashar and Udaipur, which were without roads and how these places were converted into unhealthy swamps after a little rain.

It is against this background that we are to study the trends of urbanization and the concomitant problems and prospects associated with these since the beginning of the present century. From a single town (*i.e.,* Agartala) there are at present 13 towns in Tripura including Agartala. The list of the 12 other small towns is given in Table No. 1. Upto 1951, there was only one town in Tripura, *i.e.,* Agartala. In 1961 Census, some other sub-divisional headquarters, *e.g.,* Dharmanagar, Kailashar, Udaipur, Khowai and Belonia were classified as urban areas on the basis of liberal application of the criteria of having a population of not less than 5,000 persons of which 75% of male working persons were non-agricultural. Thus the number of towns was raised to 6 in the census of 1961 and the number remained the same in 1971 census too. In 1981 census, all the 10 sub-divisional headquarters are classified as towns (including Agartala which had attained the city status). Recently, three more sub-divisions have been created. But these three new sub-divisional headquarters *e.g.*, Kanchanpur and Long-terrai in North Tripura and Gandachhera is South Tripura districts are not recognised as towns because of their predominantly rural character. Rather three new areas—*e.g.*, Kumarghat in North Tripura and Teliamurah and Ranibazar in the West Tripura districts—are declared as towns. Thus, we have at present twelve small towns in Tripura and the capital Agartala is now a city.

Table 1: List of Small Towns in Tripura

1.	Dharmanagar	Town
2.	Udaipur	Town
3.	Kailashar	Town
4.	Belonia	Town
5.	Khowai	Town
6.	Amarpur	Town
7.	Sonamura	Town
8.	Kamalpur	Town
9.	Sabroom	Town
10.	Kumarghat	Town
11.	Ranirbazar	Town
12.	Teliamurah	Town

Table 1A: Population of Agartala (now Class I) Town since 1901

Year	Population
1901	6,415
1911	6,831
1921	7,743
1931	9,580
1941	17,693
1951	42,595
1961	54,878
1971	1,00,264
1981	1,32,186
1991	1,57,358

Table 1B: Growth of Urban Population in Tripura Since 1901

Year	Tripura	Decadal Variation	West Dist.	North Dist.	South Dist.
1901	6,415	—	6,415	—	—
1911	6,831	+ 416	6,831	—	—
1921	7,743	+ 912	7,743	—	—
1931	9,580	+ 1,837	9,580	—	—
1941	17,693	+ 8,133	17,693	—	—
1951	42,595	+ 24,902	42,595	—	—
1961	1,02,997	+ 60,402	63,660	21,815	17,522
1971	1,72,360	+ 59,363	1,09,602	27,460	25,298
1981	2,25,568	+ 63,208	1,49,288	37,432	38,848
1991	4,21,721	+ 1,96,153	3,15,904	61,004	44,813

Indices of growth of Town Population of Tripura: (1901 = 100): 1991 = 106, 1921 = 121, 1931 = 149, 1941 = 276, 1951 = 664, 1961 = 1606, 1971 = 2231, 1981 = 3516 and 1991 = 6574.

From Table 1A, the pattern of the growth of population of Agartala would be evident. In 1901 the total population of Agartala town was 6,415 and the capital was planned accordingly. But in 1991 census to popualtion of Agartala alone has reached 1,57,358. Indices of growth of town population of Tripura are shown in Table 1B. If we have a close look at the above three tables (1, 1A and 1B), it would be found that there was a steady growth and in some years there was an abrupt growth of urban population in Tripura. The century began with only 6,415 urban population and in 1991 it has touched 4,21,721. Thus Agartala today has 1,57,358 and the other small towns of Tripura (exclusing the recently declared three new small towns) have 2,64,363 persons.

II

The question of local self-government became important with the growth of smaller towns. In order to make these townships self-governing and to look after construction of roads, drainage, sanitation, health etc., the state Government declared in 1978 as Notified Area Authorities (NAA). But these NAAs were nominated bodies. In consonance with the Constitution (74th Amendment) Act, popularly known as the Nagarpalika Act, elections are scheduled to be held in December, 1995 for the creation of Nagar Panchayats in the small towns of Tripura, along with the election of Agartala Municipality which had been superseded in 1988 and since then no election was held for that. It is now acknowledged by all that for effective urbanization and solution of day to day civic problems, the Nagar Panchayats should first be established and in order to make these bodies strong, large and effective devolution of power to the Local Self Governing unit is needed. True, the civic bodies are usually plagued by lack of resources; but a community participation particularly participation by women and other weaker sections of the society which the Nagarpalika Act ensures—may perhaps alter the urban scenario, although it is very difficult to evoke people's participation for the cause of the upliftment of the urban people.

In the 74th Amendment of the Constitution, the Twelfth Schedule (Article 243W) is included where the following functions of the new urban bodies are outlined—1. Urban Planning including town planning, 2. Regulation of land-use and construction of buildings, 3. Planning for economic and social development, 4. Roads and bridges, 5. Water supply for domestic, industrial and commercial purposes, 6. Public health, sanitation, conservancy and solid waste management, 7. Fire services, 8. Urban forestry, protection of the environment and promotion of ecological aspects, 9. Safeguarding the interests of weaker sections of society, including the handicapped and mentally retarded, 10. Slum improvement and upgradation, 11. Urban poverty alleviation, 12. Provision of urban amenities and facilites—such as parkas, gardens, playgrounds, 13. Promotion of cultural, educational and aesthetic aspects, 14. Burials and burial grounds, cremations, cremation grounds and electric crematoriums, 15. Cattle pounds: prevention of cruelty to animals, 16. Vital statistics including registration of births and deaths, 17. Public amenities including street lighting, parking lots, bus stops and public conveniences, 18. Regulation of slaughter houses and tanneries.

All the above mentioned 18 functions of the Nagar Panchayats will be followed in Tripura and accordingly steps are now being taken to frame rules and laws as the direct election is sheduled to be held in December 1995. A detailed discussion is needed to outline the following features of each town of Tripura: *e.g.*, the population of the area, the density of the population therein, the revenue generated for local administration, the percentage off employment in non-agricultural activities, the economic importance of each town in the past and present, the geographic location, the urban fringe, peculiar nature of problems of some towns and the master plans for over-all development, the impact and consequences of urbanization etc. But due to the lack of proper adequate upto-date information, it is not possible here to discuss the prolems of all the 12 small towns of Tripura.

Let us now cast a glance at Table 2 to have an idea about different classes of towns in Tripura (from Class I to Class VI) in different phases of time since the biginning of the present century. As the present details regarding small towns in the 1991 census is not yet available, we confine our attention upto 1981 census only. The decennial censuses constitute the basic source of quantitative information on urbanization and its various facets.

In Tripura, the most conveniently placed villages ultimately took the shape of small towns either because

Table 2: Different classes of Towns in Tripura from 1901 to 1981

Year	Class I		Class II		Class III		Class IV		Class V		Class Vi		All Classes	
	No.	Popu	No.	Popu	No.	Popu	No.	Popu	No.	Popu	No.	Popu	No.	Popu
1901									1	6,415			1	6,415
1911									1	6,831			1	6,831
1921									1	7,743			1	7,743
1931									1	9,580			1	9,580
1941							1	17,693					1	17,693
1951					1	42,595							1	42,595
1961			1	54,878			1	13,240	4	34,879			6	1,02,997
1971	1	1,00,264					4	52,758	1	9,338			6	1,62,360
1981	1	1,32,186			1	20,806	4	52,018	2	13,530	2	7,028	10	2,25,568

Source: Census of India, Series 21, Tripura, Part II-A. p. 191.

Thus in 1981, there were 10 towns (all classes) in Tripura:

West Tripura District	3
North Tripura District	3
South Tripura District	4
Total	10

Table 3: Literacy Rates and Ranks by Rural-Urban Residence for Tripura in 1981 and 1991

	1981 Rural	1991 Urban	Rank Rural Rural	Urban Urban	1981	1991	1981	1991
India	36.09	67.34	44.54	73.01				
Tripura	45.78	83.36	56.08	83.09	11	12	3	6

Table 3A: Literates and Literacy Rates in Tripura, 1991

	Total Popu..	Popu. (0-6)	Population (7+)			Literate (7+)			Literacy Rate (7+)		
			Persons	Males	Females	Persons	Males	Females	Persons	Males	Females
Tripura	27,57,205	4,97,122	22,60,083	11,65,206	10,94,877	13,65,980	8,22,402	5,43,578	60.44	70.58	49.65
R.	23,35,484	4,40,461	18,95,023	9,78,731	9,16,292	10,62,635	6,56,440	4,06,195	56,08	67.07	44.33
U.	4,21,721	56,661	3,65,060	1,86,475	1,78,585	3,03,345	1,65,962	1,37,383	83.09	89.00	76.93
Agartala Town	1,57,358	17,764	1,39,594	70,378	69,216	1,24,268	66,026	58,242	89.02	93.82	84.15

Source: Census of India, 1991, Series-I, India, Paper-2 of 1992, pp. 61, 214, 215, 328, 329.

these were administrative centres or commercial places or market places. These market centres sometimes served the demands of the nearby tea gardens, which are euphimistically called the 'isolated foci of modernisation'. The pace of the growth of small towns in Tripura in not linked with industrialization. In fact, there is no industrial town in Tripura. Other than Udaipur once the capital of the State in the past-there is not a single temple town in Tripura. In fact, the story of the growth of small towns in Tripura is an interesting chapter and it requires separate discussion.

IV

Urban areas are usually associated with higher literacy rates. Table No. 3 gives a detailed picutre of Tripura and a comparative estimate between 1981 and 1991 censuses. As the data on literacy may be used as yardstick of development; it needs a little bit discussion.

V

Big cities generate big problems. It is now asserted by ecologists that metropolitan centres and mega-cities are undesirable. As there is a growing trend towards urban decentralization and Nagar Panchayats etc., emphasis should now the given on the growth of small towns and in Tripura, because of various reasons, there is no other alternative.

these were administrative centres or commercial places or market places; these market centres of commerce served the demands of the nearby tea gardens, which are [illegible] in the [illegible] of North Tripura. Some small towns in Tripura are not the results of industrialization. In fact, there is no industrial town in Tripura, other than Udaipur, once the capital of the State in the past; there is not a single temple town in Tripura. In fact, the story of the growth of small towns in Tripura is an interesting chapter and it requires separate discussion.

IV

Urban areas are usually associated with higher literacy rates. Table No. 3 shows a detailed picture of Tripura and a comparative estimate between 1981 and 1991 censuses. As the data on literacy may be used as yardstick of development, it needs a little discussion.

V

Big cities generate big problems. It is now asserted by ecologists that metropolitan centres and mega-cities are undesirable. As there is a growing trend towards urban decentralization and Nagar Panchayats etc., emphasis should now be given on the growth of small towns and in Tripura, because of various reasons, there is no other alternative.